Traveling with the Turtle

Traveling with the Turtle
A program of Pace e Bene Nonviolence Service
2501 Harrison St., Oakland, CA 94612
Phone: (510) 268-8908 Fax: (510) 268-8799
turtle@paceebene.org
www.turtle.paceebene.org

ISBN: 0-9669783-7-4

Library of Congress Control Number: 2006934507

Pace e Bene Nonviolence Service

Pace e Bene (pronounced *pah-chay bay-nay*) means "peace and all good" in Italian. St. Francis of Assisi used this expression as a greeting and as a means of proclaiming the way of peace in the midst of a violent world.

Pace e Bene Nonviolence Service is based in Las Vegas, Nevada, with offices and program staff in Oakland, California; Chicago, Illinois; Montreal, Quebec, Canada; Perth, Western Australia, Australia; and a growing network of collaborators in North and South America. Pace e Bene offers resources to assist in the journey of personal and social transformation, such as retreats, workshops, presentations, classes, and a variety of publications, including *The Wolf*, its quarterly newsletter. Pace e Bene's staff and animating group engage in nonviolent action and work with a wide range of nonviolent movements for justice and peace.

Nevada Office	**California Office**
1420 W. Bartlett Ave., Las Vegas, NV 89106	2501 Harrison St., Oakland, CA 94612
Phone & Fax: (702) 648-2281	Phone: (510) 268-8765 Fax: (510) 268-8799
www.paceebene.org; paceebene@paceebene.org	pbcal@paceebene.org

Artist: Pamela Falkowski, © 2006. Graphic art produced by "Hildegard's Delight," the artistic arm of Sunrise Ruby Ministries. These graphics are the result of Pam's conversations with the authors and editor and her own contemplation and prayer over the years of living the vow of nonviolence.

Traveling with the Turtle

A Small Group Process in Women's Spirituality and Peacemaking

Cindy Preston-Pile and Irene Woodward

Pace e Bene Press, Oakland, California

The turtle is a rich symbol. We have entitled this manual *Traveling with the Turtle* because, among other things, the turtle symbolizes women's wisdom and strength. For Native Americans, the turtle was associated with the lunar cycle, menstruation, and the power of the female energies. Some turtles have a total of thirteen markings or sections on their shells. These thirteen markings were thought to represent the thirteen full moons or thirteen new moons that alternated each year in the lunar calendar. Many believe this is where the association with the female energies originated—the turtle's shell revealed both the natural cycle of the planet and the fertility period of females. Women's ability, her power to create new life, was intimately connected to the rhythm of nature itself. Thus, the turtle symbolizes Mother Earth, the primal mother, Womb of All.

Table of Contents

The Odds

A storm is up.
The wind chases
whatever it can unhinge
with its force for miles,
sets the sea panting
against a jetty
and agitates to gracelessness
the bare lilac branches.
The wind disturbs
those at home with gravity;
stirs what is sleeping
to the surface, pitching
bits of shells and sea glass
to the shore. There,
women are wiping
sand from their eyes,
collecting what is necessary,
what is beautiful. A storm
is up. A lone gull
shifts and presses its weight
to stay, to hover above
a circle of women
who are trying to light
a fire. They are
lighting a fire.

L.R. Berger, from "As Rains Enter Rivers."

Introduction

Dear Sisters,

Greetings of Peace and All Good—and welcome. We honor the sacred journey that you are embarking on by entering into this small group process together. We are filled with hope in knowing that you are forming community where you can share stories about the gifts and graces you have experienced, as well as the struggles you have encountered along the way, as women seeking to make peace with yourselves, your families, your communities, and in our society. With the turtle, ancient symbol of feminine wisdom and power as your guide, we are grateful that you are claiming your power and imparting your wisdom, wisdom that our world badly needs to hear.

In her poem, L.R. Berger observes that a storm is up! Violence and injustice swirl around us—but so does the Spirit. She calls to us, "Follow me." She "stirs what is sleeping to the surface," those qualities and values that we possess as women that our world so desperately needs to recognize and embrace to be made whole. Jean Shinoda Bolen summarizes this need: "Empowered maternal concern [*in its broadest sense*] is an untapped feminine force that the world needs to balance and transform aggression."

In the midst of this impending storm, the women go around faithfully "collecting what is necessary, what is beautiful," what is compassionate and loving. You are gathering in circles as women have done throughout the ages, trying to light the fire—a fire within that ignites a holy love of self, a fire that burns brightly with a passion for peace, beckoning others to come close and warm their hands and hearts. May this manual help kindle the fire that you are lighting as you begin this journey together. As you gather, know that the goals of the *Traveling with the Turtle* process are:

- To explore the values and practices of women's spirituality
- To see how these values and practices help you heal and make peace with yourself, in your relationships, in your communities, and in society.

Therefore, in this manual, you will consider women's experiences of violence and conflict and habitual responses to them, and then learn concrete ways of making peace that are practical, creative, inclusive, and nonviolent. You will be one of an increasing number of circles of women that are acting together for peace.

The History of Traveling with the Turtle

Traveling with the Turtle draws from the work of *Engage: Exploring Nonviolent Living,* a program of Pace e Bene Nonviolence Service that invites participants to discover the power of nonviolence for personal and social change. After facilitating *Engage* workshops for several years, we began to hear the need for a similar resource designed specifically for women. At one workshop, several women raised questions and concerns such as: "How do I feel and constructively express my anger?" and "Are you equating staying in an abusive relationship with nonviolence?" No, we are not.

Unexpressed or inappropriately expressed anger. Always trying to smooth things over. These are deeply ingrained responses that women have learned to use in the face of conflict and violence. *Traveling with the Turtle* is a response to these and other questions and concerns that women are raising as part of their peacemaking journeys.

Women are struggling with similar issues globally. Cindy Preston-Pile, one of the authors, participated in *Asking the Right Questions: Nonviolence Training and Gender Consultation*, a conference held in Thailand in 2004. There she met women from Africa, Asia, Eastern and Western Europe, the Americas, and Canada, who were seeking to convey in their nonviolence trainings they offered for women, and many times men, the belief that ending violence and discrimination against women is an integral part of peacemaking. These trainers sought to empower women to break out of roles that were often narrowly defined for them by their societies. Women who participated in such trainings felt more confident, valued, and liberated in their lives as they began to reclaim the power that a violent, male-dominated system had stripped from them. *Traveling with the Turtle* is an attempt to stand in solidarity with women and men, who are working to end violence—both internalized messages of oppression and external forms of violence—against women.

Her life-long endeavors of accompaniment as a professor and a spiritual director led Irene Woodward, the other author, to further discoveries. She met numerous women thirsting for a greater understanding of women's spirituality, for a validation of their own experience of themselves and of the Divine. She found that as these women probed more deeply the experience of this Spirit, they discovered others from many religious traditions and backgrounds asking the same questions, and found a connectedness, indeed a sisterhood, in this spiritual search. As part of this journey, the women whom Irene met embraced inclusiveness and mutuality as ways of being in the world, as well as the common desire for healing the wounds of our Earth and of other people.

Traveling with the Turtle is based on the premise that women's spirituality is a powerful force for peacemaking. Throughout the thirteen sessions you will reflect on different aspects of this spirituality, and how they heal, support, and empower you on your peacemaking journey.

Spirituality

What is spirituality? This is a rather elusive term. Sometimes it is equated with formal religious worship. Other times it is viewed as an alternative to such a structured practice. In this manual, we believe that spirituality pervades the entirety of our lives. Our life pilgrimage, our journey toward wholeness, is a spiritual undertaking. We encounter Spirit as we delve deeply into our own lives, into that inviolable part of ourselves sometimes called soul, and discover our own beauty, strength and goodness, our passions, and life's purpose. We encounter Spirit as we form relationships both with those whom we love deeply and with those who are different from us, who perhaps challenge us, as they help us to grow and enable us to glimpse the Divine who resides within us all.

We encounter Spirit in the presence of creation, of Earth and all of her glorious creatures. And, we encounter Spirit as we come together as families, as communities, and in movements for social change to struggle for justice and peace or, as Carter Heyward writes, "to re-create the world." Our lives are holy. We are sacred beings. Spirituality embraces all of this. It is the ground upon which we walk, the deep well from which we draw throughout this process.

Important Elements of Women's Spirituality

Women's spirituality believes that it is important that we, as women, acknowledge that we, too, are created in the image of the Holy One whom, throughout this manual, we sometimes refer to as Her, the Feminine Divine. Many other times we simply say "the Divine" or "the Holy One."

In addressing the Divine as feminine, our intent is not to exclude but rather to include women who perhaps have felt that addressing the Holy One in exclusively masculine language has meant that they cannot relate to this divinity, that they are not made in His image. New language seems to be needed to express the multitude of ways that women experience the Divine, and so we hope that, in the spirit of inclusivity embraced by women's spirituality, we will open ourselves to an array of ways of imaging the Divine.

Another important feature of women's spirituality is the understanding of power that it offers in both intimate relationships and political realities. A question that often arises with respect to power is whether or not power is a bad thing, as when one person exerts control over, another's life. Drawing on Starhawk's and Pamela Cooper-White's schemas, we call such control power-over, domination of another person, an entire people, or of Earth. This is an abuse of power.

At the same time, power can be an extraordinary, wonderful, creative, life-giving energy. The New Oxford American Dictionary offers us the following definitions of power: 1) the ability to do something or act in a particular way; 2) the capacity or ability to direct or influence the behavior of others or the course of events. Women's spirituality seeks the empowerment of women, the ability to make decisions that affect our lives—at home, in the workplace, in matters of religion, and in many other areas. In order to do this, we draw on our power-within, that deep wisdom and intuition that wells up inside of us. In listening to this voice deep within us, as Audre Lorde writes, "we begin to demand from ourselves and from our life-pursuits that they feel in accordance with that joy which we know ourselves to be capable of."

Power-with or power-sharing "carries the dignity of power-within into relationship." Peacemaking. Nonviolence. We seek to enable other people to experience this same power, strength, freedom, expression of our truest self, that we have felt. As the circle widens, power-with blossoms into community power and, eventually sisterhood—or people power. These thirteen sessions are structured around these four themes—Power-Within, Power-With, Community Power, and Sisterhood. As you move through this process, we invite you to delve deeply into your own power, to consider how you want to use it—and then act—that together we might transform the domination, the power-over that we have experienced in our lives as women and in the life of our world.

The Structure of This Process

Traveling with the Turtle is a process developed by women for women. It is comprised of 13 two-hour sessions.

Session1 introduces you to women's spirituality.

Session 2 explores empowering images of the Divine.

Part I (Sessions 3-5) helps you claim your power-within.

Part II (Sessions 6-8) explores your familiar responses to conflict and violence, as well as creative, nonviolent ways of making peace.

Part III (Sessions 9-10) considers how you can build inclusive communities.

Part IV (Sessions 11-13) honors the many social change movements initiated by women and guides the group through the process of developing and carrying out a nonviolent action. Session 13 concludes with a celebration of your lives that commissions you to go forth and continue to make peace.

Each session uses a variety of learning styles and methods to explore women's spirituality and peacemaking: ritual, story-telling, role-plays, small and large group discussions, meditation, creative imagination exercises, movement, singing, and action. Throughout the process, you are encouraged to express yourselves in a variety of ways using images, movement, song, as well as written or spoken words.

In between sessions, you are asked to engage in a Life Practice, respond to journal questions, and reflect on several readings.

The Elements of Each Session

Opening Ritual You will honor the sacredness of each other and your time together by beginning each session with a ritual that may include meditation, prayers, music, movement or symbolic gestures. We invite you to savor this time of centering and re-collection.

Sharing, Reflections on Life Practice, Journal Questions, or Readings

At the beginning of each session there will be time to share with a partner insights, questions and concerns that arose between sessions through engaging in a life practice, journaling, or from the readings for that session.

One or Several of the Following Activities:

Creative imagination exercises

Sharing in pairs, small and large groups about exercises or readings

Guided meditations

Role-play

Movement

Closing

You will end your time together with a closing ritual or circle activity.

Life Practice

Life practices help you embody what you have learned in each session.

Journal Topics and Questions

We offer questions and topics to reflect on before the next gathering.

Readings

Each session will include several articles that may be read in preparation for the following session.

Using This Process

It is our hope that this material will be adapted for an array of groups, so please adapt *Traveling with the Turtle* to meet the needs of your group or community. (Keep in mind, however, that this process is not designed to be used as the main resource for a therapy or support group.)

If you wish to concentrate on certain parts of a session because you feel that those areas are most important for your group or you need to change the agenda as stories are told and important issues and conversations arise, please do so. If you want to bring in new resources, again, do so. You may want to go through all 13 sessions or you may wish to do fewer. (For instance, you could do Parts I and II that address personal and interpersonal power and then close with the Sending Forth ritual in Session 13.) You may also want to gather for a preliminary session, perhaps over a meal, to share personal stories so that group members will get to know each other before beginning the *Traveling with the Turtle* process. Or, you may want to meet an hour before the first session.

Your group can meet every week, every other week, or once a month. We cannot say it often enough—make this process your own to whatever extent you desire. And, if you adapt a session, or sessions in a way that worked well, let us know.

Blessings

During the time Cindy was surrounded by the incredible group of women who gathered in Thailand, she dreamt of visiting a zoo filled with vibrantly colored turtles who came in a vast array of shapes and sizes. This dream turned out to be relevant because, as the title of this process explains, the turtle symbolizes women's wisdom and strength. Here again, we stand in the midst of circles of amazing, beautiful, courageous, passionate women— all of you. We pray that this turtle will walk with you as you slowly and faithfully travel this new, yet familiar path. May you be blessed by the wisdom and power of all of the women who have gone before us, all of the women who now walk with us, and all of those yet to be born.

Cindy and Irene

In Gratitude

We thank the many women who have walked with as we have struggled to give birth to this book:

> Members of our Consultative Body— Marilyn Wilson, BVM, Rev. Cynthia State-man, Brenda Vaca, Liz Sweet, Joi Morton-Wiley, and Miriam Cooney, CSC. Sister Miriam also assisted us generously in our fundraising projects.

> The many women who participated in pilot groups in Orinda, Berkeley, San Mateo, Oakland, and Guerneville, California; St. Louis, Missouri; Hartford, Connecticut; Boston, Massachusetts; Canberra, Australia; and, in particular, the women at the Federal Correctional Institute (FCI) in Dublin, California. We especially mention those women who facilitated these groups: Rose Elizondo and Katherine McCarron; Faith Madzar and Catherine Pfieffer; Laural Lantz, Lydia Ferrante-Roseberry, Kim Andrews and Peggy Dillon; Miriam Casey, Betty Till, and Ann Hadden-Corne-lius; Elizabeth Hearn and Marylee Fithian; Diana Wear, Candace O'Bryan, Carol Bialock, RCSJ, Susan Vanderburgh, and Patricia Bruno, OP; Margaret Bearlin and Thea Gaia; and Laura Magnani from the American Friends Service Committee who helped adapt and facilitate the process at FCI Dublin.

We offer special thanks to our layout, design, and computer specialist, copyeditor, proofreader, and hand-holder par excellence throughout the entire production process, Diana Wear. Our gratitude goes out, as well, to our graphic artist, Pam Falkowski, our consultants, Dr. Erica Britton and Colleen Nakamoto; our reader, Gina Sconza; and the intern who assisted us with permission rights, Lara Duncan.

We are especially appreciative of our associates at Pace e Bene: our guide with permis-sion rights, Laura Slattery; the Pace e Bene editorial committee, Peter Ediger, L.R. Berger and Veronica Pelicaric; and the ever-present assistance of Lindsay Martin. We offer a special thanks to Ken Preston-Pile who helped us every step of the way as we adapted parts of *Engage: Explor-ing Nonviolent Living*.

We thank all of the women's religious orders who helped to fund this manual, especially the Sisters of Charity, BVM; the Sisters of St. Joseph of Carondelet, St. Louis Province; the Sisters of the Holy Cross; and the Sisters of the Holy Names of Jesus and Mary.

Finally, thank you to the entire Pace e Bene community for believing in and supporting the unfolding of this vision: Peter Ediger, Veronica Pelicaric, Ken Butigan, Lindsay Martin, Mary Litell, OSF, Rosemary Lynch, OSF, AJ Johnston, Patty Caramagno-Robertson, Laura Slattery, Ken Preston-Pile, and Louie Vitale, OFM.

And to all of the strong, beautiful, good and holy women out there making this world a better place. Thank you!

Session 1

Women's Spirituality:
A Force for Nonviolent Peacemaking

Session 1
Women's Spirituality:
A Force For Nonviolent Peacemaking

In this Session We Will

- Get to know each other
- Learn about the goals of *Traveling with the Turtle* and the format for each session
- Begin to explore women's spirituality and its relationship to peacemaking

Agenda

Welcome and Introductions — *5 min*
Opening Ritual — *20 min*
Getting to Know Each Other — *15 min*
Shared Agreements — *10 min*
Our Experience of Women's Spirituality — *50 min*
A Description of Women's Spirituality — *10 min*
Closing — *5 min*
Looking Ahead — *5 min*
        Life Practice
        Journal Topics and Questions
        Readings

Materials Needed

- ☐ Name badges
- ☐ Felt tip pens or markers for writing names and recording the Shared Agreements
- ☐ Sign-in sheet
- ☐ Compact disk or audiotape player
- ☐ Recorded music
- ☐ Small prayer table
- ☐ A colorful cloth to cover the table, perhaps one that has special meaning for the group
- ☐ A candle for each woman, large enough so that she can take it home and light it regularly
- ☐ Matches
- ☐ A bell for the "babbling" exercise
- ☐ Flipchart
- ☐ Easel paper
- ☐ A basket
- ☐ Sheets of white 8 ½ x 11 paper, cut into small strips, two for each participant

Facilitator Notes
Session preparation — A month before
- Consider gathering for a preliminary session, perhaps over a meal, dedicated to sharing personal stories so that group members will get to know each other before beginning the *Traveling with the Turtle* process.
- Or, you may want to meet an hour before the first session.
- Let participants know about an earlier gathering if you choose to hold one.

Session preparation — The week before
- Review the Facilitation Guidelines found near the end of this manual.
- Review the entire session. Practice reading any visualizations or meditations, and role-play or practice setting up and facilitating exercises beforehand. Whenever possible, put material into your own words. Feel free to make notes on 3x5 cards or in the book next to the written instructions.
- Write "Women's Spirituality" at the top of a piece of easel paper and then the bullet points describing it. (Found in A Description of Women's Spirituality, Session 1, page 19).

Session preparation — The day of
- Arrange the chairs, including your own, in a circle, with a small table in the center. Place the cloth, candles and matches on the table.
- As people arrive, ask them to sign in with their contact information (at some point, group members may need to be in touch with each other).
- Make sure everyone has a copy of *Traveling with the Turtle*.
- Play some background music as people arrive, if desired.

Session 1
Women's Spirituality:
A Force for Nonviolent Peacemaking

Welcome and Introductions — *5 min*

Convey in your own words:

Welcome to our first gathering of *Traveling with the Turtle*! My name is (or we are) _____ and _____, and we will be facilitating this process.

We will be meeting for thirteen sessions to reflect on women's spirituality and its contribution to peacemaking. The goals of the *Traveling with the Turtle* process are:

- To explore the values and practices of women's spirituality
- To see how these values and practices help us heal ourselves and make peace with others
- To consider women's experience of conflict and violence and habitual responses to them
- To continue to learn concrete ways of making peace that are creative, practical, inclusive and nonviolent
- To form an increasing number of circles of women that are acting together for peace

Each session will include an opening; time to share insights that arose between gatherings; activities such as guided meditation, creative expression exercises, role-plays and small and large group reflection; a closing; and a life practice or action, journal questions, and readings for the next session. In the second to last session, our time together will include planning and carrying out a group action for peace.

During this session, we will be introduced—to each other, to the general approach of this series, and to an understanding of women's spirituality as a powerful force for healing ourselves and for making peace in our families, our communities, and our world.

Explain any housekeeping details.

Opening Ritual — *20 min*

Begin by inviting group members to take a few minutes to center themselves and become present to this time, this circle, by paying attention to their breath. Breathe in and out, in and out.

If you desire, play a song in the background.

Then share the following in your own words:

> We gather in the presence of the Holy One who comes to us in many forms—Creator, One Who Brings Peace, Companion, She who is woman like us, the Divine Feminine. Be here with us now, O Mother. Fill us with your presence, your passion, your peace. Guide us in the weeks and months ahead, showering the Wisdom of your way upon us that we may walk in beauty, embracing our sacredness and recognizing the sacredness of our sisters and brothers throughout the world. As we open this holy circle, we thank you for the gift of this time together. (*Pause for a moment.*)
>
> As we embark on our journey together, I invite you to come forward, light a candle, and share with the group your reason for wanting to enter into this process—a hope, a need, or an intention you have as we begin this exploration of women's spirituality and peacemaking.

You may wish to model this by going first. After each woman has shared her response and lit a candle, conclude with:

> We gather up these hopes and desires and acknowledge how sacred they are. We will take these candles home with us to light each time that we write in our journal, or reflect on each session's theme. During those times may we remember both our own hopes and needs and the hopes and needs of the other women in this group. Like these candles before us, may you, O Holy One, burn brightly in our hearts, lighting before us the path to peace.

Getting to Know Each Other — *15 min*

Tell the group:

> We will now get to know each other better through an exercise called "Babbling," which comes from a process called InterPlay. Find a partner. Decide who is person #1 and who is person #2. *If there is an uneven number of people, simply group the remaining folks into a triad.*

Then say:

> Person #1, I am going to give you a word and you are going to talk about that subject—whatever you have to say about it—for 30 seconds. What you say doesn't have to be interesting, or logical, or even fast. Person #2 will just listen. Your word is_____.

Give them a common, concrete subject such as dust, flowers, hair, or spoons. Be creative!

After 30 seconds or so ring a bell or say "Stop." Give person #2 the same instructions:

I'll give you a word and you talk for 30 seconds. The word is_____.

After 30 seconds or so ring a bell or say "Stop."

Do this again, being creative with your choice of words.

Repeat the same sequence once more. This time the words will be "woman" and "peacemaking." After both partners have had a turn, ask them to share anything they noticed with their partner for about 30 seconds, either about what they shared or about the exercise itself—or anything else that came up.

Have them stay with the same partner for the fourth round. Give the following instructions:

Share your name and a word that describes you, something you would like the group to know about you, with each other. Again, begin with Person #1.

Have them thank their partner, remain sitting next to each other, and face the circle. Invite all of the pairs to introduce each other to the circle.

Source: Adapted from Phil Porter and Cynthia Winton-Henry, *Leading Your Own Life: The InterPlay Leadership Program. Secrets of InterPlay I.*

Shared Agreements — 10 min

Making Agreements

Read or put in your own words:

> We have created a sacred space. We have gotten to know each other a little bit. We are now going to develop some shared agreements together so that we can maintain this safe, sacred space in order to be able to share our stories with each other. This is an important aspect of women's spirituality: our ability to reflect deeply on our own experience and to share that experience with the group and have it received and validated. This is holy ground.
>
> What, then, do you need to feel safe and comfortable in this group?

Go around the circle and invite each participant to offer something. Record the group's responses on easel paper. After everyone who has wanted to share has a chance to speak, ask if there are any other additions. If the following agreements have not been expressed, add them to the list and explain what they mean to the group. You can also refer everyone to the Proposed Agreements found below.

During our time together:

- I agree to share and participate at whatever level I feel safe and comfortable.
- I agree to maintain confidentiality.
- I agree to Step Up/Step Back. (*You may want to explain this agreement. It encourages participants to practice speaking up if they tend to be more hesitant and to step back and give others the opportunity to speak if they tend to share often in groups.*)
- I will strive to appreciate and honor our differences.

Ask if the group will agree to use these guidelines. When agreement is reached, post the list on a nearby wall for this and all of the following sessions. Also explain that since the facilitator(s) may or may not notice when one of these agreements is broken, all participants should feel empowered to interrupt the process if they notice this happening and ask that the situation be addressed.

Proposed Agreements

I agree to share and participate at whatever level I feel safe and comfortable.

- I will share what I want to share. If I choose not to share, or to share a little, that's fine. If I want to share more, that's fine. Together we will create an environment where our feelings and thoughts are respected.
- While I have the opportunity always to share at whatever level I feel safe and comfortable, I may be open to voluntarily take opportunities as they arise to feel uncomfortable when that might help facilitate my growth. In every case, this is up to me.
- The facilitators are not acting in the capacity of professional psychotherapists or counselors. They are ordinary people helping us explore alternatives to the violence in our lives and the larger world. If something comes up for me during our time together that would warrant or benefit from consulting with an appropriate health professional, I am encouraged to do so.

I agree to maintain confidentiality about personal stories or experiences shared in my small group or in the large group, unless I have been given permission to share them with others.

- In this process we work in small and large groups. I will not share a story or experience that someone else has shared in either small or large groups unless she has given her permission. When in doubt I will err on the side of caution and not share the story or experience. I will feel free, however, to share any insights that this story or experience may have stimulated.

I agree to Step Up/Step Back—to try to speak up if I tend to be more hesitant and to step back and give others the opportunity to speak if I tend to share often in groups.

- I will listen with my full and complete attention when others are speaking, and wait until a person has completed her thoughts before I speak.
- I will allow silence and accept space for various forms of communication.

I will strive to appreciate and honor our differences.

- Diversity is an opportunity for me to grow and learn in a new way. I will try to nurture an openness to, and celebration of, persons, approaches, and ways of being that are different from mine.
- As part of this, I recognize that there are power dynamics in every group, including this one. I will do my best to be sensitive to the use of power based on race, ability, sexual preference, money, or class. If someone uses power over someone else in this group (for example, if someone discounts another person's experiences), I will try to respond to this situation in a clear and loving way.

Source: Adapted from Slattery, Butigan, Pelicaric, and Preston-Pile, *Engage: Exploring Nonviolent Living.*

> *When you get Jewish, Catholic, Buddhist, Hindu, and Sufi women all practicing their faith in the same room another religion emerges, which is feminine spirituality.*
>
> Carol Lee Flinders

Our Experience of Women's Spirituality — 50 min

Beginnings — *15 min*

Introduce this exercise by sharing the following in your own words:

Woman. Peacemaking. We began our exploration of women's spirituality and its relationship to peacemaking as we "babbled" and when we stated our hopes and intentions for entering into this process. We will now spend a more extended period of time reflecting on and expressing what a spirituality embraced by women looks like to us.

Place the basket in the middle of the circle on the prayer table. Give each woman two strips of paper and then ask the group:

> When you hear the phrase "women's spirituality" what do you feel? What words, phrases, images, or beliefs arise for you? Write or draw two of your responses to these questions on these pieces of paper.

Give everyone several minutes to complete this task. When they are finished, invite them to place their pieces of paper in the basket. Pass the basket around the circle and ask each woman to take out two strips of paper. Go around the circle and have the women, one at a time, read or share whatever is on their pieces of paper. Then have them place their strips of paper on the prayer table.

Sharing in Pairs — *15 min*

Invite everyone to find a partner and ask them to reflect on what they have heard so far or on what they wrote or drew as a description of women's spirituality. Tell them you will ring a bell midway, so that both partners will have time to share.

Large Group Reflection — *20 min*

Invite everyone to return to the large group. Ask them to respond to the following question:

> How does your spirituality, as a woman, influence your desire to heal that which is broken, to act for peace?

A Description of Women's Spirituality — *10 min*

Convey the following:

> We have shared our personal experiences of women's spirituality and the influence that that spirituality has had on our desire to be women, and people of peace. As a further contribution to this conversation, here is one description of women's spirituality that we have found helpful because it makes clear the connection between this spirituality and this desire. In each session we will highlight a different aspect of this spirituality.

> Listen to the description and then add any other aspects of women's spirituality that came up during the previous exercise that are not already listed.

Tape the following description to the wall and then read it:

Women's Spirituality is: a worldwide awakening of womanpower whose vision is the transformation of our selves and our societies. The ancient spiritual voice of woman now speaks its long-hidden wisdom....

This emerging voice speaks of:
* a deepening appreciation of the Feminine Divine in whose image we are
* the empowerment of ourselves as women
* the possibility for both women and men to become whole human beings
* the loving of our bodies, emotions, minds, and spirits
* the importance of stories of our lived experience that are gateways to self-knowledge, wisdom, and self-validation
* the awareness that everything and everyone is sacred, especially ourselves
* the recognition and release of our creative power, individually and communally
* the necessity of community
* reverence for the Earth, the celebration of her seasons and cycles, and those of our lives
* the recognition that all life is interconnected
* the creation of world peace, social justice, and environmental harmony

Source: Quoted and paraphrased from *Woman of Power*.

If the group has other aspects of women's spirituality to add to the list, write them on the easel paper.

Closing — *5 min*

Conclude by saying:

> Let us close our time together by expressing with our bodies what women's spirituality means to us. We are going to create a group sculpture, a still, nonverbal (and, perhaps joyful) pose.

> I invite one woman to enter the circle and choose a pose that embodies women's spirituality for her. Then, as you feel moved, I invite the rest of you to join your pose with hers until we have created a beautiful piece of group artwork.

Hold this group pose for a few moments.

Or, the group may simply close by gathering in a circle, offering thanks for being together and then saying together: We are women of spirit. We are women of peace. We seek healing and wholeness for ourselves and our world.

Looking Ahead — *5 min*

Share the following in your own words:

> At the end of each session, we will conclude by offering suggestions for reflection and action between now and the next session. These include a Life Practice, topics and questions for journaling, and readings in preparation for the next session.

Life Practice

> Life Practice will help you embody what you have learned and reflected on during each session. Before the next session:
>
> 1) Choose one or two aspects of women's spirituality that most speak to you. Each evening, reflect back on the ways that you have lived out or expressed these values during the day.
>
> 2) Choose an object that is special and, possibly, sacred to you. Bring it with you to the next session. To open Session 2, the group will create an altar together with the objects that each woman brings. You will have the opportunity to share why this object is important to you.

Journal Topics and Questions

> You are encouraged to keep a journal as a part of the *Traveling with the Turtle* process. Journaling is a valuable vehicle for self-discovery and self-knowledge.
>
> You may use the pages provided in this book or your own notebook to record your response to the topics and questions that are provided at the end of each session. Feel free to express your responses in whatever form you are most comfortable with—words, images, a collage, doodling, etc.
>
> What you write can be just for you or you might want to share some of your reflections with other group members during each session. You will be given the opportunity to do this with a partner at the beginning of each session.

Next Session's Readings

> To prepare for the next session, read the selections found at the end of this session.

Journal Topics and Questions

1) Why did you decide to enter into this process? Reflect further on what you shared with the group. Is there anything in particular that you would like to learn or do during the next 13 sessions? Any special needs you have? Keep these desires and needs in mind as you continue this journey.

2) If you have, how did you come to know the Holy One? What have been some of your most significant experiences?

Readings for Session 2

Guadalupe: The Path of the Broken Heart
By Clarissa Pinkola Estés

Listen young ones…you write to me because you have heard of our La Sociedad de Nuestra Senora, Guadalupe, our group of social activists dedicated to being contemplatives in the world. And you wish to know what to call the experiences you have been having. The old fashioned words are appearances and apparitions. But I advise you to just call them by simple words. They are visits, as from a great and beloved sistermother….

Now you write that all around you everything seems often in complete mayhem and this causes you great sadness. I would agree completely. Our own sorrows seem heavy enough…. But watching others hurt and hurting is the breaker of most any heart….And so here are your hearts still unruined. This is a very good sign…there is great power in the broken heart….The heart broken open can be a blessing beyond compare. It not only allows you to see others, it allows you to constantly see her….

When I was seven years old, the grownups from my home and school life told me that I had at last reached "the age of reason." Apparently, in spite of my many childhood jailbreaks, running away from the house to be in the massive cathedrals of the forest, or baptizing flowers and children smaller than I in the creek, or staying late in the forest at night to see the eerie swampfire, in spite of these semi-terrible transgressions, I, the little ecstatic childwanderer, was now qualified to be "reason-able."…

My aunt having told me that in the next thirteen days I would see thirteen things that would affect me for life, "that will call for your help, your hands, your heart for the rest of your life," I now tried to keep my eyes truly open. She had said, "You are a little child and you can still see what most who are older no longer care to see, you can see what needs help."….

So, many things did I see during those thirteen holy days that my aunt had prepared me for. But one of the most startling I saw [was] as I wandered down a dirt road through the far woods. A little ways down the road a big sheriff's car, in an even bigger cloud of dust, skidded to a stop off to the side of the road where a little deeper in the woods was a stick-pole encampment of some of the hobo people who regularly jumped from the freight train uproad and stayed for periods of time in our neck of the woods.

I think there are times when you can smell mal-intention coming. I quickly jumped into the field at the roadside and lay down to hide….The deputies jerked aside the canvas flap of the stick-pole tent and charged right in. Less than a minute later, amidst all hell breaking loose and with terrible sounds of cook pots clanging and falling and scuffling sounds, and much crying out and epithets, one deputy dragged a half-naked man in manacles from out of the canvas hovel.

He was dressed like many who lived hidden in that part of the woods, many who came up from the hills, some of whom I had made best friends with. His torn strappy T-shirt was gray with oils, his trousers were stained with paint and dirt. He was unwashed, unshaven, uncombed, and, like a bull roped to the ground, his eyes were rolling, his mouth slobbering as he cried out what sounded to me like, "Milady! Milady!" The deputy shoved the disheveled man into the patrol car and slammed the door and ran back to the tent.

As I watched frightened and horror-stricken, I thought I heard in my head a calm and gentle voice asking, "Do you love me?"

"Love you? Love you?" I thought. My anguish over what I was seeing was so great I could hardly comprehend the words being spoken into the ear of my heart.

"If you love me, comfort them."

"What?" I thought, trying to understand. Before I could react, the deputies dragged a screaming woman from the tent. She struggled against their manhandling of her. She had a short lit cigarette between two fingers, and she wore only one shoe, a broken-down black flat....The men had hold of her so-thin arms, like a corpse's almost, and right before my eyes they bent her arms backwards to angles not truly possible. And she was all flaming words and flailing limbs. She screamed and screamed and for one breathtaking moment I felt she looked directly at me, appealing directly to me, though surely she could not have seen me in the dense field across the road, "Help me, help me," she screamed again and again.

I heard a calm voice in my panicked heart ask:

"Do you love me?"

"If you do, then help me."

I felt deeply confused, yet I shot up like a quail. I had sudden turbines in my legs, my arms reaching ten feet ahead of me, my lungs filling with a gigantic thundercloud. My head back, I ran like a crazy child the distance down and across the road. The deputies were pushing her into the car, they were slamming the door on the couple. The officers piled into the front seat and slammed their own doors. I could still hear the woman screaming.

"Help me, help me."

Completely panicked but somehow able, I thought, "Yes, I will help you." Agonized still, but in a new way, I thought, "But how? How?"

I came up alongside the back end of the big sedan just as the car began pulling away. I yelled out loudly—I hope I called out in a voice that could be heard from earth to the heavens, but I am afraid that I was so filled with fear that maybe I only croaked. Yet, I felt I pulled in the breath of windstorms and that I thundered out as strongly as I could....."In Her name and all that is holy, do these people no harm!"

The deputies startled and braked the car. I just had enough time to throw myself across the trunk where the faces of the two haggard and manacled souls gazed up at me with what seemed like excellent wonder. I just had enough time, one split second, to use three of my fingers at once to make the Sign of the Cross on the dusty back window and cry out, "These souls are under my protection." Now the car window was rolling down on the driver's side. I skidded off the car and fell to the road....Now the door was opening on the driver's side. I scrambled to my feet, and ran as though a demon were chasing me....

I did not know what I enacted then or later. I am not ever certain yet these many years later. I only know I followed rather than led....

I do not know what the man and woman did wrong. Likely nothing. Vagrant. Talking too loud, making love too loud, or just by their presence disturbing the gentry who had come to build big houses out in the woods and who we knew were made uncomfortable by us, the truly rustic. I only know that the sounds of thuds of fists on bone is a truly sickening sound and the sound and feel of these were not unfamiliar to me before or after. Life went on. But for me, not as before....

Though I could go on as before, pick self up for thousandth time, millionth time, and go on because there was nothing else to do...—still, I could never forget. I had a strange moment in time, what I someday would come to understand as the transformative moment, as when lightning strikes, and all vision and knowing is changed in an instant. On the road with the people in the woods, I thought I had seen the holy people being manhandled. Through the back of the car window, those poor imprisoned innocents, I thought I saw for a moment, both of them, man and woman, as mi Guadalupe. I thought for a split second, I saw in both of them mi Guadalupe suffering. I thought I saw Her being assaulted. This was the end of my life as I had known it to that time. "Do you love me? Then help me." This was one of my thirteen post-consecration callings.

When I told my aunt what had happened, she cried and took my hands. "You do not have to ask who says, 'They are under my protection,'" she said. "You already know."

I felt I did know.

Twelve years later, when I was nineteen, I heard this from Her:

"Do you love me, my sister?"

I answered, "Yes, my Dear One, I love you."

"How much do you love me?"

"With all my heart, my Beloved."

"Will you then visit me in prison?"

"In prison?"

I was afraid to go to prison. But I went, as I would go on pilgrimage in the ensuing years to other prisons, those made by government, and those many, many soul prisons, human-made, and to my own imprisonments, as well, some of choice, some by fate.

I promised then that if I kept hearing Her call, I would try to keep going where sent. As you can see, I am a fool for Her completely. I am still going. This time it is the immigration jail; other years, it has been pilgrimages several times a year to other places—the locked institution for boys aged eighteen to twenty-one, the locked institutions for girls and boys aged twelve to eighteen, the men's penitentiary, the women's federal prison, the city and the county jails, the state prisons, sometimes ministering to patients at city hospitals brought in chains for a needed surgery.

It goes on, as it always has. Do you love me?

Yes, I love you.

Will you then come visit me in the home for unwed mothers? I would—and there the next sword was run through my heart.

Do you love me?

Yes, I love you.

Will you help run a shelter for battered women? Will you lick the wounds of the wounded?

Yes. Another sword. Do you love me?

Yes, I love you, my Dear.

Will you walk with me through skid row with alcohol swabs and wipe hands and feet teeming with bacteria, the cuts and hurts of the men and women who can hardly be told apart. Will you do that for me?

Yes. A big sword.

Do you love me? With all that I am.

Will you stand in the cold of a Chicago night in the dead of the winter listening to me dressed as an old man telling his life's tale with the worst breath you could ever imagine?

Yes, this I can do.

Do you love me? Do you love me?

Yes, yes, a thousand times yes.

So, m'hijas y m'hijos, now I am at the end of this missive to you. You have asked me the way to continue and to deepen your devotion to Her. I have this great feeling in my bones that you already well know the way and just need a tiny little reminder: She comes in untidy ways mostly, often in very big and very bold form rather than demure. You will recognize Her on sight, for She is a woman who looks just like you and all that you love.

Mi Guadalupe is a girl gang leader in heaven.
She is unlike the pale blue serene woman.
She is serene, yes, like a great ocean is serene.
She is obedient, yes, like the sunrise is obedient to the horizon line.
She is sweet, yes,
like a huge forest of sweet maple trees.
She has a great heart, vast holiness and like any girl gang leader ought, substantial hips.
Her lap is big enough to hold every last one.
Her embrace can hold us,
All.

Source: Ana Castillo, ed., *Goddess of the Americas.*

History of the Goddess

"In the beginning, people prayed to the Creatress of Life....At the very dawn of religion, God was a woman. Do you remember?" So wrote Merlin Stone in a book that inspired many to seek to uncover the history of the Goddess.

Paleolithic Era

The first evidence of religious ritual originates several million years after the famed "Lucy" and her ancestors—thought to be the first humans—appeared in Africa. From 70,000 to 50,000 B.C.E., Neanderthal peoples often buried their dead in the fetal position, perhaps returning them to the Mother of the Living and the Dead.

From 32,000-10,000 B.C.E., the late Old Stone Age, many carved female statues were produced. Images of animals were painted deep within well-known caves. Historian G. Rachel Levy proposes that Paleolithic people understood the cave to be the womb of the Creatress, the Great Mother. In Neolithic and Bronze Age Crete, rituals were celebrated in caves, entering into the darkness of the womb in order to be reborn.

The Neolithic "Revolution"

During the Neolithic Era or the New Stone Age (10,000-8000 B.C.E.) women's status was high because they played central roles in farming, weaving, and the making of pots. These new discoveries, such as the invention of agriculture where seeds grew to be plants that in turn became food eaten by the community, were seen as mysteries brought by the Goddess. The primacy of the Goddess in Neolithic religion was a reflection of the indispensable roles of women in this society.

Old Europe

Archaeologist Marija Gimbutas uses the term Old Europe to differentiate the Neolithic and Copper Age cultures of southern and eastern Europe from 6500 to 3500 B.C.E., from the patriarchal societies that came after them. Gimbutas describes the first culture as matrifocal, where power and possessions are passed down through women, and peaceful, while the second one is patrifocal and warlike. In Old Europe, the Goddess was worshiped as the Giver, Taker, and Renewer of Life. In this worldview, all of nature was seen as part of her body and symbolic of her power. Women played central roles in the creation of Old European religion and probably in its rituals.

Catal Huyuk

Archaeologist James Mellaart found a culture similar to that of Old Europe in the Neolithic town of Catal Huyuk (c. 6500-5650 B.C.E.) where central Turkey is now located. Mellaart suggests that there, too, women played important roles in the cultural and religious life of the town. The Great Goddess was worshiped and no evidence of warfare was found.

The Rise of Patriarchy and War
In a survey of sex roles and power based on information from 150 different societies, Peggy Reeves Sanday discovered a strong contrast between societies that celebrated "female power" and those based on male domination. She found that in societies where nature is considered sacred, women have more power but are not dominant. There is a strong correlation between Goddesses or female Creators, the participation of women in religious roles, and female power in society.

Societies based on male domination are organized around hunting, animal husbandry, and larger-scale agriculture. These societies are not egalitarian. Women and nature are viewed as objects to be exploited or ruled. A male priesthood leads to worship of male gods.

In keeping with these findings, the peaceful and egalitarian matrifocal societies of the Neolithic Period came to an end as nature was harnessed through centrally organized agriculture. This development allowed some individuals to control large areas of land. The invention of deadly weapons and the establishment of warfare as a way of life, perhaps to protect one's land, hastened this process. Other societies were attacked by warrior groups. Carol Christ states, "In my opinion, the institutionalizing of warfare as a way of life (however it occurs) is the single most important factor leading to the subordination of women." (p. 61) Men are trained to become violent and dominant and are rewarded by the right to rape "enemy" women.

Slaying the Goddesses
In classical Greek and Near Eastern myths, Goddesses of the Neolithic and Paleolithic eras are slain or made subordinate to the new Gods of the patriarchal warriors—e.g., Zeus. "The goal is to dethrone the Goddess and to legitimate the new culture of the patriarchal warriors." (p. 62) In the Judeo-Christian tradition, as well, Scripture attempts to halt worship of the Goddess. In Genesis 2-3, Eve is called "The Mother of All the Living." She and the snake, an ancient symbol of the Goddess, are blamed for bringing suffering into the world.

Contemporary Goddesses
The Goddess, the Divine Feminine, lives on in the Jewish image of Shekinah, in Sophia/Wisdom in Judeo-Christian Scripture and in Mary in the Christian tradition. In Mexico, the shrine of the Virgin of Guadalupe is built on a hill sacred to a pre-Aztec Goddess. In Ireland, the sacred fire of the Goddess Brigid was kept burning by nuns living at a monastery said to be founded by St. Bridget.

Today in India, Hindus worship the Goddess Kali, as the one who brings both life and death. In Buddhism, Tara, the Mother of All Deities, is prayed to for an end to human suffering, and Kuan Yin, the Goddess of Compassion, is a source of deep understanding and compassionate wisdom.

Source: Adapted from Carol Christ, *Rebirth of the Goddess: Finding Meaning in Feminist Spirituality*.

Ritual
By Patricia Mathes Cane

From earliest times, the clan, group, or community gathered together to ritualize significant moments of life, death, and passage. With the advance of modern culture the focus of ritual shifted away from the circle of community, and the power to lead was taken over by priests or leaders….In many cultures ritual has been a resource for people to deal with grief, loss, and emotional pain. Rituals and gatherings in the circle have provided ways to reclaim the healing power of community and to make meaning out of difficult moments that people have experienced individually or as a group….

The power of the gathered circle is recognized by Christina Baldwin in *Calling the Circle: The First and Future Culture*. Baldwin describes meetings in a circle as challenging five thousand years of enculturation. In the gathering "power will be shared, opened up, dealt with differently, so that we may find a new way of being together." The ritual circle also offers a way of moving from being a passive spectator to being a creator of the ritual experience. Maria Harris, writing on feminist spirituality, says that it is important to create rituals that "do include us, speak for us, and place us in the position of celebrants and full participants in the community work of acknowledging the continuing Presence of Goodness gifting our lives…"

Besides formal religious ceremonies, there are also many other kinds of rituals that touch the ordinary moments of life. One definition of the word "ritual" is "a pattern of activity that is repeated over and over again," like a ritual afternoon cup of tea, a ritual bath, or the way some families eat their main meal together. Elinor Gadon in *The Once and Future Goddess* describes another aspect of the word: "'Ritual' comes from 'rtu', Sanskrit for menses. The earliest rituals were connected to the woman's monthly bleeding….Women's periodic bleeding was a cosmic event, like the cycles of the moon and the waxing and waning of the tides. We have forgotten that women were the conduit to the sacred mystery of life and death." With mindful attention to the many human and ordinary moments of life, ritual can imbue them with extraordinary meaning.

Personal Rituals

- Candle Rituals: Lighting a candle to connect with the Light within—at a difficult moment, a time of distress or depression, at a time of joy, for a dinner celebration, to honor the memory of a loved one.
- Cleansing Rituals to cleanse negative energy or difficult memories: a ritual prayer; a ritual shower or bath; a cleansing diet or fast; use of water, salt, music or incense to clear negative energy.
- Forgiveness Rituals to forgive and let go of the past: a prayer, a ritual gesture with another person.
- Thanksgiving Rituals to acknowledge the blessings of life: a prayer, candle, flower, gesture.
- Rituals of Remembrance to connect with: persons who have died, events of the past, special moments.
- Creation of a Sacred Space: an altar or some simple place in the home where images, flowers, photos of loved ones, momentos, elements of nature, and written prayers may be reverently placed.

Source: Patricia Mathes Cane, *Trauma Healing and Transformation: Awakening a New Heart with Body Mind Spirit Practices.*

Feminist spirituality:

- *Regards the human race as one humanity in [varied] genders and sets out to make the fullness of humanity available to [all] of them.*
- *More than that, it undertakes to release the energy of the human race. When female talents, gifts, and ideas become accessible to the human enterprise unhindered by social barriers or official limitations, then and only then...will we get a glimpse of the full face of [the Divine]....*
- *Commits itself to the equality, dignity, and humanity of all persons to such an extent that it sets out to secure the societal changes necessary to achieve that reality for both women and men....*
- *The real development of the human race...depends on the equal partnership of women and men, not the oppression of one for the indulgence of the other. Feminism makes humans of us all.*

Source: Joan D. Chittister, *Heart of Flesh: A Feminist Spirituality for Women and Men.*

Session 2

Empowering Images of the Divine

Session 2
Empowering Images of the Divine

In this Session We Will:

- Explore our images of the Divine, especially feminine ones, some of which may be new and different to some of us
- Reflect on which of these images most empower and heal us as women
- Consider the role that ritual plays in our lives

Agenda

Introduction — *2 min*
Reflections from the Last Session — *10 min*
Opening Ritual: Creating a Group Altar — *20 min*
Exploring Our Images of the Divine — *60 min*
What Rituals Do You Practice? — *20 min*
Closing — *5 min*
Looking Ahead — *3 min*
        Life Practice
        Journal Topics and Questions
        Readings

Materials Needed

- ☐ Shared Agreements
- ☐ Small prayer table
- ☐ A colorful cloth to cover the table
- ☐ A candle
- ☐ Matches
- ☐ Objects that each woman brings for the altar
- ☐ Flipchart
- ☐ Easel paper
- ☐ Markers
- ☐ Books that have feminine images of the Divine—pictures, photographs— such as *Rebirth of the Goddess: Finding Meaning in Feminist Spirituality* by Carol Christ or *The Mother's Song: Images of God the Mother* by Meinrad Craighead or statues, artwork, etc. (if available)
- ☐ Compact disk or audiotape player (if desired)
- ☐ Recorded music (if desired)

Facilitator Notes
Session preparation — The week before
- Review the entire session. Practice reading any visualizations or meditations, and role-play or practice setting up and facilitating exercises beforehand. Whenever possible, put material into your own words. Feel free to make notes on 3x5 cards or in the book next to the written instructions.

Session preparation — The day of
- Arrange the chairs, including your own, in a circle, with a small table in the center. Place the cloth, candle, and matches on the table.
- Tape the Shared Agreements to the wall.
- Play some background music as people arrive, if desired.

Session 2
Empowering Images of the Divine

Introduction — 2 min

Convey in your own words:

> Welcome to Session 2. In Session 1, we began our exploration of women's spirituality and peacemaking. Now we turn to the Holy One who walks with us on our journey toward wholeness, illuminating our way. We will share with each other our different images of the Divine, deepening our appreciation of the Feminine Divine in whose image we are made. We will reflect on which of these images are the most empowering and healing for us as women. And, we will explore what role ritual plays in our lives.

Remind everyone about the Shared Agreements.

Reflections from the Last Session — 10 min

Explain the following:

> At the beginning of each session, we will find a partner. Perhaps we could pair with a different woman each time. We will then share with our partner any insights that came up or experiences we had between sessions, or reflections we had on the life practice, journal questions, or readings.

Invite the women to do this now.

Opening Ritual — 20 min
Creating a Group Altar

Light the candle. Then convey the following in your own words:

> Take several deep breaths. Let go of any distractions and worries that you are carrying with you so you can enter into this precious time and space.
>
> You were invited to bring to this gathering an object that is sacred and special to you to place on a group altar that we will create together. When you are ready, I invite you to place your object on the altar and share with the group why it is important to you.

After everyone has shared, say:

> Take a moment to gaze upon this beautiful altar that we have created together. (*Pause*)

As we look at these objects that are sacred to us, let us close our ritual by saying together: We are women of spirit. We are women of peace. We seek healing and wholeness for ourselves and our world.

Exploring Our Images of the Divine — 60 min

Brainstorm: Names of the Divine — *10 min*

Say:

> We created a group altar to honor the Divine who is with us now. Throughout our lives, we have probably been taught to address the Holy One by a variety of names. Let us briefly brainstorm images or names of the Divine (some of which may now have negative connotations for us) that come to mind spontaneously, images that were instilled in us by church, family, or society.

As each woman calls out her response, record it on easel paper.

Creating a Personal Altar Visualization — *20 min*

Then say in your own words:

> We have before us many names of the Divine, some of which resonate with us and some that don't. Now we are going to visualize who the Divine, the One whom we find in the core of our sacred selves, is for us now at this point in our lives. We are going to envision creating a personal altar for the Holy One.

> Find a partner. Sit next to each other and close your eyes. Take time to enter into the visualization and then, if you desire, share with each other what you discovered during your meditation.

Read this meditation slowly:

> Imagine that you are going to create a personal altar.

> - Where would this sacred space be?
> - What cloth would you drape on a table, on a shelf, or on the floor?
> - What objects, images, or pictures would you place on it?
> - Most importantly, what image of the Divine would you put on the altar among these other items that are so dear to you? Enter into the deepest part of yourself and engage all of your senses: sound—of music playing or of silence, touch—the feel of dark, rich soil or of a human hand, taste, smell, and sight.

Source: "Creating a Group Altar" was developed with Colleen Nakamoto.

Invite group members to share with their partner what they discovered during this visualization. When everyone is finished, ask them to return to the large group.

Large Group Reflection — *30 min*

Then, share:

> We are going to spend a little more time exploring our images of the Divine.

If you have pictures that portray the Divine as feminine, pass them around the circle and give the group time to look at them. If you do not have pictures, say:

> In some religious or spiritual traditions, the Divine has been portrayed as feminine—as the Bearer of all Life, as Mother Wisdom, as Woman Spirit, as a Many-Breasted Goddess.

Then say:

> Take a moment to gaze upon these pictures consider such images that depict the Holy One as feminine. These images are important because women's spirituality emphasizes how necessary it is that we as women come to believe that we, too, are created in the image of the Divine, that She is woman like us.

YHVH Giving Birth
By Lynn Gottlieb

YHVH giving birth
At the shores of the Red Sea
Squatting over the waters
Spreading her legs wide.
Women dancing in the salt seawaters
Midwives at Her occasion
YHVH's birth cries
Sounds of jubilation
As a people is born
YHVH midwife woman
With strong arms and outstretched hands
Opening Her womb,
Giving birth to freedom...

Source: *She Who Dwells Within: A Feminist Vision of a Renewed Judaism.*

Ask the group to reflect on the following questions:

- Do images of the Feminine Divine speak to you or are you unfamiliar or uncomfortable with them?
- Given the array of images of the Divine that we have brainstormed and then visualized on our altar, which images of the Divine do you find to be the most healing and empowering for you as a woman?

What Rituals Do You Practice? — *20 min*

Introduce this reflection in your own words:

> We have shared the myriad ways that we image the Divine. Whatever our image of the Holy One is, how do we draw closer to Her or Him, to the Source of Creation? Ritual is one way of connecting with the Divine or with our deepest, most authentic selves. Ritual can be defined, writes Patricia Mathes Cane, as "a pattern of activity that is repeated over and over again," like a ritual afternoon cup of tea, a ritual bath, or the way some families eat their main meal together. Both individual and communal rituals (such as creating a group altar) are an important expression of women's spirituality.

Any ritual is an opportunity for transformation. To do ritual, you must be willing to be transformed in some way. That inner willingness is what makes the ritual come alive and have power. If you aren't willing to be changed by the ritual, don't do it. Starhawk

---

Then ask the group:

- What rituals do you practice?

For example:

- What brings you healing?
- How do you mark special occasions?
- What brings you closer to the Holy One and yourself?

Invite the women to find a partner and respond to some of these questions. Then, bring the group back together and conclude with two or three sharings from participants.

Closing — *5 min*

Invite everyone to return to the large group and then read the following poem together:

On Being a Woman

Great Spirit
I am woman
Reflecting the great feminine side of you
I am fortunate because
I am close to you in this way

I have power to create, flowing through every particle of me
I share with all women this powerful gift of giving
And I don't mind the discomfort I bear for having this nature
The great basket of your love is my basket

Your powerful listening presence is my listening
The grand bowl of your potential is my bowl
Your great womb of creation is my womb
Where my greatest power lies

And I will give all of me in your name
And I will nurture and care for this world
Because that is what you do

And I will nurture and care for myself
Because I represent you
And I require honor and respect
Because I represent you

I will allow no abuse of myself or others
Because I represent you
And I will love my masculine side
Because that too is you

And I will love and respect men and children
Because you are in everyone
And I will support and uplift other women
Because you are in everyone
And I will treat animals and plants with respect
Because they too are you

And I will walk with nature and care for her
Because that is the incubator you have given us.

Source: Jose Luis Stevens, *Praying With Power.*

Images of the Divine Feminine in the Judeo-Christian Tradition

Hebrew Scripture

- Wisdom/Sophia (Greek word for Wisdom) is the female personification of God in the Hebrew Scriptures. More is written about Sophia in the Hebrew Bible than about Adam, Noah, Abraham, and Sarah.
- What She does is already portrayed elsewhere in the Scriptures as the field of action of Israel's God. Sophia is the creator of the cosmos, pervading it with her spirit: "When God set the heavens in place, I was present…when God established the foundations of the earth, I was by God's side, a master craftswoman." (Proverbs 8:27-31)
- She works in history to save Her chosen people, using Moses to lead the people of Israel to freedom. (Wisdom of Solomon, 10)
- She is all-knowing and all-powerful. She speaks as the Divine, claiming that listening to Her words will bring salvation.
- Sophia is portrayed as mother, sister, female lover, hostess, preacher, and an array of other roles.
- "Sophia is a significant symbol for contemporary women because she portrays the assertive, dynamic, activist woman….Sophia is an angry preacher who awakens us to the anger of [the Divine] and helps us to express our anger with patriarchy in church and society. Sophia, Woman of Justice, challenges us to work in solidarity with the poor and oppressed for the transformation of unjust structures. Sophia, the Liberator, who sets free the oppressed and the oppressors…empowers us to participate in her saving action in our local communities….As Birther of Creation, Sophia reveals our connectedness with one another and all earth's creatures. Sophia, the Caring Mother, nurtures us and shows us how to nurture ourselves and others."

Christian Scripture

- In many New Testament texts, Jesus is Sophia. "As…wisdom Christology shows, Jesus was so closely associated with Sophia that by the end of the first century he is presented not only as a wisdom teacher, not only as a child and envoy of Sophia, but ultimately even as the embodiment of Sophia herself." Source: Elizabeth Johnson, *She Who Is*.

- What Judaism said of Sophia, Christian hymn makers and epistle writers came to say of Jesus. "He is the one through whom all things are made." (1 Cor 8:6) Jesus acts as Sophia did, gifting those who love him with life. (Jn 17:2)

- The Gospel of Matthew in particular depicts Jesus as Sophia's child who befriends the outcast and communicates Her prophetic message.

- Paul calls Jesus the Christ, and then identifies Christ with Sophia. "We are preaching a crucified Christ who is the Wisdom of (Sophia) of God." (1 Cor 1:24-25) Divine Sophia is here manifest in solidarity with the one who suffers.

- John's entire Gospel, particularly the Prologue, is suffused with wisdom themes. The description of Jesus as Word or Logos is similar to the description of Sophia. John changes Sophia's name to Logos, Word of God, and then identifies this pre-existent, co-creator with Jesus. For John, Jesus is Sophia. Like Sophia, Jesus was present "in the beginning," is active in the creation of the world, and gives life to those who seek it." (Jn 1:1-18)

- "Since Jesus the Christ is depicted as divine Sophia, then it is not unthinkable—it is not even unbiblical—to confess Jesus…as the incarnation of God imaged in female symbol." Source: Elizabeth Johnson, *She Who Is*.

Sources: Excerpted and adapted from Bridget Mary Meehan, *Delighting in the Divine Feminine* (Elizabeth Johnson, *She Who Is* is quoted in Meehan).

Looking Ahead — *3 min*

In preparation for the next session, remind participants to do the Life Practice, journal topics and questions, and the next session's readings, found at the end of this session.

Life Practice

Take time to make some kind of altar at home if you don't already have one. Or create a simple ritual that affirms your beauty as a woman.

Journal Topics and Questions

1) When in your life have you acted in response to your "gut" feeling, your intuition, or drawn on a strength that seemed to just well up inside of you?

2) Spend some time reflecting on your relationship to your body. How do you feel about your body? Do you listen to what your body tells you—through its wisdom, intuition, passions and creative urges, through illness or fatigue?

Readings for Session 3

The Erotic as Power
By Audre Lorde

There are many kinds of power, used and unused, acknowledged or otherwise. The erotic is a resource within each of us that lies in a deeply female and spiritual plane, firmly rooted in the power of our unexpressed or unrecognized feelings....

As women, we have come to distrust that power which rises from our deepest and nonrational knowledge. We have been warned against it all our lives by the male world, which values this depth of feeling enough to keep women around in order to exercise it in the service of men, but which fears this same depth too much to examine the possibilities of it within themselves. So women are maintained at a distant/inferior position to be psychically milked, much the same way ants maintain colonies of aphids to provide a life-giving substance for their masters.

But the erotic offers a well of replenishing and provocative force to the woman who does not fear its revelation, nor succumb to the belief that sensation is enough....The erotic is a measure between the beginnings of our sense of self and the chaos of our strongest feelings. It is an internal sense of satisfaction to which, once we have experienced it, we know we can aspire. For having experienced the fullness of this depth of feeling and recognizing its power, in honor and self-respect, we can require no less of ourselves.

It is never easy to demand the most from ourselves, from our lives, from our work. To go beyond the encouraged mediocrity of our society is to encourage excellence. But giving in to the fear of feeling and working to capacity is a luxury only the unintentional can afford, and the unintentional are those who do not wish to guide their own destinies.

This internal requirement toward excellence which we learn from the erotic must not be misconstrued as demanding the impossible from ourselves nor from others. Such a demand incapacitates everyone in the process. For the erotic is not a question only of what we do; it is a question of how acutely and fully we can feel in the doing. Once we know the extent to which we are capable of feeling that sense of satisfaction and completion, we can then observe which of our various life endeavors bring us closest to that fullness.

The aim of each thing which we do is to make our lives and the lives of our children richer and more possible. Within the celebration of the erotic in all our endeavors, my work becomes a conscious decision—a longed-for bed which I enter gratefully and from which I rise up empowered....

When I speak of the erotic, then, I speak of it as an assertion of the life force of women; of that creative energy empowered, the knowledge and use of which we are now reclaiming in our language, our history, our dancing, our loving, our work, our lives....

The erotic functions for me in several ways, and the first is in providing the power that comes from sharing deeply any pursuit with another person. The sharing of joy whether physical, emotional, psychic, or intellectual, forms a bridge between the sharers that can be the basis for understanding much of what is not shared between them, and lessens the threat of their difference.

Another important way in which the erotic connection functions is the open and fearless underlining of my capacity for joy. In the way my body stretches to music and opens into response, hearkening to its deepest rhythms, so every level upon which I sense also opens to the erotically satisfying experience, whether it is dancing, building a bookcase, writing a poem, examining an idea.

That self-connection shared is a measure of the joy that I know myself to be capable of feeling, a reminder of my capacity for feeling. And that deep and irreplaceable knowledge of my capacity for joy comes to demand from all of my life that it be lived within the knowledge that such satisfaction is possible, and does not have to be called marriage, nor god, nor an afterlife.

This is one reason why the erotic is so feared, and so often relegated to the bedroom alone, when it is recognized at all. For once we begin to feel deeply all the aspects of our lives, we begin to demand from ourselves and from our life-pursuits that they feel in accordance with that joy which we know ourselves to be capable of. Our erotic knowledge empowers us, becomes a lens through which we scrutinize all aspects of our existence, forcing us to evaluate those aspects honestly in terms of their relative meaning within our lives. And this is a grave responsibility, projected from within each of us, not to settle for the convenient, the shoddy, the conventionally expected, nor the merely safe.

During World War II, we bought sealed plastic packets of white, uncolored margarine, with a tiny, intense pellet of yellow coloring perched like a topaz just inside the clear skin of the bag. We would leave the margarine out for a while to soften, and then we would pinch the little pellet to break it inside the bag, releasing the rich yellowness into the soft pale mass of margarine. Then, taking it carefully between our fingers, we would knead it gently back and forth, over and over, until the color had spread throughout the whole pound bag of margarine, thoroughly coloring it.

I find the erotic such a kernel within myself. When released from its intense and constrained pellet, it flows through and colors my life with a kind of energy that heightens and sensitizes and strengthens all my experience.

We have been raised to fear the yes within ourselves, our deepest cravings. But, once recognized, those that do not enhance our future lose their power and can be altered. The fear of our desires keeps them suspect and indiscriminately powerful, for to suppress any truth is to give it strength beyond endurance. The fear that we cannot grow beyond whatever distortions we may find within ourselves keeps us docile and loyal and obedient, externally defined, and leads us to accept many facets of our oppression as women.

When we live outside ourselves, and by that I mean on external directives only, rather than from our internal knowledge and needs, when we live away from those erotic guides from within ourselves, then our lives are limited by external and alien forms, and we conform to the needs of a structure that is not based on human needs, let alone an individual's. But when we begin to live from within outward, in touch with the power of the erotic within ourselves, and allowing that power to inform and illuminate our actions upon the world around us, then we begin to be responsible to ourselves in the deepest sense. For as we begin to recognize our deepest feelings, we begin to give up, of necessity, being satisfied with suffering and self-negation, and with the numbness that so often seems like the only alternative in our society. Our acts against oppression become integral with self, motivated and empowered from within.

In touch with the erotic, I become less willing to accept powerlessness, or those other supplied states of being which are not native to me, such as resignation, despair, self-effacement, depression, self-denial.

Recognizing the power of the erotic within our lives can give us the energy to pursue genuine change within our world, rather than merely settling for a shift of characters in the same weary drama.

For not only do we touch our most profoundly creative source, but we do that which is female and self-affirming in the face of a racist, patriarchal, and anti-erotic society.

Source: Audre Lorde, *Sister Outsider*.

Sentenced to Be Raped
By Nicholas D. Kristof

MEERWALA, PAKISTAN—I'm still trying to help out President Bush by tracking down Osama bin Laden. After poking through remote parts of Pakistan, asking for a tall Arab with a beard, I can't say I've earned that $25 million reward.

But I did come across someone even more extraordinary than Osama.

Usually we journalists write about rogues, but Mukhtaran Bibi could not be more altruistic or brave, as the men who gang-raped her discovered. I firmly believe that the central moral challenge of this century, equivalent to the struggles against slavery in the 19th century or against totalitarianism in the 20th, will be to address sex inequality in the third world—and it's the stories of women like Ms. Mukhtaran that convince me this is so.

The plight of women in developing countries isn't addressed much in the West, and it certainly isn't a hot topic in the presidential campaign. But it's a life-and-death matter in villages like Meerwala, a 12-hour drive southeast from Islamabad.

In June 2002, the police say, members of a high-status tribe sexually abused one of Ms. Mukhtaran's brothers and then covered up their crime by falsely accusing him of having an affair with a high-status woman. The village's tribal council determined that the suitable punishment for the supposed affair was for high-status men to rape one of the boy's sisters, so the council sentenced Ms. Mukhtaran to be gang-raped.

As members of the high-status tribe danced in joy, four men stripped her naked and took turns raping her. Then they forced her to walk home naked in front of 300 villagers.

In Pakistan's conservative Muslim society, Ms. Mukhtaran's duty was now clear: she was supposed to commit suicide. "Just like other women, I initially thought of killing myself," said Ms. Mukhtaran, now 30. Her older brother, Hezoor Bux, explained: "A girl who has been raped has no honorable place in the village. Nobody respects the girl, or her parents. There's a stigma, and the only way out is suicide."

A girl in the next village was gang-raped a week after Ms. Mukhtaran, and she took the traditional route: she swallowed a bottle of pesticide and dropped dead. But instead of killing herself, Ms. Mukhtaran testified against her attackers and propounded the shocking idea that the shame lies in raping, rather than in being raped. The rapists are now on death row, and President Pervez Musharraf presented Ms. Mukhtaran with the equivalent of $8,300 and ordered round-the-clock police protection for her.

Ms. Mukhtaran, who had never gone to school herself, used the money to build one school in the village for girls and another for boys—because, she said, education is the best way to achieve social change. The girls' school is named for her, and she is now studying in its fourth-grade class.

"Why should I have spent the money on myself?" she asked, adding, "This way the money is helping all the girls, all the children."

I wish the story ended there. But the Pakistani government has neglected its pledge to pay the schools' operating expenses. "The government made lots of promises, but it hasn't done much," Ms. Mukhtaran said bluntly.

She has had to buy food for the police who protect her, as well as pay some school expenses. So, she said, "I've run out of money." Unless the schools can raise new funds, they may have to close.

Meanwhile, villagers say that relatives of the rapists are waiting for the police to leave and then will put Ms. Mukhtaran in her place by slaughtering her and her entire family. I walked to the area where the high-status tribesmen live. They denied planning to kill Ms. Mukhtaran, but were unapologetic about her rape.

"Mukhtaran is totally disgraced," Taj Bibi, a matriarch in a high-status family, said with satisfaction. "She has no respect in society."

So although I did not find Osama, I did encounter a much more ubiquitous form of evil and terror: a culture, stretching across about half the globe that chews up women and spits them out. We in the West could help chip away at that oppression, with health and literacy programs and by simply speaking out against it, just as we once stood up against slavery and totalitarianism. But instead of standing beside fighters like Ms. Mukhtaran, we're still sitting on the fence.

Source: Nicholas D. Kristof, "Sentenced to be Raped," op-ed in *The New York Times*.

PART ONE

POWER-WITHIN

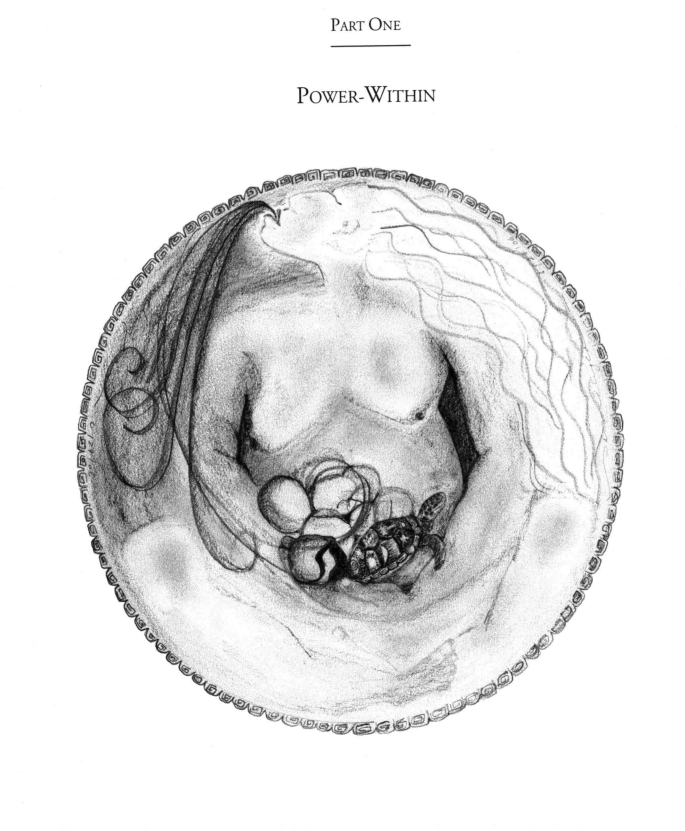

Session 3

Unleashing Our Power-Within

Session 3
Unleashing Our Power-Within

In this Session We Will:
- Discover the power, gifts, and body wisdom we each possess as women
- Recognize that accessing such power is an act of peace
- Reflect on ways to nurture our power-within

Agenda
Introduction — *2 min*
Reflections from the Last Session — *10 min*
Opening Ritual — *5 min*
Personal Power Place Meditation — *10 min*
Individual Reflection and Large Group Sharing — *40 min*
Nurturing Our Power-Within — *35 min*
Closing — *15 min*
Looking Ahead — *3 min*
      Life Practice
      Journal Topics and Questions
      Readings

Materials Needed
- ☐ Shared Agreements
- ☐ Prayer table
- ☐ A colorful cloth
- ☐ A candle
- ☐ Matches
- ☐ A mirror for the Closing
- ☐ Compact disk or audiotape player (if desired)
- ☐ Recorded music (if desired)

Facilitator Notes
Session preparation — The week before
- Review the entire session. Practice reading any visualizations or meditations, and role-play or practice setting up and facilitating exercises beforehand. Whenever possible, put material into your own words. Feel free to make notes on 3x5 cards or in the book next to the written instructions.
- You may wish to record the Personal Power Place meditation ahead of time for the group. If you choose to do so, be sure to read it slowly so that everyone can enter deeply into the meditation.

Session preparation — *The day of*

- Arrange the chairs, including your own, in a circle, with a small table in the center. Place the cloth, candle, and matches on the table.
- Tape the Shared Agreements to the wall.
- Play some background music as people arrive, if desired.

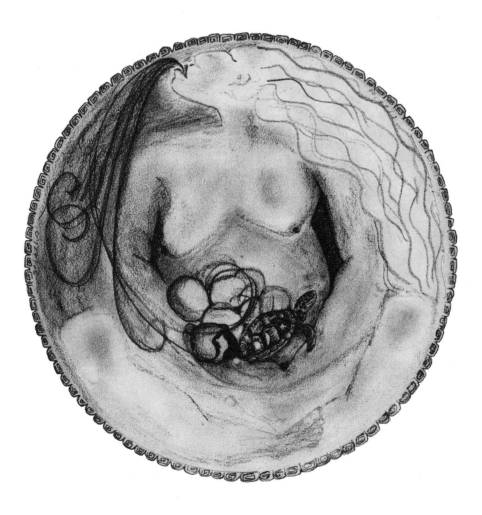

Session 3
Unleashing Our Power-Within

Introduction — *2 min*

Convey in your own words:

> Welcome to Session 3. In Session 2, we shared with each other our images of the Divine and the various rituals that we practice. Now we will discover and nurture our power-within that Pamela Cooper-White describes as "the power of one's own inner wisdom, intuition, self esteem, even the spark of the divine." The empowerment of ourselves as women is a cornerstone of women's spirituality. It stands in stark contrast to the way we often understand or experience power—as domination of or control over others. Claiming our power and voices as women is a subversive act of peacemaking in a society that primarily employs power-over.

> Source: Adapted from Pamela Cooper-White, *The Cry of Tamar: Violence Against Women and the Church's Response.*

Remind everyone about the Shared Agreements.

Reflections from the Last Session — *10 min*

Share the following:

> Find a partner and share with her any insights that came up or experiences you had between sessions, or reflections you had on the Life Practice, journal questions, or readings.

Opening Ritual — *5 min*

Light the candle. Say:

> Let us take a few moments to breathe. *(Pause)* Let us open our sacred space by saying together:

> We are women of spirit. We are women of peace. We seek healing and wholeness for ourselves and our world.

Read the following reflection:

Imagine a Woman

Imagine a woman who believes it is right and good she is woman,
   A woman who honors her experience and tells her stories,
      One who refuses to carry the sins of others within her body and life.

Imagine a woman who believes she is good,
   A woman who trusts and respects herself, who listens to her needs and desires,
      And meets them with tenderness and grace.

Imagine a woman who has acknowledged the past's influence on the present,
   A woman who has walked through her past
      Who has healed into the present.

Imagine a woman who authors her own life,
   A woman who exerts, initiates, and moves on her own behalf,
      Who refuses to surrender except to her truest self
         And to her wisest voice.

Imagine a woman who finds [the Divine] in herself,
   A woman who imagines the Divine in her image and likeness,
      Who designs her own spirituality and allows it to inform her life.

Imagine a woman in love with her own body,
   A woman who believes her body is enough, just as it is,
      Who celebrates her body, its rhythms and cycles
         As an exquisite resource.

Imagine a woman who honors the face of [the Divine] in her changing face,
   A woman who celebrates the accumulation of her years and her wisdom,
      Who refuses to use precious energy
         Disguising the changes in her body and life.

Imagine a woman who values the women in her life,
   A woman who sits in circles of women,
      Who is reminded of the truth about herself when she forgets.

Conclude by proclaiming together:

Imagine yourself as this woman!

Source: Patricia Lynn Reilly, "Imagine a Woman," in *A God Who Looks Like Me: Discovering a Woman-Affirmative Spirituality.*

Personal Power Place Meditation — *10 min*

Tell the group:

> We are going to imagine that we are the woman described in the opening reflection by doing a guided meditation that leads us to that deepest place within ourselves where we can experience ourselves as enough, as good, as holy.
>
> You will travel to that place where your power and the gifts that you have to offer our world reside. You will be invited to think of one particular time when you sensed that inner power.
>
> Find a comfortable position—either sitting or lying on the ground. Close your eyes. Again, pay attention to your breathing.

Either play the tape of this meditation or read the meditation, slowly:

> Remember a time when you felt empowered. *(Pause for a significant amount of time.)* Breathe deep. Remember how you felt. How did you move? How did you breathe? Where do you carry that feeling in your body? Breathe into that place, let your breath carry you down like waves, flowing in and out, and let yourself rock on three deep waves, going deeper into yourself.
>
> Feel the flame you guard. Feel the spark at the core. Enter into it.
>
> It is like a landscape you can travel in. It is a place of power alive in you. Breathe here, feel your power. This is your place—make it real.
>
> Breathe deep….Look….In the center of this place, your place of power, is a gift. Feel it, touch it, hold it, look at it. This is your gift. Feel how you move with it, dance with it, carry it in your place of power….
>
> Your gift can sustain you. Your gift can heal you. Know how to use it.
>
> Take your time, explore this place, find what is in it for you. *(Pause)*
>
> When you are ready to leave, return to the center of your place.
>
> Breathe deep…and say goodbye and thanks….Say goodbye and thanks to anyone you have met here. Remember your gift and know how you will carry it back with you. And remember what is at the center of your place of power so you can find it again just by breathing and remembering.

Feel your breath now, like waves flowing in and out of that place in your body where you carry power. Feel yourself ride the waves. Say goodbye, and come back on three deep breaths, coming back, bringing back knowledge and memory and gifts, and feel yourself fully present again in the circle, in this room.

Breathe deep, move, stretch, open your eyes, and say your own name out loud.

Source: Starhawk, *Truth or Dare: Encounters with Power, Authority and Mystery.*

Individual Reflection and Large Group Sharing — *40 min*

Invite the women to return to the large group. Ask them:

- What power or gift did you discover?
- How did you feel as you discovered this gift, this power?
- Where do you feel it in your body?

Reflect in silence for a moment. *(Pause)*

When or if you are ready, share your discovery with the group. This might include indicating the part of your body where this power resides.

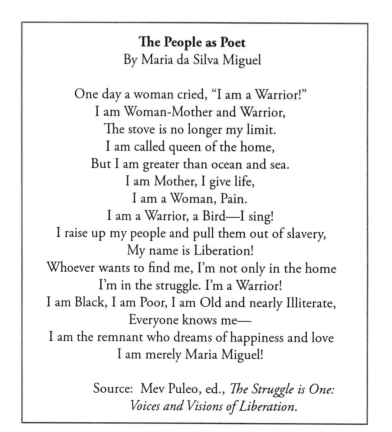

The People as Poet
By Maria da Silva Miguel

One day a woman cried, "I am a Warrior!"
I am Woman-Mother and Warrior,
The stove is no longer my limit.
I am called queen of the home,
But I am greater than ocean and sea.
I am Mother, I give life,
I am a Woman, Pain.
I am a Warrior, a Bird—I sing!
I raise up my people and pull them out of slavery,
My name is Liberation!
Whoever wants to find me, I'm not only in the home
I'm in the struggle. I'm a Warrior!
I am Black, I am Poor, I am Old and nearly Illiterate,
Everyone knows me—
I am the remnant who dreams of happiness and love
I am merely Maria Miguel!

Source: Mev Puleo, ed., *The Struggle is One:
Voices and Visions of Liberation.*

Nurturing Our Power-Within — 35 min

Share the following in your own words:

> We have shared with each other the power or gift we discovered within ourselves. How do we nurture what we have just discovered? How do we cultivate our power-within so that, as Audre Lorde writes, we can "begin to live from within outward, in touch with the power of the erotic within ourselves, and allowing that power to inform and illuminate our actions upon the world around us"?

> How do we learn to listen to and trust that internal sense of satisfaction, our capacity for experiencing joy, that *yes* that Lorde speaks of?

Invite the women to form groups of three and respond to these questions:

1) In your daily life, what helps you listen to and affirm your deepest feelings, your power-within, your erotic power? (For example: Do you exercise? Do you spend time in nature? Do you talk with close friends?)
2) Which of your life activities bring you the most satisfaction and joy?

Ask everyone to return to the large group. Take a few minutes to see if there are any further insights or reflections that anyone would like to share.

Closing — 15 min

Share the following in your own words:

> We have touched our power-within as women. We have touched our joy. Let us close by affirming that each of us is brilliantly beautiful in our own unique way. We are going to pass around a mirror. Hold the mirror, gaze into it if you want and the group will say to you: "(Name of the woman), you are good, beautiful, strong, and holy." After the group has spoken to you, you are invited to say the same phrase either in a whisper, or a shout, or, if you prefer, simply hold the mirror in silence.

After the mirror has been passed around the circle, say:

> We will close by saying together: "We are good, beautiful, strong, and holy."

Caring for Ourselves: Salute to the Sun or the Moon

You may wish to include this body movement at some point during the session, or group members can simply read and practice it on their own.

This body movement meditation, based on the Yoga Salute to the Sun, helps us release tension and stress. It re-energizes our body-mind-spirit through re-connecting us to the cycles of nature, to the sun's energy. The Salute to the Sun can be a healing practice and used as a daily meditation, adapting each reflection to meet one's own needs.

The group can face the sun if it is out. If it is evening, the group can do a Salute to the Moon. Since the movement involves stretching, do the exercise carefully. If any participant has difficulty standing, she can do the movement seated.

1) **Connection with the Energy**: Stand with feet separated shoulder-width, knees bent. Before you start the Salute, look at your hands and rub them together for a few moments to feel the warmth of your energy. Then join your hands together at the level of your heart in prayer and gratitude. Center yourself and return to your sacred personal power place, grateful for the unique gift of your life.

2) **Greeting and Welcoming the Sun**: From a centered position, exhale and stretch your arms straight forward, palms facing down toward the Earth, thumbs crossed. Inhale deeply and move your arms upward to the sun until they are over your head. Being careful of your back, arch slightly backwards, opening in gratitude and joy to greet and welcome the sun's energy as it merges with your own energy.

3) **Basking in the Sun**: Open your hands to the heavens, arching your neck and back. Feel energy moving up from the earth through your body and into the heavens. Breathe in, receiving the fullness of the sun, breathe out all tension and fear. As you bask in the sun, open yourself to be bathed and nourished. Feel light and grace flooding through you. Feel fully alive as you bask in the light of the sun.

4) **Touching the Earth**: With arms stretched out slowly bend forward, hands and arms arching downward until your fingers touch the earth. (Be careful of your back and stretch only as far as is comfortable.) Inhale and then exhale as you begin to move toward the ground. Feel Her solidness beneath you, supporting you, loving you. Relax.

5) **Letting Go**: As you bend downward and touch the earth let go of all tension and stress in your body, mind, and spirit. Let go of any negative voices that speak to you from within or without. Breathe out completely all problems, fears, worries, and anxieties you may be carrying, letting these be absorbed and transformed in the earth. Surrender completely in this moment in deep faith and trust.

6) **Rebirth to New Life**: From the bent position gradually begin to move back upward inhaling fully the energy of the earth, filling yourself with new life. As you move back upward feel the new energy pulsing through your body, renewing you.

7) **Here I Am:** Come back to full standing position moving your arms upward and outward until your hands are at shoulder level, palms facing forward. Hold this position

for a moment. As you open to the new life pulsing within you, connect with the unique calling that you have in this lifetime. Open yourself to give this gift in full commitment. Yes! Here I am!

8) The Blessing: Bring your hands back again to chest level, palms together in the posture of prayer. As you feel the unique gift of your being, take a moment to feel gratitude and then return to the eternal silence of your soul. Bless the sun, bless yourself, and bless all beings.

Repeat the Salute a few times. As you complete the last series of movements, roll back up to straight position, while at the same time using your arms and hands to pull energy up from the Earth to cleanse and bless your body. Finish the movement by bowing to the sun, yourself, and to all of the people in the circle.

Personal Experience

Staff from a women's prison in Honduras found this to be wonderful exercise for the women prisoners, whom they respectfully refer to as women "deprived of their liberty."...Many of these women felt helpless in the face of...Hurricane Mitch...overwhelmed by worry for their families outside the prison. Elements of nature to them became terrifying. With the Salute to the Sun the women were able to reconnect with elements of nature, to let go of their emotional pain and fear, and to experience the healing of themselves as part of the cycles of the earth and the sun.

Source: Adapted from Patricia Mathes Cane, *Trauma Healing and Transformation: Awakening a New Heart with Body Mind Spirit Practices.*

Looking Ahead — *3 min*

In preparation for the next session, remind participants to do the Life Practice, journal topics and questions, and the next session's readings, found at the end of this session.

Life Practice

1) Re-read "Imagine a Woman" and continue to recite to yourself the mantra: "I am good, beautiful, strong, and holy."

2) Do something that nurtures your body and spirit, something that cultivates your power-within.

Note: Session 4 may be a challenging session for those of us who have experienced extreme forms of violence. You may want to glance at it ahead of time. Take care of yourself. If you need to excuse yourself from certain activities, or from the entire gathering, feel free to do so.

Journal Topics and Questions

1) Next time we will be looking at the emotion of anger. Before we meet again, take notice when or if you become angry. What physical sensations do you experience? What triggered this emotion? If you are not sure you are angry, check-in with your body to see what it is telling you.

2) Choose one of these experiences and reflect on what you did with your anger. First of all, did you know you were angry at the time? Did you express your anger in an indirect way (through sarcasm, blaming, sulking, etc.) or a direct way? Did you keep it stuffed inside?

Readings for Session 4

The Feminine Wound
By Sue Monk Kidd

[A] woman's awakening begins...as she experiences emptiness, self-negation, disillusionment, a deep-felt recognition of the limitation placed on women's lives, especially her own.

An experience of nothingness was what I encountered....In tasting what it meant to be female in my culture and faith, I felt, for the first time, a hidden despair lodged inside....

I had delusions that I was probably the only woman in the world with a wound like that. Later I would be surprised to discover that most women carry this wound, though it is usually buried and unnamed. Psychotherapist Anne Wilson Schaef's name for this wound is "the original sin of being born female." She writes,

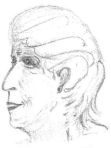

"To be born female in this culture means that you are born 'tainted,' that there is something intrinsically wrong with you that you can never change, that your birthright is one of innate inferiority. I am not implying that this must remain so. I do believe that we must know this and understand it as a given before it can be worked through."[14]

Of course, being female is not inferior at all, but that doesn't change the fact that women have often experienced it that way. Messages of inferiority and self-denial are passed to us all our lives, messages that we should deny our own experiences, feelings and needs. We absorb them in an ongoing process of osmosis that creates and enlarges the wound's core...

Peggy Orenstein's 1994 book, *Schoolgirls*, draws on a 1991 survey by the American Association of University Women, which suggests that parents and teachers seem to have lesser expectations for girls than for boys. Orenstein showed that girls' self-esteem is lost as they "dumb themselves down" and conform to lesser expectations to avoid being threatening. The girls in her study learned by adolescence not to be too outspoken, too aggressive, or too smart. They learned to balance drive with deference. The boys, by contrast, were rewarded for their drive and discouraged from showing deference. Girls learned to negate themselves through simple experiences: On the playground calling a boy "a girl" was the worst slur possible...

At church girls fare no better. A young girl learns Bible stories in which vital women are generally absent, in the background, or devoid of power. She learns that men go on quests, encounter God, and change history, while women support and wait for them. She hears sermons where traditional (nonthreatening) feminine roles are lifted up as God's ideal. A girl is likely to see only a few women in the higher echelons of church power...

She also experiences herself missing from pronouns in scripture, hymns, and prayers. And most of all, as long as God "himself" is exclusively male, she will experience the otherness, the lessness, of herself; all the pious talk in the world about females being equal to males will fail to compute in the deeper places inside her.

As a girl absorbs her culture, for instance as she watches movies and television, she may also come to understand that her real importance derives from her relationship with men and boys by how good she looks for them or how well she takes care of them. She will notice the things traditionally assigned to women—keeping a home, cleaning, cooking, laundry, child rearing—and grow aware of how little value these things seem to have in the world compared to things men typically do.

When she grows up and enters the workplace, she will likely plunge into the stagger-ing dilemma that is often hers alone—working while caring for children and keeping a house. She'll likely encounter ceilings, networks, and traditional assumptions that work against her as a woman. She will arrive at the disconcerting realization that success comes only as she learns to modulate and adapt her feminine self to a man's world....

The feminine wound is created as we *internalize* all these experiences—the voices we hear at church, school, home, work, and within the culture at large suggesting (in ways both bold and subtle) that women and feminine experience are "less than."

If you receive often enough the message that women are inferior and secondary, you will soon believe you are inferior and secondary. As a matter of fact, many experts tell us that "all women in our society arrive at adulthood with significant feelings of inadequacy."[16]

Once on an airplane I sat beside a thirty-year-old woman with a briefcase. As we chat-ted, a female voice came over the loudspeaker and said, "This is your captain." The woman stopped midsentence. "Oh no," she said, "a woman pilot." "I'm sure she's well trained," I said. "Right," she said, "but she's still a woman." Her feminine wound—her personal concentration of female inferiority had made a brief appearance...

Recognizing the feminine wound is important because in the end it's the only way we can stop being victims. We can't change anything until we acknowledge the problem. I'd been an unconscious victim before my awakening began. Discovering the truth was waking me up to my victimization, but it was also making it possible for me to move beyond it...

While holding onto the awareness, then, that we must not fall into shaping our identity as victims, we have to tell ourselves the "flat-out truth," as my grandmother used to call it...

But seeing such truth can be dangerous. Philosopher Mary Daly reminds us, "It isn't prudent for women to see all of this. Seeing means that everything changes: the old identifica-tions and the old securities are gone."[21]

The question, she says, is whether women can forgo prudence in favor of courage. That was the question that followed me as I made my way into the new year.

Source: Sue Monk Kidd, *The Dance of the Dissident Daughter*.

Working With Our Anger

What is Anger?
Anger is an emotion that tells us something is wrong. Anger can be a response to pain, hurt,

betrayal, or being ignored. Anger can be feeling out of control. It can be a feeling of rage or a response to injustice.

In Buddhism, anger is a mental state not a physical one. You become unable to bear a person, situation, or idea and so harbor ill will towards it or wish to harm it. Anger includes a whole range of emotions: annoyance, frustration, spite, resentment, and hatred.

Negative self-talk can contribute to anger. You blame other people for the way you feel. You label other people as bad. Or, you believe that, when they acted, other people intended to hurt you. In Buddhism, this is called "inappropriate attention." We exaggerate the negative qualities of a person, situation, or idea, or project onto them negative qualities that they do not possess.

How Can I Deal With My Angry Feelings?

1) *Learn to recognize your feelings*
One way of identifying anger is to notice your physical sensations. What emotions lie beneath your tight muscles or clenched jaw? Or, you can notice if you're in a bad mood and, again, ask yourself: "What am I really feeling? What happened to prompt these feelings?"

2) *Owning your feelings*
Your anger is your responsibility. Other people are not responsible for your feelings even if they said or did something that set you off. You can learn to accept your anger if you can let go of judging it. Anger is simply what you are feeling at the moment.

3) *Responding to your feelings*
If you are able to recognize and then own your anger, you will have a choice of when, where, and how, or if, you express it.

When My Buttons Are Pushed

In order to take more responsibility for your anger, you need to become aware of your anger buttons. In *The Anger Workbook for Women*, Laura J. Petracek reveals that there are three common themes that trigger women's anger: powerlessness, injustice, and the irresponsibility of other people. She lists several other things that also might trigger your anger: interpersonal relationships, being treated unfairly, unmet expectations, feeling stressed out, criticized, tired, or harassed.

Your sense of self-esteem or self-worth also affects how you handle anger. If you have high self-esteem, you are less likely to consent to feeling unnecessarily angry or bad about yourself. If you do not value yourself, you will get angry more easily at yourself and at others, and then react in unhealthy ways. You can build your self-esteem by taking responsibility for your relationships, expressing your anger and its underlying emotions the best you can, and, gradually, experiencing success in your communication with others.

Finally, it is also helpful to let go of the "Rules of the Universe." These include: "Everyone should like and appreciate me," and "Everyone should agree with my opinions." If you view people with these beliefs in mind you will more likely get into conflict with them and feel misunderstood, unappreciated, and unloved. These feelings are not coming from others but from your view of them. These "Rules" are some of your buttons.

What Can I Do With My Anger?

If you choose to express your anger or other emotions surrounding it, in Session 6, we will look at a four-step process for doing this. This process will enable you to address and transform a conflictual situation.

Buddhism offers a way for preparing for this nonviolent interaction. Buddhism believes that there is an alternative to expressing or suppressing anger. You can transform it within yourself. Buddhism teaches that each time you express anger, you strengthen the habit of feeling and then act out its violent energy. Suppressing anger doesn't get rid of it either, and may damage you mentally and physically.

Patience is an alternative—the ability to remain internally calm in the face of harm or conflict. Patience dissolves the anger-energy so that it no longer resides in you. It creates mental space so that you can choose the most appropriate behavior for a situation. Patience is not the action that you take; it is your attitude. *Nor is patience passivity.* Sometimes you might choose to respond strongly. Other times you might decide not to respond.

Buddhist Techniques for Working With Anger

Observing Our Anger
While sitting quietly, become aware of the physical and mental sensations that arise and pass as the anger flows through you. You may notice that your heart is pounding. You may realize that beneath the anger is hurt, pain, or betrayal. You can simply observe all of this, without reacting to any of the feelings by pushing them away. As you do this, you will be able to more easily recognize when you are feeling angry and, eventually, will watch these sensations arise and fade of their own accord.

Reframing the Situation (Can be done when you are not upset)
Again, sit quietly and remember a situation in which you responded in anger or an event that

brings back feelings of hurt or hostility. Try to view the situation from a new perspective. Evaluate your thoughts, feelings and perceptions to see if they are accurate. Envision yourself responding to the other person differently. This practice helps us dissolve past hurt and grudges, and prepares us to act the way we want to in situations of conflict. Focus on transforming your emotions and attitudes, rather than on what you should say or do. As you begin to transform your feelings, it will become easier to decide how to act.

Cultivating Love and Compassion

We can also learn to subdue our anger and cultivate positive emotions such as patience, love, and compassion. For helpful meditations see "The Ball of Light" in Session 4 and the Buddhist Practice of LovingKindness in Session 7.

Source: Adapted from Laura J. Petracek, *The Anger Workbook for Women* and Thubten Chodron, *Working with Anger.*

The Violence in Ourselves
By Dorothy Samuel

Ms. Samuel, while writing specifically to pacifists, speaks to us all about how to channel anger effectively. One can understand her essay also as an attempt to call those who have rejected violence also to embrace nonviolence as a positive action.

Consider the Richard Nixons, the My-Lai participants, the rapists brutally assaulting our freedom of movement, the stubborn and unethical bosses—even the husbands, wives, (lovers) and children who continually grate on our nerves. Pacifists though we may be, we are constantly reminded that there are surges of hatred, impulses of violence, within our own natures. And just because we are pacifists, people dedicated to love and compassion and tenderness, we are often paralyzed by these emotions in ourselves. Often we know no other response but to straitjacket them, even to deny them. We are ashamed of feeling fury, of experiencing violent anger, of the occasional mounting within us of a desire to see someone actually hurt.

It is my belief, based on years of experience with my own anger supplemented by recent exploration into the angers of other nonviolence adherents, that much of the ineffectiveness of peace people stems from their sense of shame. We are often incapacitated by our own angers, even by the remembrance that we have felt anger—real, nasty, pervasive anger. This shame can make us too tolerant of others—the criminal on the streets or the bully-child on the playground. Frequently, we hesitate to confront these people with the firmness they need—the very firmness their actions may be begging for. We are paralyzed by our own sense of guilt.

When this occurs, we actually become pliant victims of the vicious and the violent lest we loose our own anger, lest we become as coercive as they. We acquiesce to the less overt domineering and manipulation practiced by bosses or club associates or even self-selected pacifist leaders in the fear that confrontation might lead us to violence, if only psychic violence. We at times pamper and encourage the ruthless and insensitive behaviors of our own family members by giving positive, accepting feedback to negative and unacceptable affronts.

We feel that love means inoffensiveness at all costs. And we worship love, we pacifists, sometimes identifying love with a kind of patience and long-suffering quite unlike the personal example of that St. Paul whose 13th chapter of First Corinthians we quote. We may forget, in judging our own angers, that the love demonstrated by St. Paul and Jesus and Gandhi and Martin Luther King was a tough, firm, outspoken honesty that demanded the best from people; a love more accurately described by the Quaker injunction "speak truth to power" than by the passive acquiescence of "never make anyone unhappy."

I believe these great people accepted their anger, learned to use their anger. To "use" anger releases one from the destructive effects of anger—upon oneself and upon others. It is only diffuse, blood-heating, unfocused and unexpressed anger which short-circuits our rational powers, constricts our physical muscles, and makes us prisoners of fear—if only the fear of our own incapacity to act in a manner we consider worthy.

In my own experience, though I have not since I was a child touched anyone with physical violence, I have most certainly offered verbal and psychic violence to others at a level which appalls me. And I have found, on looking back, that this occurred only when I bottled up the anger in me with all the strength of my being. At such times, if the provocation continued too long for my powers, I finally exploded in nasty, vicious, and totally unredemptive abuse of the people involved. Unwilling to admit my anger, I was unable to use that anger, and the anger took control of me.

I am no longer ashamed of my angers and I no longer deny the existence of anger. I have, in fact, learned from less guilt-ridden areas just how effectively anger can be used.

I am not a large woman, nor an unusually strong one. Yet throughout my life, I have deliberately used anger to enable me to accomplish physical tasks otherwise beyond my strength—moving a piano, stretching a broken clothesline, lifting an injured child. In all these cases, I focused my anger on the situation—not on myself or my weakness, not on the person who "caused" the need, or the person who "should have been there." I focused my anger on the demands of the situation: I enjoyed the rush of adrenaline and the surge of strength; and I exulted when I had accomplished an "impossible" task. My anger was transformed into a tool under my conscious control, and its use as a tool left me with a kind of glory.

At first, of course, I did this without conscious understanding. But having experienced my own physical strength when angry, I began deliberately to call anger up when such strength was needed. Only much later did I recognize the same pattern in cases where I had used my anger constructively to meet violence or threat from the world around me. And I began to see the same use of anger in the great pacifists—and in the great acts of pacifists around me.

They used their angers; they were not engulfed by them. Neither were they incapacitated by a sense of guilt over feeling anger. They did not retreat in shame before their anger at persecution of German Jews, or the lynching of black people, or the carpet bombing of Vietnamese. They used that anger to confront an otherwise overwhelming situation. And in one-to-one situations, they did not deny their own anger at bullying of peaceful demonstrators or senseless attacks offered them on the street. They did not draw back in fear that their own anger might hurt the feelings of those caught up in violence.

Instead, they spoke truth to violence—in the home and on the job as well as in Washington. They stood up to attack—in the meeting houses and the conferences as well as on the protest lines. Their anger at the situations became a source of strength, an energizing power for creative response, for initiative action.

Anger is not the only source of strength, fortunately, nor is it the only motivating force, for creative response to attack. But when anger springs up as a natural response to an intolerable situation—not at individuals—it releases one from passivism, to creative pacifism—aggressive good will by which situations are transformed, and sometimes people too. It was anger-at-the situation which moved the retired school teacher in New York to draw herself up and tell the young hood, "You put that gun away!" Anger-at-the situation wiped out fear in a younger teacher in a large suburban high school when a boy she had just corrected slipped up behind her and held a gun at the back of her head. Turning at his call, she told him smartly, "School is no place for guns. Give that to me!" Both attackers obeyed. Confronted by a positive response empowered by fully controlled and focused anger—anger at the situation, not anger threatening them personally—their shoddy, diffused violence evaporated.

Gandhi, we all know, used his anger at the treatment of Indians in South Africa to launch a campaign which not only freed hundreds of thousands eventually from oppressive laws, but which immediately freed those who accompanied him from the corrosive inner decay and self-doubt of frustrated, repressed anger. Martin Luther King did the same for American blacks, and in the process both leaders actually did more for the oppressors' ultimate well-being than had generations of subservient encouragement to be their worst selves.

But I am not only thinking of the leaders of vast movements. I recall one instance when anger turned a thief's purposes inside out. A mother was cooped up in a hot car with three small, protesting children when a man came up to the open window, hand in pocket, and demanded her pocketbook. Out of her frustration and pain and absorption in her own life-style, she burst out, "Pocketbook! Do you know what's in my pocketbook? I haven't even enough money to buy the baby's milk, and the rent is due, and my husband just got laid off. My God! The price of eggs has gone up again."...On and on it flowed as she poured out her troubles as she might have to a friend or neighbor. The thief entered her scenario so fully that he dropped a ten-dollar bill into the car before he left.

Violence is never redemptive, never healthful. We are right to deny it a part in our lives. But we must not confuse violence with anger. Anger is a normal, human response to outrage, a bio-chemical marshalling of our forces and our strength. It is a response pattern to be admitted, controlled, and used like any other human quality—even, in time, to be enjoyed as one enjoys second wind. It is in the frustration of anger, the repression and denial of anger as something shameful, that it turns into an explosive force of destruction and violence.

Source: Dorothy Samuel, "The Violence in Ourselves," in *Fellowship Magazine*.

Session 4

What Gets in the Way?

Session 4
What Gets in the Way?

In this Session We Will:
- Consider what negative messages we have internalized about ourselves and the impact these voices have on our ability to claim our power-within
- Banish these negative voices
- Reflect on how we relate to our anger

Agenda
Introduction — *2 min*
Opening Ritual — *5 min*
What are My Negative Inner Voices Telling Me? — *35 min*
Banishing These Negatives Voices — *15 min*
How Do I Relate to My Anger? — *35 min*
Closing: Drumming Circle — *30 min*
Looking Ahead — *3 min*
       Life Practice
       Journal Topics and Questions
       Readings

Materials Needed
- ☐ Shared Agreements
- ☐ Prayer table
- ☐ A colorful cloth
- ☐ A candle
- ☐ Matches
- ☐ Sheets of construction paper cut into squares (four per sheet, one square for each woman)
- ☐ Markers and colored pencils
- ☐ Talking stick for How Do I Relate to My Anger? (if desired)
- ☐ A bowl in which you can burn pieces of paper, perhaps containing sand or rocks.
- ☐ Drums for everyone—either real ones or empty garbage cans, coffee tins, oatmeal boxes, an extra small table, etc., as well as spoons for those who would like to use them for drumming.
- ☐ Timer
- ☐ Compact disk or audiotape player (if desired)
- ☐ Recorded music (if desired)

Facilitator Notes
Session preparation — The week before

- Review the entire session. Practice reading any visualizations or meditations, and role-play or practice setting up and facilitating exercises beforehand. Whenever possible, put material into your own words. Feel free to make notes for this purpose on 3x5 cards or in the book next to the written instructions.
- Cut sheets of construction paper into four squares so that each woman will have one square for the exercise "What are My Negative Inner Voices Telling Me?"

Session preparation — The day of

- Arrange the chairs, including your own, in a circle, with a small table in the center. Place the cloth, candle, and matches on the table. Also place the bowl on the table.
- Tape the Shared Agreements to the wall.
- Play some background music as people arrive, if desired.

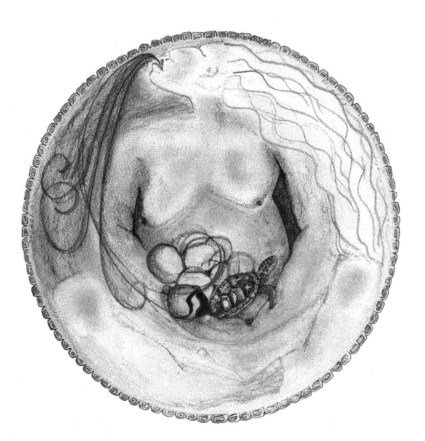

Session 4
What Gets In The Way?

Introduction — *2 min*

Convey in your own words:

> Welcome to Session 4. In Session 3, we discovered and nurtured our power-within. This time, as we gather, we will reflect on what keeps us from claiming this awesome power. We will consider what negative messages we have internalized about ourselves and the impact these voices have on our ability to claim our power-within. We will then banish these negative voices. We will also reflect on how we relate to our anger, considering what lessons we have been taught about expressing or not expressing this powerful emotion. Let us remember that women's spirituality invites us to love our emotions, bodies, minds, and spirits.

Remind everyone about the Shared Agreements.

Note: This may be a challenging session for those of us who have experienced extreme forms of violence. Take care of yourself. If you need to excuse yourself from certain activities, or from the entire gathering, please do so.

Reflections from the Last Session

Share the following in your own words:

> During this session we will be sharing what might be more intimate and sensitive areas of our lives with each other, so we need as much time and space as possible. Therefore, we will not share our reflections from the last session with a partner.

Opening Ritual — *5 min*

Light the candle. Say:

> Let us take a few moments to breathe. *(Pause)* Let us open our sacred space by saying together a mantra. It will become our group mantra that will open each ritual:

> We are good, beautiful, strong, and holy. We are women of spirit. We are women of peace. We seek healing and wholeness for ourselves and our world.

Then say:

> Now let's go around the circle and each clap a brief rhythm. We'll repeat whatever you clap.

After everyone has done that, invite everyone to clap together—beginning slowly and then more quickly as if you are applauding yourselves.

What are My Negative Inner Voices Telling Me? *— 35 min*

Share in your own words:

> In the last session, we listened to a reading by Patricia Lynn Reilly that invited us to imagine ourselves as "a woman who believes she is good, a woman who authors her own life, a woman in love with her own body, a woman who finds the Divine in herself."

> When you heard that you are this woman, were there "voices" inside of you arguing with you, telling you the opposite? Did you feel self-doubt or self-rejection? Find a partner and reflect on what Sue Monk Kidd calls in her selection "The Feminine Wound:" negative messages about yourself that you have internalized, messages that tell you that you are not "good, beautiful, strong, and holy."

After the women have reflected on these questions for awhile, give each of them a piece of construction paper. Ask each woman to write on it one of these negative messages that influences what she believes about herself.

Then say:

> I invite you to share your message with the group. What is your inner negative voice telling you?

After all of the women have read their statements, give these instructions:

> I now invite you, one at a time, to place your message on the floor in the center of the circle. Each time one message has been placed on the ground, everyone please position yourself—place your body—either close to or far away from the piece of paper depending on whether or not this is one of your internal negative voices. E.g., Stand on or close to the paper if you also often tell yourself this message, or further away from it, if you do not hear this inner voice.

Continue this exercise until all of the women have had the opportunity to place their messages in the middle of the circle and group members have positioned their bodies in response to them. If time permits, you may ask members of the group to share why they have chosen to stand where they are standing.

Banishing These Negative Voices — *15 min*

Share the following in your own words:

> These internalized negative messages come from somewhere. Perhaps we remember hearing them from a parent or a teacher, or in church. Maybe we were influenced by what we heard and saw in the media. Maybe these critical messages just seemed to be in the air around us.
>
> This is one way that the male-dominated society—patriarchy—that we live in exercises power-over us, by devaluing who we are as women. These messages criticize our emotions, our bodies, our abilities, our very being.
>
> We listened to these messages so long that we began to believe them. But this is not who we are! We are good, beautiful, strong, and holy women created in the image of the Divine.
>
> Let us banish these messages once and for all!

Place the bowl on the prayer table. Invite each woman to come forward and burn her message, using the lit candle and placing her piece of paper in the bowl.

How Do I Relate to My Anger? — *35 min*

Say:

> We have banished some of our negative voices. What other messages have we received that keep us from being the powerful women we are? When we have tried to express one of our strongest emotions, anger, what have we been told? Or, have we given up trying to say what we really need to say? Can we even feel our anger?
>
> An important part of our healing process and our journey as peacemakers includes reflecting on our relationship to our anger. Let us ask ourselves the following questions.

- What was I taught about anger as a girl and then as a woman?
- Was I told to be nice to everyone, not to make waves, or was I taught to speak up?
- Am I comfortable with my anger, or afraid of or unsure what to do with it?

Give these instructions:

Take a moment to reflect on your responses to those questions. *(Pause for a moment.)* We will go around the circle two times, each time completing a different sentence.

The first time we go around the circle, we will complete this sentence: "Growing up, I was taught that_____." For example, "I was taught that anger is…" or "I was taught that I should or shouldn't…"

The second time we will respond to this statement: "Today as a woman I have learned that_____."

Go around the circle twice, giving everyone the chance to finish these two statements. You may want to use an object as a talking stick, something that each woman can hold while she is speaking.

After everyone has completed these two sentences, share the following in your own words:

Learning how to accept and then express our feelings of anger is one of the greatest challenges that we face as women. Some of what we have learned has led us to believe that anger is a negative, unacceptable emotion and that, especially because we are women, we should not let others see its many faces. Let us remember what Dorothy Samuel wrote in her reflection: "We must not confuse violence with anger….It is in the…repression and denial of anger as something shameful that it turns into an explosive force of destruction and violence."

Let the group know that further resources for dealing with anger and strong emotions are found in the reading "Working with Our Anger," in the sidebar in this session, "The Ball of Light," and in the Opening Ritual for Session 7, "The Buddhist Practice of LovingKindness."

Closing: Drumming Circle — *30 min*

Ask everyone to choose a drum.

Getting To Know Your Drum — *10 min*

Convey the following in your own words:

> Because some of us have been taught to be silent, we are going to give ourselves permission to make some noise. We are going to make some noise together! You can make whatever kind of noise you want. You don't need to have any special intent around this noise you will make.
>
> We are going to start by getting to know our drums. Place your hands on your drum. Hold them there. See how that feels. *(Pause)* Now move your hands around. How does that feel? *(Pause)*
>
> Now I will set the timer for one minute. During that time I invite you to explore your drum, get to know it. Touch your drum again with your hand, spoon, or mallet. Try different beats—you don't need to make or create a rhythm. Do it for yourself. Listen to its vibration.

Set the timer. When one minute has passed, ask the group:

- How was that for you?
- Was it fun or hard for you?
- Have you drummed before?

Then say:

> Now we are going to drum again for two minutes. Remember you can stop and start whenever you want.

Set the timer. When two minutes have passed, ask the group how that was for them.
Say:
> Now we are going to drum with our eyes closed for two minutes. Go!

Set the timer. When two minutes have passed, again ask the group how that was for them.

Giving Voice — *10 min*

Share these instructions in your own words:

> Now that we are more familiar with our drums we are going to begin to give voice to our anger. Drum your anger. Or just drum and see what comes out.

Remember that you can start and stop at any time. You can drum the whole time. You can sit in silence and listen to others' drumming.

If you do not want to express your anger here—or are unable to—think about what it would be like to drum if you were angry. Or, you can drum a friend's story or a response to something you read in the newspaper. Or, you can drum support for someone else being angry, perhaps someone in this group.

This time I will set the timer for 5 minutes.

Set the timer and invite everyone to begin.

When 5 minutes have passed, hold the silence of the circle for 30 seconds to a minute. Let the group have that experience. Ask if anyone wants to share how that felt in her body.

Letting Our Anger Be Transformed — *10 min*

Then say:

How does my anger change when it is okay to make sound, when it is okay to express it? We will drum again for 5 minutes, letting our anger slowly be transformed into a powerful, constructive, life-giving response.

Set the timer for 5 minutes and invite everyone to begin.
When 5 minutes have passed, hold the silence of the circle for one to two minutes. Thank everyone for drumming.

The Ball of Light

This Tibetan Buddhist meditation will help pacify our anger and develop love and compassion. In this meditation, begin by imagining that you are feeling love and compassion for all living beings. Love is the wish that all beings have happiness, and compassion is the wish for them to be free from suffering and its causes. Visualize this love and compassion appearing as a ball of light in the space in front of you. See the light flowing into you from this radiant sphere, purifying all of your anger, hurt and bitterness. Let the brilliant light fill your body completely, making your body and mind calm and blissful. Concentrate on feeling free from all disturbing emotions.

After awhile, imagine light again flowing from the radiant sphere into you, this time filling you with patience, love, compassion, and all the good qualities you wish to develop. Focus on feeling that you have generated these positive qualities and can express them easily and appropriately in your daily interactions with other people. To end this meditation, imagine that the ball of light, which contains all of these good qualities, comes to the top of your head and dissolves into you. Envision it coming to rest at your heart center, in the center of your chest and feel that your heart/mind has become inseparable from this love and compassion.

Source: Adapted from Thubten Chodron, *Working With Anger.*

Looking Ahead — 3 min

In preparation for the next session, remind participants to do the Life Practice, journal topics and questions, and the next session's readings, found at the end of this session.

Life Practice

Practice the technique "Reframing the Situation" from one of the last session's selections "Working With Our Anger" (reprinted here).

1) Sit quietly and remember a situation in which you responded in anger or an event that brings back feelings of hurt or hostility. Then, try to view the situation from a new perspective during your meditation. Evaluate your thoughts, feelings, and perceptions to see if they are accurate. Envision yourself responding to the other person differently. This type of practice helps us dissolve past hurts and grudges, and prepares us to act the way we want to in situations of conflict. Focus on transforming your emotions and attitudes, rather than on what you should say or do. As you begin to transform your feelings, it will become easier to decide how to act.

If you feel that the situation or event you reflected on needs further resolution and you are ready and able to engage with this person or group, do so, using what you just learned in this meditation.

2) Read about the fingerholds in the readings for Session 5. Practice using them when you feel strong emotions, such as anger, arising. Also practice them so that you can use them during Session 5, if you need to, when we will reflect on a time when you either were violent toward someone or someone was violent to you.

Note: Session 5 may also be a challenging session for those of us who have experienced extreme forms of violence. You may want to glance at it ahead of time. Take care of yourself. If you need to excuse yourself from certain activities, or from the entire gathering, please do so. You can always rejoin the group for the following session.

Journal Topics and Questions

None for this session.

Readings for Session 5

Fingerholds to Manage Emotions
By Patricia Mathes Cane

The following practice is a simple way to work with emotions….Emotions are like waves of energy moving through the body, mind, and spirit. Often we judge emotions as "good" or "bad," rather than recognizing them as wise messages from the body guiding us in our response to challenges or to our environment. With overwhelming feelings, energy can become blocked or repressed, resulting in pain or congestion in the body. Through each finger runs a channel or meridian of energy connected with an organ system and related emotions. By holding each finger while breathing deeply, we can work with the flow of emotional energy and feelings to bring physical release and healing. Fingerholds are a helpful tool to use in daily life. In difficult situations when tears, anger or anxiety arise, the fingers may be held to bring calm and focus so that the appropriate response or action may be taken. The practice may also be done as a meditation with music, or used before going to sleep to release the problems of the day and bring deep relaxation to body, mind and spirit. The practice may be done on oneself or on another person.

MIDDLE FINGER Anger, Rage
INDEX FINGER Fear, Terror, Panic
RING FINGER Worry, Anxiety
THUMB Grief, Tears
SMALL FINGER Lack of Self-Esteem

Practice

Hold each finger with the opposite hand for 2-5 minutes. You can work with either hand. Breath in deeply; recognize and acknowledge the strong or disturbing feelings or emotions you hold inside yourself. Breathe out slowly and let go. Imagine the feelings draining out of your finger into the earth. Breathe in a sense of harmony, strength, and healing. And breathe out slowly, releasing past feelings and problems. Often as you hold each finger you can feel a pulsing sensation as the energy and feelings move and become balanced….

Emotions Associated with Each Finger

- Thumb: Grief, Tears, Emotional Pain (Babies suck their thumbs for comfort.)
- First finger: Fear, Terror, Panic (Perhaps how we feel when an authority figure waves his or her finger at us.)

- Middle finger: Anger, Rage, Resentment (The custom of "giving the finger.")
- Ring finger: Worry, Anxiety, Nervousness (Many people unconsciously play with the ring on this finger when they are worried.)
- Small Finger: Lack of self-esteem, Victim (Small finger equals feeling small.)

Source: Adapted from Patricia Mathes Cane, *Living in Wellness—Trauma Healing: A Capacitar Manual of Body Mind Spirit Practices for Stress, Trauma and Compassion Fatigue.*

Descriptions of Violence

John Dear:
Violence is best defined as that act of forgetting or ignoring who we are: brothers and sisters of one another....Violence is any behavior that dehumanizes us, from thoughts of self-hatred to intentional harm or physical injury done to another.

Engage:
Violence is any physical, emotional, verbal, institutional, structural, or spiritual behavior, attitude, policy, or condition that diminishes, dominates, or destroys ourselves or other beings.

Violence crosses boundaries without permission, disrupts authentic relationships and separates us from other beings.

Violence is often motivated by fear, unrestrained anger, or greed to increase domination or power over others.

Violence often provokes new violence.

Hussein Bulhan:
Violence is not an isolated physical act or a discrete random event....Any relation, process, or condition imposed by someone that injures the health and well-being of others is by definition violent.

Sources: Dear quote in Laura Slattery, Ken Butigan, Veronica Pelicaric, and Ken Preston-Pile, *Engage: Exploring Nonviolent Living*; Bulhan, *Frantz Fanon and the Psychology of Oppression.*

Session 5

Our Movement Toward Healing

Session 5
Our Movement Toward Healing

In this Session We Will:

- Explore our understanding of violence
- Share our own experiences of violence—when someone was violent toward us, we were violent to someone, or to ourselves
- Express our need for healing and receive support from the group

Agenda

Introduction — *2 min*
Opening Ritual — *25 min*
Zones of Learning — *10 min*
The Violence Spectrum — *35 min*
Sharing an Experience of Violence — *45 min*
Closing: Healing Circle — *20 min*
Looking Ahead — *3 min*
      Life Practice
      Journal Topics and Questions
      Readings

Materials Needed

- ☐ Shared Agreements
- ☐ Prayer table
- ☐ A colorful cloth
- ☐ A candle
- ☐ Matches
- ☐ Two sheets of white 8 ½ x 11 paper
- ☐ Masking tape
- ☐ Flipchart
- ☐ Easel paper
- ☐ Markers
- ☐ Art supplies—clay, Play Doh, white paper (for drawing or journaling), construction paper, crayons, colored pencils, pastels, scissors, glue, etc.
- ☐ Compact disk or audiotape player
- ☐ Recorded music

Facilitator Notes
Session preparation — The week before
- Review the entire session. Practice reading any visualizations or meditations, and role-play or practice setting up and facilitating exercises beforehand. Whenever possible, put material into your own words. Feel free to make notes on 3x5 cards or in the book next to the written instructions.
- For the Violence Spectrum, on one piece of white 8 ½ x 11 paper, write "Violent." On the other piece, write "Not Violent."

Session preparation — The day of
- Arrange the chairs, including your own, in a circle, with a small table in the center. Place the cloth, candle, and matches on the table.
- Tape the Shared Agreements to the wall.
- Play some background music as people arrive, if desired.

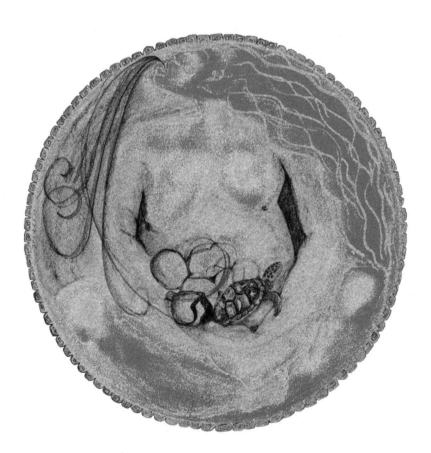

Session 5
Our Movement Toward Healing

Introduction — *2 min*

Convey the following in your own words:

> Welcome to Session 5. In Session 4, we reflected on what gets in the way of claiming our power-within, and then banished our internal negative voices and drummed our anger, watching it change. In this session, we continue on our peacemaking journey, seeking the healing that we all need. We will first explore our understanding of violence and then share with each other our own experiences of violence, honoring the importance of telling our stories because they are gateways to self-knowledge, wisdom, and self-validation. We will conclude by expressing our need for healing and receiving support from the group.

Remind everyone about the Shared Agreements.

Note: This may be a challenging session for those of us who have experienced extreme forms of violence. Take care of yourself. If you need to excuse yourself from certain activities, or from the entire gathering, please do so. You can always rejoin the group for the following session.

Also encourage participants to use the fingerholds that they practiced earlier.

Reflections from the Last Session

> During this session we will be sharing what might be more intimate and sensitive areas of our lives with each other, so we need as much time and space as possible. Therefore we will not share our reflections from the last session with a partner.

Opening Ritual — *5 min*

Light the candle. Say:

> Let us take a few moments to breathe, to return to this safe and welcoming place. *(Pause)* Let us again open our sacred space by saying together our group mantra:

> We are good, beautiful, strong, and holy. We are women of spirit. We are women of peace. We seek healing and wholeness for ourselves and our world.

Have the group read this poem together:

One Day My Soul Just Opened Up

One day my soul just opened up
and things started happenin'
I mean
I cried and cried like never before
I cried tears of ten thousand mothers
I couldn't even feel anything because
I cried til I was numb.

One day my soul just opened up
I felt this overwhelming pride
what I was proud of
only God knows
Like the pride of a hundred thousand fathers
basking in the glory of their newborn sons
I was grinnin' from ear to ear!

One day my soul just opened up
I started laughing
and I laughed for what seemed like forever
wasn't nothin' particularly funny goin' on
but I laughed anyhow
I laughed the joy of a million children playin' in the mud
I laughed til my side ached
Oh God! It felt so good!

One day, my soul just opened up
There were revelations, annihilations, and resolutions
feelings of doubt and betrayal, vengeance and forgiveness
memories of things I'd seen and done before
of places I'd been, although I didn't know when
there were lives I'd lived
people I'd loved
battles I'd fought
victories I'd won
and wars I'd lost.

One day, my soul just opened up
and out poured all the things
I'd been hiding
and denying
and living through
that had just happened moments before.

One day, my soul just opened up
and I decided

I was good and ready!
I was good and ready!
To surrender
my life
to God.

So, with my soul wide open,
I sat down
wrote Her a note
and told her so.

Source: Gemmia L. Vanzant, *One Day My Soul Just Opened Up.*

Zones of Learning — 10 min

Say:

As we explore violence, and the healing that we seek, the Zones of Learning can be a useful tool to help us monitor how much we want to share with the group. Let's look at this diagram:

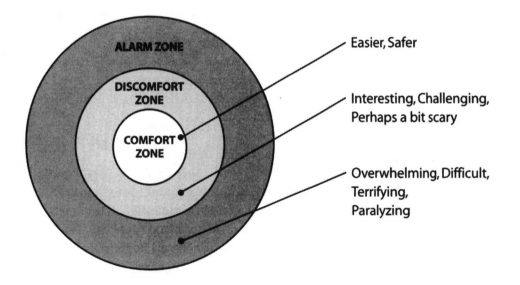

Point to circles and explain diagram. Then share in your own words:

When we have positive experiences that we're used to and we've had many times before, we are in our comfort zone. This can mean anything from reading a good book, to spending time with friends, to doing a familiar job task. Even though we're comfortable with this experience, we can learn and grow from it.

Sometimes we have experiences that are newer, that make us a little nervous, we may be in our discomfort zone. It may be a brand new job assignment or a new stage in a relationship. It's an event that's not too far outside your experience, but makes you uneasy. It provides you with a good opportunity to grow and learn.

Sometimes things happen to us that really scare and possibly traumatize us. It's so sudden, so unfamiliar or so painful that you find yourself feeling paralyzed, overwhelmed, confused, afraid, even terrified, and generally wanting to hide in bed. Perhaps it may be an emergency you witness on the street or an extremely short deadline on a very tough job assignment.

Learning and growth can take place in our *comfort zone* but it is more likely to occur when we step into our *discomfort zone*.

Experiences that are too challenging or disturbing, however, can move us into our *alarm zone*, where fear and distress shut down our learning, growth, and transformation. We can end up in a depressed, negative place.

Our comfort zone can offer us a center and a base for learning and action. Our discomfort zone can offer us new ways to grow and change. The alarm zone can overwhelm us. We want this to be a safe circle where everyone shares only at the level where she is comfortable. As we begin to reflect on violence, practice becoming aware of what zone you are in so that this is an experience for learning and growth, not one that causes alarm.

Ask for questions. If you are unsure of the answer, don't hesitate to say so or to ask the rest of the group for their thoughts.

Source: Slattery, Butigan, Pelicaric, and Preston-Pile, adapted from a handout, "Using Discomfort Zones for Learning, by *Future Now: A Training Collective*, which incorporated ideas first developed by "Training for Change," *Engage: Exploring Nonviolent Living*.

> *Only when women and children are safe from violence, deprivation, and abuse will the cycle of violence begetting violence, which underlies terrorism and wars, end.*
>
> Jean Shinoda Bolen

The Violence Spectrum — 35 min

Clear a large space. (If necessary, move chairs and other objects to the side.) Place the piece of paper with "Violent" on the wall on one side of the room, place the paper with "Not Violent" on the wall on the other side of the room. Place some masking tape on the floor in a line from the "Violent" to the "Not Violent" side. Ask people to get up and move into this open space. Then share:

Now we are going to explore our understanding of violence with an exercise called the "Violence Spectrum." We will reflect on a variety of situations and think about to what degree the actions of the people in these situations are "Violent."

To help us, we are designating one side of the room as "Violent" (*point to it*) and the other side (*indicate it*) as "Not Violent."

The closer you position yourself to the "Violent" side of the room along the line, the more violent you think the person is being in this situation.

The closer you position yourself to the "Not Violent" side of the room, along the line, the less violent you think the person is being in this situation.

If you are undecided, stand in the middle of the room, off the line.

I will now give you a situation, and then ask you to decide if the person in the situation is being violent or not violent. When you hear this, move to a place relative to the center line that indicates what you think or feel. Then I'll ask you why you are located where you are. If you hear something from someone else that you had not considered but that makes you change your point of view, feel free to move from your position.

Note: Everyone's decision or position is equally valid. Let us respect everyone's opinions.

Read one of the situations from the list below:

- Gloria spray-paints "this insults women" on a sexist billboard. From your point of view is Gloria's action violent or not violent?
- Hank drains the oil from his car and pours it into the gutter. From your point of view is his action violent or not violent?
- A person does nothing as a man on a nearby street repeatedly slaps a woman who appears to be his wife or girlfriend. From your point of view is the onlooker's action violent or not violent?
- Alice has greatly insulted John. In turn, John refuses to talk to Alice. Is John's action violent or not violent? (After the initial discussion you might change it a bit by saying "John has shut Alice out of his life. From your point of view is John's action violent or not violent?")
- A bartender serves a customer another drink even though she knows the customer is an alcoholic and is drunk. From your point of view is the bartender's action violent or not?
- A waste incinerator is releasing toxic waste into the air in a low-income neighborhood. An environmental rights group protests at the incinerator, eventually causing it to shut down. From your point of view are the group's actions violent or not violent?
- Beverly shoots a burglar who comes into her house. From your point of view is her action violent or not violent?
- A character on a TV police show is murdering other people. From your point of view is the police show violent or not violent?
- A junior high teacher shows a tape of the beheading of a person in Iraq to his class. From your point of view was the teacher's action violent or not violent?
- During the Summer Olympics of 2004 the U.S. media often showed and interviewed spouses of competing athletes. No U.S. media covering the Olympics ever showed or interviewed a partner of a homosexual athlete. From your point of view is the media's lack of coverage violent or not violent?
- David puts mouse poison out in his house. Is David's action violent or not violent?
- A company decides to move to Mexico to save labor costs. This costs a small town in the United States 200 jobs, while creating 250 jobs for Mexicans. From your point of view are the company's actions violent or not violent?
- Greg spanks his child who is misbehaving. From your point of view is his action violent or not violent?

Ask participants whether the actions of the person or group are "violent" or "not violent." Invite everyone to move to a space in the room that represents her thinking. Then:

Why have you located yourself where you did?

Call on people by alternating between participants on opposite ends of the line. Because participants are given limited information in the scenario, they will often make certain assumptions about it. During the discussion, ask people to pay attention to their assumptions. As the energy starts to wane for a particular scenario, ask the following:

What could have been a different response by the person acting in this situation that would have resulted in a "win-win" situation, where both parties benefit and get their needs met?

Do two or more other scenarios in the same way.

Debriefing the Violence Spectrum

After you have finished with all the scenarios you wanted to present, invite everyone to return to their chairs. Debrief this exercise by asking the following question. Write the responses on a piece of easel paper.

What did you learn in this exercise?

In concluding this exercise, sum up briefly in a sentence or two the lessons of the group. If the following points were not made, consider making them at this time.

This exercise often:
- Shows some of the different types of violence that exist
- Reveals the wide range of opinions people hold about violence
- Highlights that we often bring our assumptions and biases to the decisions we make;
- Allows us to begin thinking about how to respond more nonviolently in different situations

Source: Adapted from Slattery, Butigan, Pelicaric, and Preston-Pile, *Engage: Exploring Nonviolent Living.*

Sharing an Experience of Violence — 45 min

Creative Reflection — 5 min

Invite participants to use the creative supplies to reflect on an experience of violence:

The Violence Spectrum exercise gave us an opportunity to reflect on some examples of violence. We will now have the opportunity to personalize our exploration of violence by sharing our stories and our own experience of violence with each other.

Reflect on a time, that you'd feel comfortable sharing in a small group, when you either were violent to someone or to yourself, or someone was violent to you. You may want to focus on an experience or situation that has been resolved, at least in a very basic sense.

We will take about 15 minutes to reflect on a personal experience of violence using a creative medium, for example, crayons, markers, clay, and so forth. You can express this experience or your feelings about it in images, colors, a drawing, or by journaling.

This will be a quiet, reflective period, time just for you. After you reflect on this experience you will have the opportunity to share with two other people.

Again, reflect at whatever level you feel comfortable. Remember, this process is not psychotherapy or counseling, but an opportunity for furthering our own healing so that we might be a healing, peaceful presence in our relationships and in our world. I invite you to focus on an experience in light of this.

If any of you need referrals for help with healing, there are some listed at the end of the session.

Play background music during this creative reflection period.

Small Group Reflection — *30 min*

When the women are finished with their creative reflection, invite them back to the circle. Divide the large group into smaller groups of three people. Invite each group to gather in a separate part of the room. Have the 1's gather in one part of the room, the 2's in another place, and so on. It is all right if not all the groups have the same number of participants.

Then, again in your own words:

I invite you to relax and be aware of the presence of those in your circle. Now, one at a time, share at whatever level you feel comfortable, either the personal experience of violence that you drew or wrote about, or about the reflection you had as you were drawing or journaling. Each person will have about eight minutes.

Keep track of the time and let the groups know when they should be shifting to the last person. Call everyone back into the large group after 25 minutes. Once seated, share:

I invite you to come to the center of the room and place your artwork on the prayer table.

After everyone has placed her contribution on the table, invite group members to take a moment of silence to hold and honor the sharing of their experiences of violence gently.

Source: Adapted from Slattery, Butigan, Pelicaric, and Preston-Pile, *Engage: Exploring Nonviolent Living.*

Gender Violence Worldwide, Throughout the Life Cycle

Phase	Type of Violence
Prebirth	Sex-selective abortion (e.g., in China, India, Republic of Korea); battering during pregnancy (emotional and physical effects on the woman; effects on birth outcome); coerced pregnancy (for example, mass rape in war).
Infancy	Female infanticide; emotional and physical abuse; differential access to food and medical care for girl infants.
Girlhood	Child marriage; genital mutilation; sexual abuse by family members and strangers; differential access to food and medical care; child prostitution.
Adolescence	Dating and courtship violence (for example, acid throwing in Bangladesh, date rape in the United States); economically coerced sex (African secondary school girls having to take up with "sugar daddies" to afford school fees); sexual abuse in the workplace; rape; sexual harassment; forced prostitution; trafficking in women.
Reproductive age	Abuse of women by intimate male partners; marital rape; dowry abuse and murders; partner homicide; psychological abuse; sexual abuse in the workplace; sexual harassment; rape; abuse of women with disabilities.
Elderly Abuse	Of widows; elder abuse (in the United States, the only country where data are now available, elder abuse affects mostly women).

Source: Heise, Pitanguy, and Germain, "Gender Violence Worldwide, Throughout the Life Cycle," in *Violence Against Women: The Hidden Burden.*

Closing: Healing Circle — 20 min

Place a chair next to the prayer table with everyone's artwork on it and then describe the healing circle in your own words:

We have listened to and gently held each other's stories of violence. In our small groups, we found listening ears and open, compassionate hearts. We are not alone. In this larger circle, this community, we can find the same support. This circle can help us begin to or continue to heal from what we have experienced. Now is an opportunity for you to receive the support you need from this group explicitly.

Then ask group members:

What further healing do you need to experience as a result of this session? What do you need or want from this group?

If you would like, I invite each of you, one at a time, to come into the center of the circle and sit in this chair and share your need with the group—or simply ask to be held in silence. The rest of us will extend our hands toward you or touch you if you are comfortable with that and ask, silently or out loud, that you be healed.

Let the group members know that if they feel more comfortable remaining in their own seats, they may do so. Or you may want to all hold hands and then go around the circle, focusing the group's energy on each person—and possibly extending your hands toward them—for several minutes. Do whatever is most comfortable for the group.

If you would like people to enter the circle, you may wish to model this by going first. Then, after everyone has had the opportunity to sit in the chair and express her needs, invite group members to extend their hands toward each other, or hold hands, and send healing energy to each other.
Thank everyone for being courageous enough to seek healing as they continue on their journey toward wholeness.

Looking Ahead — *3 min*

In preparation for the next session, remind participants to do the Life Practice, journal topics and questions, and the next session's readings, found at the end of this session.

Life Practice

Reflect back on your own or a group member's experience of or need for healing. Think of ways that you can further the healing process for yourself or this woman. Chant the group mantra regularly: "I am good, beautiful, strong, and holy. I am a woman of spirit. I am a woman of peace. I seek healing and wholeness for myself and our world." Add something new to your altar, create a ritual or drum on behalf of yourself or others.

Journal Topics and Questions

1) All of us have experienced conflict in our lives. During the period before the next session, try to become aware of some of the types of conflict that you experience or face.

2) Do you have a typical way of responding to conflict? Are you afraid of conflict or does it energize you? Do you view conflict as a natural part of life's interactions, or something to flee?

Resources for Healing

National Domestic Violence Hotline, 1-800-799-SAFE, 1-800-787-3223, www.ndvh.org.

National Coalition Against Domestic Violence (NCADV), (303) 839-1852, www.ncadv.org.

Institute on Domestic Violence in the African-American Community, www.dvinstitute.org, (612) 624-5357.

National Latino Alliance for the Elimination of Domestic Violence (the Alianza), www.dvalianza.org, (646) 672-1404.

Communities Against Violence (415) 333-HELP, www.cuav.org.

> *Works to end violence against and within lesbian, gay, bisexual, transgender and queer/questioning (LGBTQ) communities.*

Rape, Abuse, and Incest National Network, 1-800-656-4673.

Readings for Session 6

The Two Hands of Nonviolence
By Barbara Deming

The Two Hand of Nonviolence metaphor comes from the writings of the late Barbara Deming, a feminist writer and activist. In her book Revolution and Equilibrium, *Deming's metaphor of the two hands underscores the creative tension that fuels both interpersonal transformation and social change.*

With one hand we say to one who is angry, or to an oppressor, or to an unjust system, "Stop what you are doing. I refuse to honor the role you are choosing to play. I refuse to obey you. I refuse to cooperate with your demands. I refuse to build the walls and the bombs. I refuse to pay for the guns. With this hand I will even interfere with the wrong you are doing. I want to disrupt the easy pattern of your life."

But then the advocate of nonviolence raises the other hand. It is raised out-stretched —maybe with love and sympathy, maybe not—but always outstretched with the message that "No, you are not the other; and no, I am not the other..." With this hand I say, "I won't let go of you or cast you out of the human race. I have faith that you can make a better choice than you are making now, and I'll be here when you are ready. Like it our not, we are part of one another."

Two Hands in North Carolina
By J'Ann Schoonmaker Allen

"Don't go a step farther," yelled a gruff male voice as a group of fourteen people, ranging in age from 17 to 65, cautiously walked around the end of a chain link fence that bordered the Aero Contractors building in Smithfield, North Carolina at the Johnston County Airport, "unless you want to be arrested."

My heart pounded. I was afraid. This was my first act of civil disobedience. I'd joined Stop Torture Now (STN) in order to express my concern for the violence I had read that the U.S.A., my country, was participating in throughout the world. The atrocities taking place in Guantanamo convinced me to join in demonstrating my concern. But that was in the early spring of 2005. Since then the *New York Times* and multiple other media had reported that U.S. aircraft were carrying prisoners from the U.S.A. to foreign countries where torture was permitted. Some of these flights, known as extraordinary rendition, reportedly began in North Carolina. Aero Contractors denied responsibility, but we wanted an investigation of the company and their actions. We wanted to present an indictment to company officials.

We'd practiced this action the Saturday before around the flagpole near the skating rink at Forest Park in St. Louis, Missouri. Another woman and I had the task of talking to the police, sheriff's department, and other law enforcers in order to diffuse any potential violence. We had no idea how we'd be treated by the police. Although part of the group hailed from the Raleigh area and had participated in other acts of civil disobedience, none of us were familiar with the police in this county.

As the group of fourteen continued to walk slowly toward the flagpole in front of Aero, I and the rest of the support group positioned ourselves along the fence. And then I realized how scared I was. The pounding in my heart continued. I told myself that I had a job to do. And then I remembered to breathe.

I breathed in. I breathed out. My heart-beat slowed. I began to speak to the deputy blocking the path the fourteen had taken. I knew that I was babbling, but I allowed the language of my breathing to speak. I began talking about the lovely weather and then I remembered that I hadn't introduced myself. The sheriff's officer replied that he'd read my name on my blue-and-white letter jacket.

I laughed and told him that it was my daughter's jacket. My name was J'Ann, not Jessica as monogrammed on the front. I chatted about the pine trees and how the last time I'd been in this area was in the late 60s when my husband was in basic training at Ft. Bragg. I'd noticed the sign for Fayetteville, the town housing Ft. Bragg, on our drive into Raleigh the afternoon before as we drove along the interstate to our rendezvous in Raleigh. As I chattered away, I noticed that my fear had subsided and this sheriff had begun to smile at me.

Although my husband Jim felt much guilt about staying in the Army after his draft commitment as a social worker ended, I began to use Jim's twenty years of military service as a way to connect with this law enforcement officer. I told the sheriff that I'd been an Army wife for twenty years. And as I babbled, I realized that I had established common ground. I was practicing the "two hands of nonviolence" encouraged by Pace e Bene that I'd learned in the *Traveling with the Turtle* women's group I had joined in the Fall of 2005.

Jean, the other woman charged with diffusing tension, and Louise, our media contact, began passing out press releases to the sheriff's deputies, as other deputies walked towards the fourteen. We were trying both to serve an indictment to Aero and offer a prayer of lament for the wrongs we'd committed in torturing others. We told the deputies that we were not going to harm or deface any property. We simply wanted to make people aware of the "torture taxis" operating out of the Johnston County airport and to ask Aero to desist their practice of performing extraordinary renditions.

The deputies listened as we watched the arrests taking place in the early morning sunlight. We sang: "We shall not be moved. We shall not be moved. Like a tree standing by the water, we shall not be moved." One of the reporters heard a sheriff's officer join in our singing. As the van carrying the fourteen trespassers pulled away, we quietly walked down the road to our cars and continued our mission.

I joined a group delivering indictments to various members of the board of Aero Contractor and the Johnston County Airport commissioners. For most of the day we had a police escort. At the County office where we met with the chair of the commissioners board, several of the sheriffs told us that if what we claimed was true, that Aero was carrying out missions of rendition in order to torture suspects, we needed to stop those flights. The community was listening to us. I was not afraid.

The years I spent meditating and the Pace e Bene course encouraged me to listen to my own self, through my body, while listening to the other. I know that I don't have all the answers. I know that I need to work with others. And I find that when I really listen to the other while listening to myself, presenting my views while acknowledging the other, I become a peacemaker.

Source: J'Ann Schoonmaker Allen wrote this piece for *Traveling with the Turtle*.

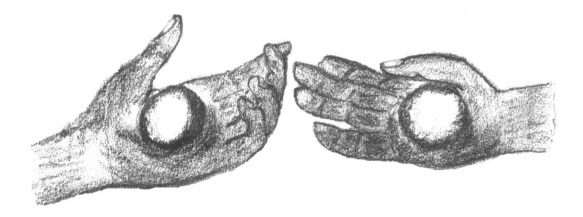

Creating True Peace
By Thich Nhat Hanh

The night before his enlightenment, the Buddha was attacked by Mara, the Tempter, the Evil One. Mara and his army of demons shot thousands of arrows at the Buddha, but as the arrows neared him, they turned into flowers and fell harmlessly at his feet.

This is a powerful image. We can all practice so that we can receive the violent words and actions aimed at us and, like the Buddha, transform them into flowers. The power of understanding and compassion gives us the ability to do this. We can all make flowers out of arrows.

During the war in Vietnam, one of my closest students, Sister Chan Khong, who is also a professor at a university in Saigon, wrote a petition for peace. She persuaded seventy of her fellow teachers to sign it. Shortly afterward, there were widespread attacks on South Vietnam by troops from the North, and the atmosphere became very tense. As a result, the local authorities made a public broadcast calling all the professors who had signed the petition to come to the Ministry of Education to sign a statement recanting their support for the peace petition. All of the professors except Sister Chan Khong complied.

The Sister was called in to speak with the minister himself, who said that if she did not withdraw her statement for peace, she would lose her position at the university and possibly be put in jail. Using her mindfulness training, Sister Chan Khong calmed her emotions and declared that she was determined to bear all responsibility for her act of initiating the petition. Then, she said, "Mr. Minister, as a teacher I believe the most important thing we can do during this time of killing and confusion is to speak out with courage, understanding, and love. That is a precious gift that we can give to our students. That is what I did. You, the Minister of Education, were a teacher, too, before having a high position in the government. You are like a big brother to us younger teachers." When he heard this, the minister's heart softened. He understood and apologized and did not take any more action against Sister Chan Khong.

It is possible to water the seed of compassion even in such a situation of adversity. When we see clearly with the eyes and heart of understanding and compassion, we no longer feel that we are the victims of the other's violence. We can even open the heart of the person we feel is trying to hurt us. We can turn our enemies into friends.

As you begin your practice of nonviolence, this may seem very difficult to do. You become aware that violence is all around you. You become aware of the seeds of anger, fear, and hatred in your own unconsciousness. You may feel a huge block of suffering inside you and feel that you are unable to transform the anger and fear within you and the violence that is directed at you. For many of us this is the situation. We have allowed violence to accumulate in us for too long because we have had no strategy to deal with it. When we cannot handle our suffering, we spew forth our frustration and pain onto those around us. We are victims of our own suffering, but because we do not know how to handle it, we hurt others while we are in pain. We—each of us—must become responsible for our own pain and work to transform it in order to save ourselves and those we love.

As you begin to transform your own inner pain, you also transform other people's anger and hatred into flowers. You soon see that arrows shot at you come out of other people's pain. You do not feel injured by their arrows or actions; instead, you have only compassion. Your compassion transforms the speech and actions of the other person. Together these practices provide real self-protection, which is necessary before we can protect others.

Every time you smile away your irritation and anger, you achieve a victory for yourself and for humanity. Your smile is like the smile of the Buddha when he defeated Mara. Mara is within us in the form of suspicion, jealousy, a misperception, but with a good understanding of yourself and others, you will avoid getting caught by Mara and making mistakes. Instead of watering the seeds of violence, you will cultivate the seeds of compassion and bring relief to yourself and others.

Source: Reprinted with the permission of The Free Press, a Division of Simon & Schuster Adult Publishing Group, from *Creating True Peace: Ending Violence in Yourself, Your Family, Your Community* by Thich Nhat Hanh. Copyright © 2003 by The Venerable Thich Nhat Hanh. All rights reserved.

PART TWO

POWER-WITH

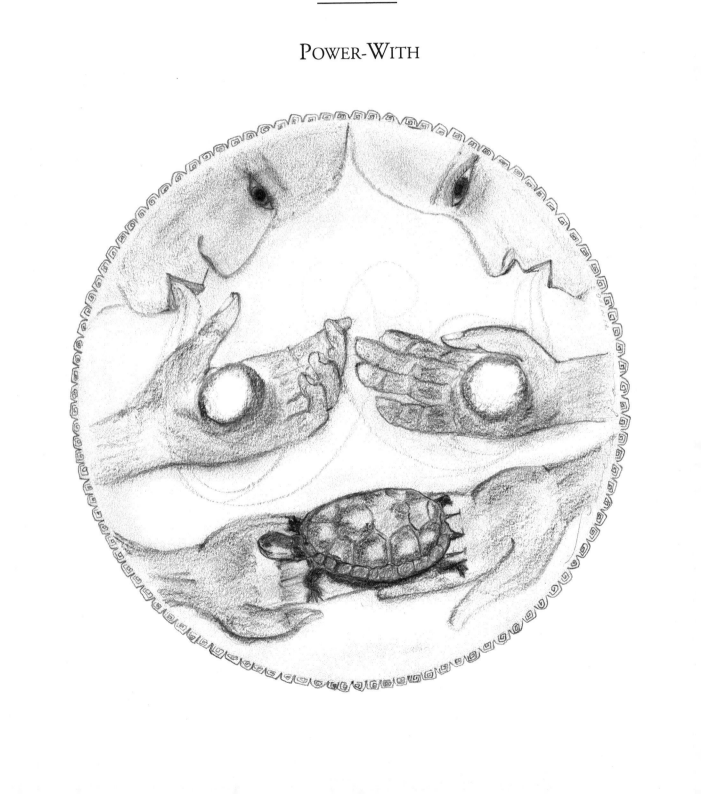

Session 6

Discovering New Responses to Conflict

Session 6
Discovering New Responses to Conflict

In this Session We Will:
- Reflect on the difference between violence and conflict
- Explore our familiar ways of responding to conflict
- Begin to learn new ways of responding to conflict and violence

Agenda
Introduction — *5 min*
Reflections from the Last Session — *10 min*
Opening Ritual — *10 min*
Conflict and Violence — *25 min*
Our Responses to Conflict — *30 min*
Responding Nonviolently — *35 min*
Closing — *5 min*
Looking Ahead — *3 min*
      Life Practice
      Journal Topics and Questions
      Readings

Materials Needed
☐ Shared Agreements
☐ Prayer table
☐ A colorful cloth
☐ A candle
☐ One 8 ½ x 11 sheet of paper
☐ Colored pencils/crayons
☐ Matches
☐ Flipchart
☐ Easel paper
☐ Markers
☐ Compact disk or audiotape player (if desired)
☐ Recorded music (if desired)

Facilitator Notes

Session preparation — A week before

• Review the entire session. Practice reading any visualizations or meditations, and role-play or practice setting up and facilitating exercises beforehand. Whenever possible, put material into your own words. Feel free to make notes on 3x5 cards or in the book next to the written instructions.

Session preparation — The day of

• Arrange the chairs, including your own, in a circle, with a small table in the center. Place the cloth, candle, and matches on the table.
• Tape the Shared Agreements to the wall.
• Play some background music as people arrive, if desired.

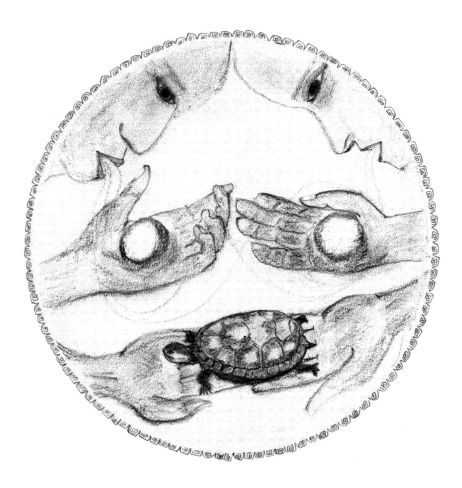

Session 6
Discovering New Responses to Conflict

Introduction — 5 min

Convey the following in your own words:

Welcome to Session 6. In Session 5, we explored our understanding of and shared our personal experiences of violence. We then received needed support from this circle. As we continue to seek healing so that we may recognize and use the power we possess as women, we now move to the next section of this process: Power-With or Power-Sharing.

Pamela Cooper-White writes: "Power-with carries the dignity of power-within into relationship. Power-with is the power of an individual to reach out in a manner that negates neither self nor other. It prizes mutuality over control and operates by negotiation and consensus." Power-with is the foundation of both conflict resolution and nonviolent action. Power-with helps us build healthy, life-giving relationships because it calls forth our best self by fostering respect and empowerment for both ourselves and our opponent.

As we consider what kinds of relationships we want to create, we will now reflect on the difference between violence and conflict, explore our familiar ways of responding to conflict, and begin to learn new ways of responding to conflict and violence.

Reflections from the Last Session — 10 min

Share the following:

Find a partner and share with her any insights that came up or experiences you had between sessions, or reflections you had on the Life Practice, journal questions or the readings.

Opening Ritual — 10 min

Light the candle and open with the group mantra: We are good, beautiful, strong, and holy. We are women of spirit. We are women of peace. We seek healing and wholeness for ourselves and our world.

Place the 8 ½ x 11 sheet of paper on the table along with the colored pencils or crayons. Let participants know that they are going to create a group doodle. Tell them that whoever feels moved to begin this group doodle can do so by picking up the piece of paper and doodling or drawing whatever she wants on it. Then pass the sheet of paper around the circle until everyone has had the opportunity to contribute to the doodle. Place it on the table and end with a moment of silence for what the group has created together.

Conflict and Violence — *25 min*

Opening Brainstorm: Types of Violence — *10 min*

Say the following in your own words:

> Let us now continue our exploration of violence by doing a brief brainstorm together of different types of violence. Call out different examples of violence.

Write the women's responses on easel paper.

What is Conflict? — *15 min*

After you have solicited several examples, share the following in your own words:

> The last session and this brainstorm both show us that there are many types of violence: personal, interpersonal, familial, communal, and societal or structural. Given what we have learned about violence, then, what is conflict? What, if any, is the difference between conflict and violence? Listening to the word "conflict" and reflecting on your own experience, what does conflict mean to you? Let us spend some time as a group sharing our responses to these questions.

Record some of the responses to these questions so that the group members can see what conflict is to them.

Our Responses to Conflict — *25 min*

Partner Sculpting — *15 min*

Convey the following in your own words:

> Now that we have a better understanding of what conflict is, we can begin to consider how we respond to it. Before we look at new ways of responding to conflict that allow us to use our power-with, to stand in our own truths while at the same time reaching out to the other person, we need to be conscious of our familiar ways of responding to conflict.

How do you react to conflict?

This next exercise will help you answer this question, as well as get in touch with the way your response feels in your body.

You will do this exercise in pairs. Each one of you is going to "sculpt" your familiar response. You are going to place your partner in a position that reflects either a specific experience of conflict you have had with someone or a general sense of the energy you feel is directed at you in a conflictual situation. You will then place yourself in a position that reflects how you generally respond to conflict.

If she is comfortable with you doing so, you can move different parts of your partner's body—her arms, her legs, etc.—ask her to make a simple gesture and ask her to make certain facial expressions in order to convey the interaction you desire.

You will have the opportunity first to describe these positions to your partner. After creating the sculpture, each pair will then hold this position long enough to notice how you each feel in this situation. You will then switch roles and the other person will create a new sculpture.

You might want to model this by creating a sculpture with a partner before beginning the exercise.

Then share:

Pair with the woman whom you partnered with during the Reflections from the Last Session. Now, decide who will go first. That person will be the sculptor.

Say to the woman who is the sculptor:

- Describe to your partner the position that you will be placing her in—a position that reflects either a specific experience of conflict you have had with someone or a general sense of the energy you feel is directed at you in a conflictual situation—and then the position in which you will place yourself.
- Place your partner, and then yourself, in these positions.
- Both of you hold that sculpture in silence as you pay attention to your body—how it feels and where you most notice your reaction. Notice what the experience tells you through your body.
- Come out of the sculpture. Both of you take a few deep breaths, remember what you have felt, and take a few more breaths.
- Share any feelings you have or anything you noticed while holding these positions, beginning with the woman who was the sculptor.

After each pair has had a chance to create a sculpture and share their responses, give the second person the opportunity to sculpt her scenario. Again, have both partners share how that felt in their bodies, or anything else they noticed.

Large Group Reflection — *15 min*

Invite everyone to thank her partner and return to the circle. Then ask:

- What did you learn from this exercise?

If you desire, write the group's responses on easel paper. Summarize the group discussion by conveying the following:

We have embodied our familiar ways of responding to conflict. There are three common ways to respond to interpersonal conflict:

- Avoiding or withdrawing from the conflict

- Accommodating to the conflict—living with it, adapting to it, accepting that this is just the way things are

- Responding to conflict in kind—for example: using power-over, being aggressive, defensive or manipulative.

Was one of these your usual response?

Source: Developed with Colleen Nakamoto

Responding Nonviolently — *35 min*

Partner Sculpting — *15 min*

Share the following in your own words:

> Now we will explore another way of responding to conflict, injustice, or violence using nonviolence. *Engage: Exploring Nonviolent Living* tells us: "Nonviolence is active and creative power for justice and well-being of all that employs neither passivity nor violence....Nonviolence is organized love." Nonviolence means that we see the humanity of the other, that we seek her or his wholeness. Thich Nhat Hanh says "Nonviolence is not a principle. It is a flower that blooms on the ground of understanding and love. Nonviolence is something to cultivate." It is a way of life.

> *Nonviolence not only allows but requires me to act from the full range of my feelings and reactions. It is about speaking the whole complicated truth... and it requires my most bitter words, my most hearty laughter, my deepest compassion, my sharpest wit.*
>
> Pam McAllister

The Latin root of the word power means "to be able." As women, we want to be able to communicate our emotions and our needs powerfully, in a manner that allows the other person to receive them. We also want to be able to hear what the other person is telling us. Nonviolence lets us do this. We will now take some time to experiment with responding in a nonviolent manner.

Ask the women to find the same partner. Invite the woman who was the first sculptor to go first again. Then, give her these instructions:

- Ask your partner to return to the same posture of conflict. Now ask yourself: How would I rather have responded? How could I have responded nonviolently? Place yourself in this position.
- Both of you hold that sculpture in silence as you pay attention to your body again—how it feels, where you most notice your response.
- Come out of the sculpture and take a few deep breaths.
- Share with each other any feelings you have or anything you noticed this time while holding these positions, beginning with the woman who was the sculptor.

Now give the second person in each pair the opportunity to go through this same process. Again, have both partners share how that felt in their bodies, or anything else they noticed.

Some Reflections on Nonviolence

Nonviolence is active and creative power for justice and well-being of all that employs neither passivity nor violence....Nonviolence is organized love. *Engage*

Peace starts in the capacity to see humanity in the other one. So, overcome the "otherness" and embrace the humanity in whoever is there. Isabel Allende

The essence of nonviolence is understanding and compassion, so when you cultivate understanding and compassion, you are practicing nonviolence...the more you can understand, the more you can be compassionate, the more you can be nonviolent....Nonviolence is not a principle. It is a flower that blooms on the ground of understanding and love. Nonviolence is something to cultivate. Thich Nhat Hanh

The call for human beings to "love your enemies" means: wanting wholeness and well-being and life for those who may be broken and sick and deadly. Angie O'Gorman

Source: Adapted from Slattery, Butigan, Pelicaric, and Preston-Pile, *Engage: Exploring Nonviolent Living.*

Large Group Reflection — *20 min*

The Two Hands of Nonviolence

Invite everyone to thank her partner and return to the circle. Then share the following in your own words:

> We just practiced responding to conflict in a healthier, more life-giving manner. We tried to interact nonviolently with our partner. This response, using nonviolence to respond to interpersonal conflict as well as to violence and injustice, is also illustrated by the Two Hands of Nonviolence, a metaphor developed by Barbara Deming, feminist writer and activist.
>
> This visual metaphor can be depicted by assuming this pose: one arm is outstretched at a 90-degree angle or parallel to the ground with the palm facing up and the other arm is straight out in front, parallel to the ground, with the palm facing out in the universal sign for stop. Finally, pull these two hands (keeping them in their same mode) closer to the body—in a relaxed but steady way.
>
> Active nonviolence is a process that holds these two realities in tension and is like saying to a person:
>
> On the one hand (symbolized by the "stop sign" hand), I will not cooperate with your violence or injustice and I will resist it with every fiber of my being.
>
> On the other hand (symbolized by the hand that is open), I am open to you as a human being.
>
> *Perform this gesture slowly and invite people to hold the pose for 15 to 30 seconds. Ask people to notice any feelings or sensations they experience as they hold this pose and imagine in front of them someone with whom they are in conflict.*

Then say:

> I invite you to practice two movements with this pose. First of all, hold out both of your hands at a 90-degree angle, palms facing up, feeling open and connected to the other person, and then slowly rotate the one arm upward into a position of resistance. Hold that pose for several seconds. Was that a difficult or easy movement for you to make?
>
> Then, hold out both hands in the posture of resistance and slowly rotate one hand downwards into the position of openness. Hold that pose for several seconds. Was that a difficult or easy movement for you to make?

Finally, ask the group:

- What did you notice as you practiced the Two Hands of Nonviolence posture?
- What did you notice as you moved from a gesture of openness to one that included resistance, or from a gesture of resistance to one that included openness and connection?

Source: Adapted from Slattery, Butigan, Pelicaric, and Preston-Pile, *Engage: Exploring Nonviolent Living*.

Conclude by saying in your own words:

In responding to conflict and violence, women's spirituality invites us to convey a sense of connectedness to our opponent, while at the same time showing strong resistance to an unacceptable, intolerable, or unjust situation. Embodying the Two Hands of Nonviolence gives us the opportunity to experience in our bodies a powerful, nonviolent way of responding to conflict and violence.

Closing — 5 min

Share the following in your own words:

We will close with the group standing in a circle, performing "the wave." (The wave has three actions: Action one is the right hand held up in resistance; action two is the left hand reaching out offering to construct a different relationship; action three is extending both arms into the air with joy and a bit of silly relief.) I will begin with one action, which the person to my right will duplicate and hold, then the next person will duplicate and hold until the action has gone around the whole circle. I will then do the second action, followed by the third.

Source: Created by Janet Chisholm.

Looking Ahead — *3 min*

In preparation for the next session, remind participants to do the Life Practice, journal topics and questions, and the next session's readings, found at the end of this session.

Life Practice

Practice using the Two Hands of Nonviolence when you are in the midst of a conflict or find yourself in a situation where you need to stand your ground and, at the same time, remain open to the other person, recognizing your common humanity. This might happen at home with your partner or your children or parents, in your workplace, at school, with your religious community, or maybe even while you are running errands, or participating in a political action.

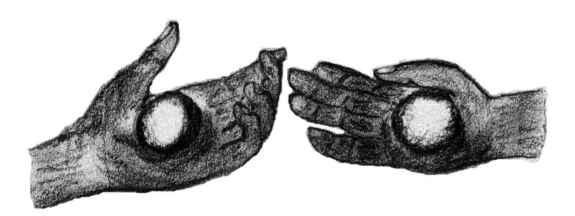

Journal Topics and Questions

1) Read the CARA four-step process for the next session (found in Session 7.)

2) Reflect on and journal about a conflict that you are either in the midst of or currently avoiding, or a situation that looks like it will become a conflict that you would like to practice dealing with. How are you dealing, or not dealing, with the conflict now? What possible ways do you see of resolving it?

We may be using this real-life conflict in an exercise for the next session. So either choose a situation that you are comfortable sharing and exploring responding to with the group or have another conflict in mind, besides the one you journaled about, that you are willing to share with the group.

Readings for Session 7

Communication: An Introduction to a Historical Model and to The New Powerful, Non-Defensive Communication Model
By Sharon Ellison

The War Model

Defensive Self-Protection: The historical use of the *rules of war* as the basis for our verbal inter-actions currently affects our lives in all realms. Using the *war motto* "To be open is to be vulner-able, and to be vulnerable is to be weak," people automatically close down, become defensive, and react to others in an adversarial manner. Such defensiveness not only inhibits our ability to understand and learn, it literally creates and accelerates conflict. Rather than protecting us, defensiveness depletes our energy and prevents us from achieving our goals.

Types of Defensive Reactions: Our defensive strategies, often not conscious, typically fall into three basic categories: *surrender, withdrawal and counterattack.* Each of these strategies includes one format designed primarily for *protection* and another to also *retaliate* against others. While a person might use any or all of six defensive reactions, most people have a habitual one; thus a common *personality type* can be associated with each type of defensive reaction....

Surrender

- **Surrender-Betray:** Co-dependent personality type. Giving into someone who treats you poorly, blaming yourself, and making excuses for the person.

- **Surrender-Sabotage:** Passive-aggressive personality type. Pretending to agree with someone who you think is treating you poorly and then doing something to undermine the person.

Withdrawal

- **Withdrawal-Escape:** Passive personality type. Avoiding talking about something you don't want to discuss in order to avoid conflict.

- **Withdrawal-Entrap:** Vindictive personality type. Refusing to respond to someone in order to draw that person into a situation where he or she may feel uncomfortable or act inappropriately.

Counterattack

- **Counterattack-Justify:** Defensive personality type. Responding to criticism by explain-ing your own behavior or making excuses.

- **Counterattack-Blame:** Aggressive personality type. Attacking the other person's position in an attempt to defend yourself.

Communication Tools Misused: Our three basic forms of communication —*questions, statements, and predictions*— are all misused when we are defensive—so dramatically that we might as well be trying to build a house by pounding nails with a saw. For example, when we ask a question, we often, through our tone, body language and wording, convey an attitude of interrogation. People are often quite unconscious of the degree to which they do this.

Power Struggles: These defensive ways of speaking and reacting are manipulative—and cause others to resist what we say. Each person involved can feel like a victim, even while lashing out in verbal attack; this dynamic causes ongoing power struggles which become addictive. Because we have never changed the basic model for how we communicate, we consider such conflict to be *normal — just human nature.*

The Powerful Non-Defensive Communication Model

Non-Defensive Communication Tools: The character and function of *questions, statements, and predictions* are very different when we use them non-defensively. For example, rather than asking questions that convey our own opinion or lead others to answer in a prescribed way, we can ask questions that are genuinely *curious, open, innocent, neutral,* and *inviting.*

Formats for Non-Defensive Communication: This part of the material covers specific formats for using each communication tool. We are using non-defensive communication when we 1) ask questions, 2) make statements, and, 3) predict consequences in an open, sincere way without trying to control how other people respond. We can gather accurate information, speak with clarity, protect ourselves, and hold others more accountable. People are more likely to respect us and we can strengthen personal and professional relationships.

1) Ask Questions: We can select from dozens of ways to use *questions* to gather accurate information quickly and to stimulate others to respond sincerely and honestly.

> **Nature:** curious, open, innocent, neutral, inviting.
> **Purpose:** To gather thorough information to understand accurately what the person means, believes, or feels.
> **Example:** If someone acts upset, the first step is to simply ask the person directly about your own assumption so he or she can *confirm, deny,* or *qualify,* for example, "Are you irritated (frustrated, angry, upset) about something?"

Avoid: Using a question to *express your own opinion* or *to entrap* others.
(**Example:** Don't you think? Didn't you like...?)

2) Make Statements: We can make *statements* using four different formats. These statements provide others with thorough information about how we interpret what they are saying and our own reactions to it.

    Nature: open, direct, vulnerable, subjective, descriptive.

    Purpose: The first three steps are to state neutrally our subjective interpretation of 1) what we hear the other person saying, 2) any contradictions we see (perceive) in the person's tone, body language, and words, and 3) our conclusions regarding the person's overt and covert messages. The fourth step is not neutral and is to 4) fully express our own reactions, our feelings, beliefs, and reasoning.

    Example: If the person continues to act irritable and yet denies it when asked, saying harshly, "I'm *fine!*," we might respond with this four-part statement:

- **Hear:** "*When* I hear you saying that you are in a good mood
- **See:** *and* (at the same time) I see that you are rolling your eyes and shrugging
- **Conclude:** *then* I believe that something is wrong but you don't want to tell me
- **Reaction:** *and* so I feel frustrated and am not sure if I should ask you more questions or leave you alone."

    Avoid: Stating *opinion* as *fact* or trying to *convince* others to agree.

3) Predict Consequences: We have two formats for making *predictions,* which we use to create security through predictability.

    Nature: protective, foretelling, neutral, definitive, firm.

    Purpose: To create boundaries and security by telling another person ahead of time how we will react if s/he does make a certain choice, and how we will react if s/he does not make that choice.

    Example: If the person still acts upset and continues to deny it, after hearing our statement, saying "I said I'm *fine*, there's no *problem!*," we can set a limit using an "If...... then" sentence: "If you would like to tell me what's going on, then I'd like to hear it." "If you don't want to tell me, then I don't want to try to make you."

    Avoid: Using a consequence prediction to *coax, punish,* or *falsely threaten* others.

Quantum Leaps: Each of us can protect ourselves without getting defensive and have greater influence without being manipulative or controlling. Using non-defensive communication, we can be honest and powerful while being compassionate and sincere.

One aspect of the *power* of non-defensive communication is that the process allows us to communicate with great clarity and walk away with increased self-esteem, even if the other person chooses not to cooperate. Anyone who uses this process can make a quantum leap in personal and professional growth. By changing how we communicate as individuals, we can work effectively toward greater understanding among diverse groups, and ultimately toward a more peaceful world.

Source: Adapted from Sharon Ellison, *Taking the War Out of Words: The Art of Powerful, Non-defensive Communication.*

Seven Hours of Terror
By Bill Hewitt, Paige Bowers, Siobhan Morrissey,
Lori Rozsa, Steve Helling, Jeff Truesdell, and Liza Hamm

Ashley Smith was unpacking—literally—for a new start when alleged killer Brian Nichols took her hostage. Faith, patience—and a determination to see her daughter again—saved her life, and possibly others.

The little girl wandered into her grandparents' home office and noticed a familiar face displayed in a news photo on the computer screen. "That's my mama, what's her picture doing there?" asked 5-year-old Paige Smith. Replied her grandfather Richard Machovec: "Your mama is a hero." "What's a hero?" asked Paige.

Paige may be too young to comprehend the extraordinary courage of her mother, Ashley Smith, but in everyone's life, it seems, there are a few moments of truth, a crossroad where character is revealed. And for Smith that time and place was the seven hours early Saturday morning that she was held hostage in her suburban Atlanta apartment by Brian Nichols, who was wanted for the vicious murder of four people in the Atlanta area. The 26-year-old widow let her compassion work its magic—and disarmed the 6'1", 210-lb. suspect with her faith. "He said he thought that I was an angel sent from God and that I was his sister," a shaken Smith later told reporters. "And that he was lost, and God led him right to me to tell him that he had hurt a lot of people."

In the days following her March 12 ordeal, Smith was proclaimed a hero by almost everyone for helping apprehend Nichols. And certainly her refusal to panic in the face of such terrifying circumstances—which in all likelihood averted further bloodshed—qualified as heroic...

Smith's nightmare unfolded with chilling suddenness. She had been busy unpacking boxes in her one-bedroom apartment in Duluth, Ga., where she had just moved two days before. Around 2 a.m. on Saturday she went to a convenience store for some cigarettes and on her return noticed a man in a truck in the parking lot....As she started to put the key in the door of her apartment, the man was right there behind her, jabbing a gun in her side. She let out a scream. "Don't scream," she says he told her. "If you don't scream, I won't hurt you."

He forced her into the bathroom and asked if she knew who he was. When he took off his hat and she saw his shaved head, she did: He was the accused rapist and killer she had seen on the news all day.

It was Nichols, 33, who on Friday morning had allegedly overpowered a guard and murdered a judge, a court stenographer and a sheriff's deputy at the Fulton County courthouse....At the time Nichols had been on trial for allegedly bursting into the apartment of his ex-girlfriend armed with a machine gun and then sexually assaulting her repeatedly over the course of three days.

During his get-away, police reported, he had hijacked at least three vehicles and later allegedly murdered an off-duty U.S. Customs agent. His escape had cast a blanket of terror over the whole Atlanta area, and now here he was in her home. "Please don't hurt me," Smith begged. "I have a 5-year-old little girl."...Whether it was the mention of the child or not isn't clear, but Smith quickly detected a glimmer of empathy—and exhaustion—from Nichols. "I don't want to hurt you," he said. "I don't want to hurt anybody else."

All the same, he tied her up. "He brought some masking tape and an extension cord and a curtain in there," Smith later recalled, "and I kind of thought he was going to strangle me." Instead he told her he wanted to "relax" and take a shower....When he got out, they sat in the bathroom and talked. Smith asked if he would let her go to see her daughter at church at 10 the next morning. At first he said no. She began to talk about her own life, about how her husband had died four years earlier. "I told him if he hurt me, my little girl wouldn't have a mommy or daddy," she said...

In 2001, with Ashley looking on, [her husband] was stabbed in the chest during a melee with more than a dozen acquaintances in an apartment parking lot....The mortally wounded Smith was lifted onto the back of a pickup truck, where he died...Smith's sister-in-law, Tanya Smith, believes Mack's death gave Ashley a chance to connect with Nichols. "You just expect to see somebody the next day, and we're just not guaranteed that next breath," Tanya says. "I really think that helped her to a degree to understand and to feel."...

Recently (her aunt Kim) Rogers had given her a copy of the Christian inspirational bestseller *The Purpose Driven Life*....Now Smith asked Nichols if she could read it. When he said yes, she picked up the book and turned to where she had left off....She began to read aloud. He suddenly said, "Stop, read that again." She did, and they talked more about their families and how he just wanted "to sit down, to watch TV, to eat some real food." He was clearly becoming more subdued. "He looked at pictures of my family," said Smith. "He asked me if he could look at them and hold them."

By that time, he had untied Smith and left his guns where she could have grabbed them. Despite those gestures of trust, the strain was wearing on her. "I really didn't keep track of time too much because I was really worried about just living." She said. At one point he asked her what she thought he should do. She gave it to him straight. "I said, I think you should turn yourself in. If you don't turn yourself in, lots more people are going to get hurt, and you're probable going to die." That didn't quite get through. "Look at me, look at my eyes," he said. "I'm already dead." Smith replied: "You are not dead. You are standing right in from of me." As Smith saw it, "He needed hope for his life."

Around 6 a.m. Nichols told her he was going to have to move the truck, which he admitted to her he had stolen from the federal agent, David Wilhelm, so that it wouldn't be spotted. He also told her he was going to need her to drive him back in her car once he had ditched the other vehicle. "Can I take my cell phone?" she asked. He had no objection and even left the guns behind. As she drove behind him, she thought about calling the police, but she feared that she might get caught in cross fire when they moved in. She also believed that she would soon have a better opportunity to summon help. "I really felt deep down inside," she said, "that he was going to let me see my little girl." After Nichols got rid of the truck about two miles from Smith's apartment complex, he was almost shocked when she swung by to pick him up. "Wow, you didn't drive off?" he asked. "I thought you were going to."

Instead she took him back to the apartment and served him a breakfast of pancakes and juice. "He was overwhelmed," she recalled. "He said, 'Real butter, pancakes?'" He asked what time she would need to leave in order to meet her daughter, who was being brought to church by Rogers. She said 9:30….."I sat down and talked to him a little bit more," she recounted. "He put the guns under the bed, like, you know, 'I'm done. I'm not going to mess around with you anymore.'" At 9:30 she got up to leave, and the strength—or the oddness—of the bond that had formed between them became apparent. Said Smith: "He asked me: 'Is there anything I can do while you're gone, like hang your curtains or something?'" She said sure, if he wanted to. "I think he knew that I was going to do what I had to do," said Smith, "and I had to turn him in."

As soon as she was out of the apartment she dialed 911. Within minutes the area was crawling with SWAT teams. Nichols opened the door and waved a white towel of surrender. At a hearing on March 15 he was told the state intended to charge him with the four murders. In the days afterward, Smith holed up with Paige, trying to recover….Mother and daughter spent their first day together watching the Cartoon Network. "What was so sweet was that Ashley was totally exhausted, so she put her head in Paige's lap and fell asleep for an hour and a half," says Rogers. "Paige was sitting there stroking her mom's head while she was watching TV."

Source: Bill Hewitt, Paige Bowers, Siobhan Morrissey, Lori Rozsa, Steve Helling, Jeff Truesdell, Liza Hamm, "Seven Hours of Terror," *People Magazine*.

Session 7

Practicing Nonviolent Responses

Session 7
Practicing Nonviolent Responses

In this Session We Will:
• Learn ways of centering ourselves
• Continue to explore ways that we can respond nonviolently to conflict or violence
• Practice these responses using situations of conflict from our own lives

Agenda
Introduction — *2 min*
Opening Ritual — *15 min*
Reflections from the Last Session — *10 min*
CARA: The Four-Step Process for Nonviolent Engagement — *20 min*
Nonviolent Engagement: Real-Play Exercise — *60 min*
Closing — *10 min*
Looking Ahead — *3 min*
        Life Practice
        Journal Topics and Questions
        Readings

Materials Needed
☐ Shared Agreements
☐ Small prayer table
☐ A colorful cloth
☐ A candle
☐ Matches
☐ Bell
☐ Flipchart
☐ Easel paper
☐ Markers
☐ Compact disk or audiotape player (if desired)
☐ Recorded music (if desired)

Facilitator Notes
Session preparation — A week before
• Review the entire session. Practice reading any visualizations or meditations, and role-play or practice setting up and facilitating exercises beforehand. Whenever possible, put material into your own words. Feel free to make notes on 3x5 cards or in the book next to the written instructions.
• Write the four steps of the CARA process on easel paper.

Session preparation — The day of

- Arrange the chairs, including your own, in a circle, with a small table in the center. Place the cloth, candle, and matches on the table.
- Tape the Shared Agreements to the wall.
- Play some background music as people arrive, if desired.

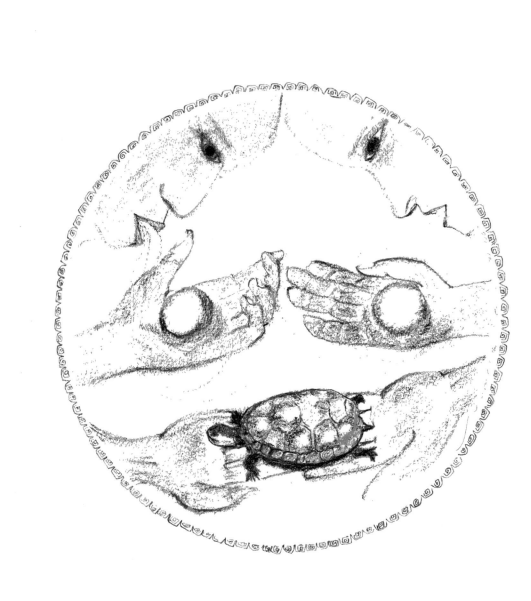

Session 7
Practicing Nonviolent Responses

Introduction — *2 min*

Convey in your own words:

Welcome to Session 7. In Session 6, we embodied our familiar ways of responding to conflict and began to learn new ways of responding to conflict and violence. In this session, we will practice peaceful, nonviolent ways of resolving conflict, using situations from our own lives. As we do this, we remember that women's spirituality believes that everything and everyone is sacred, both ourselves and those with whom we experience difficulties.

Opening Ritual — *15 min*

The Buddhist Practice of LovingKindness
Ring the bell and then convey the following in your own words:

Let us begin our session by saying together our group mantra:

We are good, beautiful, strong, and holy. We are women of spirit. We are women of peace. We seek healing and wholeness for ourselves and our world.

We will now do the Buddhist practice of LovingKindness together, knowing that we communicate best when we are calm and centered, grounded in love, and have respect and compassion for ourselves and each other.

Many of us need to relearn how to give and receive kindness and how to be kind to ourselves. Practicing kindness supports our deeper intention to heal....LovingKindness...is the active practice of sending love and kindness to ourselves and then others. We will do this practice in silence.

Source: Excerpted from Ruth King, *Healing Rage: Women Making Inner Peace Possible.*

Read each step, pausing after each phrase so participants have time to meditate on it.

Step 1:

We begin first by sending kindness to ourselves, which is often the most alien, the most difficult, and the most needed. In your mind's eye imagine yourself seated comfortably

(Pause)…Repeat these phrases slowly with your well being in mind, and until you feel the words resting softly in your body:

- May I be well, happy, and peaceful.
- May no harm come to me.
- May I be kind, understanding, and courageous in meeting the difficulties life offers.
- May my actions in the world be motivated by love.
- May I be free from suffering.

Step 2:

Again, Pause after each phrase.

Invite the faces of dear ones to appear—those closest to you, i.e., parents, teachers, ancestors, friends, family members. *(Pause)* As they appear on the screen of your mind, acknowledge their faces and their spirits in your heart. Repeat these phrases with their well being in mind:

- May you be well, happy, and peaceful.
- May no harm come to you.
- May you be kind, understanding, and courageous in meeting the difficulties life offers.
- May your actions in the world be motivated by love.
- May you be free from suffering.

Step 3:

Finally, imagine those who have caused harm and suffering to you and in the world. Unfriendly people and those full of pain, greed, and hatred. Those who have innocently or willfully misunderstood you or others. Those who have not been in their right mind. *(Pause)* Again, repeat the above phrases slowly with their well being in mind.

End the meditation by telling the group:

Let us conclude by saying together:

May we all be well, happy, and peaceful. May no harm come to us. May we all be kind, understanding, and courageous in meeting the difficulties life offers. May our actions in the world be motivated by love. May we all be free from suffering.

Ring the bell.

Source: Exerpted and adapted from Ruth King, *Healing Rage: Women Making Inner Peace Possible.*

Reflections from the Last Session — 10 min

Share the following:

> Find a partner and share with her any insights that came up or experiences you had between sessions, or reflections you had on the Life Practice, journal questions, or the readings.

CARA: The Four-Step Process for Nonviolent Engagement — 20 min

Share in your own words:

> Women's spirituality greatly values power-within, that power we tap into when we listen to and act from our deepest self. It also values power-with. Power-with seeks what is best for both ourselves and for those with whom we experience conflict.
>
> We experienced power-with in the Two Hands of Nonviolence exercise. The CARA process offers an additional way to use this power-with to make peace.
>
> As you will remember, one of our journal questions for this session included reading the CARA Four-Step Process.
>
> CARA — Center, Articulate, Receive, and Agree—is a four-step process for nonviolent engagement and transformation. CARA means "face" in Spanish. This process is a way to relate face-to-face with others in a nonviolent way, and is also a method for understanding how nonviolent action in social movements happens. It helps us to face people with whom we are in conflict in a way that does not avoid, accommodate, or respond to conflict in a like manner. Let us now go through this process step by step.

Step One: Center Ourselves

> Centering is the process of making contact with what is really happening within us, our *true selves*—that part of us where our heart, mind, and body are connected, and our heart is allowed to function unobstructed. By anchoring ourselves in our heart, we are prepared to *respond*, not simply *react*, to the conflict we are facing. We may decide to protect ourselves. We may decide to engage. In either case, we can act from a place where we are most truly who we are, and not simply from a worn-out and potentially destructive script.
>
> *Brainstorm with participants how they center and ground themselves. Some possible ways include (write these on easel paper after soliciting from group):*

- Breathing and focusing on one's breath
- Asking the other person to sit down

- Silently repeating a meaningful or sacred prayer, word, mantra, or name
- Recognizing and naming one's emotional state in that moment (fear, anger, sadness, happiness, and so forth)

Step Two: Articulate Our Truth

The goal of Step Two is to identify and share what is happening for us in the moment. This involves discovering what we are truly feeling and needing, and then sharing it with the other person. By being open, direct, vulnerable, and inviting, we are disarming ourselves so that the other person can feel less defensive. We have an attitude of interest and curiosity, trying to learn from the other. We believe in cooperation. We don't want to engage in a power struggle, but believe we can reach a win-win solution.

Brainstorm with participants how they can do this. Some examples include (write these on the easel paper):

- Relaxing body posture
- Speaking slowly and softly
- Using "I" statements such as:
  I feel...
  I believe...

Step Three: Receive the Truth of the Other Person

Step Three involves *deep listening* to the other person's truth: their feelings and what they need. It requires us to be truly curious and interested in the other, in their position and in them as persons. We are limited beings with a finite understanding of and possession of the Truth. Our commitment should be to the Truth, more than our version of the truth. This insight—the fact that we only have a piece of the truth—opens us to the piece of the truth of the other person, including our opponent. Our opponent often has a piece of the truth that we are missing, that we will only get by being curious and listening with our hearts. There is a reason that they are holding a position different from the one you are; try to get to it.

Brainstorm some possible ways to do this step. Some examples include (write on easel paper):

- Listening actively, reflecting back what we're hearing
- Asking questions with curiosity
- Asking questions by lowering your voice at the end of the sentence

- Seeing what the person means by using certain words, what she or he believes or feels
- Checking out any of your own assumptions concerning the situation
- Probe any inconsistencies you may notice between the other person's words and their non-verbal communication (for example, when someone says in a loud, forced voice, "I am fine!" we see a contradiction).
- If you need time to think through the other's sharing, ask to resume the conversation later.

Note that Steps Two and Three are reversible.

Step Four: Agree, Don't Assume

Step Four is the process of revealing the truth and untruth of both parties, and finding ways to put the "two truths together" and discover the points of agreement where the needs of both parties are met.

Realizing that truth gets revealed over time and that our learning and growing is a process, we remain constantly open to revising our understanding, as we are transforming in the truth.

Brainstorm some possible ways to do this step. Some examples include (write on easel paper):

- Point out the elements you both agree on
- Ask the other person if each of you can consider the truth of the other and can agree on any of those additional pieces of the truth
- Agree to disagree on the elements that are clearly in opposition to each other

Ask if there are any questions.

> I really see no other solution than to turn inward and to root out all the rottenness there. I no longer believe we can change anything in the world until we have first changed ourselves.
>
> Etty Hillesum

The Habits of Mutuality
By Katherine Zappone

A spirituality for feminists affirms mutual relationship as the most appropriate way of living interdependence. Reciprocal respect and care for every other establishes the possibility of living from our own center while creating a life-supportive environment for others....

A spirituality for feminists will include the following habits, to be practiced regularly:

1. Self-love
2. Taking our selves and one another seriously
3. Being present to our selves and others
4. Seeing the sacred in our selves and others
5. Acknowledging and respecting differences
6. Facing conflict
7. Participating in supportive communities

We have already seen that self love is the starting point of mutual love....To see the sacred in ourselves and others is to declare the inherent goodness and equal worthiness of all. Feminist thealogy declares that we are the living body of the sacred; the Goddess is within. Mary Daly writes of the divine spark in each woman's Self. Perceiving sacredness as part of humanity is one spiritual habit that leads to another. As Janet Kalven states, "Seeing God/dess in the other, seeing the other as sacred, is the theological basis for respecting differences." Valuing and receiving others as they are in themselves means to receive, love, and celebrate the differences. This no doubt generates conflict. Our participation in supportive communities provides safe space to face the conflicts and mend the brokenness that they cause.

Interdependent "love of neighbor" sunders our illusion of separateness. We cannot be healed by ourselves. The healing happens now, even as we anticipate future wholeness. Mutual relationships empower imagination of a new world, even as we live in the present one. Friendship animates politics; we cannot transform the world alone. In a spirituality for feminists, [the Holy One] can't do it alone either.

Source: Katherine Zappone, *The Hope for Wholeness: A Spirituality For Feminists.*

Nonviolent Engagement Real-Play Exercise — *60 min*

Now we will work with the CARA process ourselves. Again, the CARA four steps are:

1) Center yourself
2) Articulate your truth
3) Receive the truth of the other person, and
4) Agree, don't assume

We will now have an opportunity to practice the Four Steps by performing a "real-play" exercise. A "real-play" is a role-play exercise that practices nonviolent responses to a challenging, concrete, and real-life conflict or situation. (This process often has many benefits, including helping us get a feel for how our adversary may see our position.)

Convey the following in your own words:

We will practice the Four-Step process by having one person share a conflict she is dealing with. Some of you will volunteer to be the other person or people involved in this conflict scenario. The rest of you will be observers.

Who has a conflict she would like to work on? You will be the main actress.

You may need to first solicit several scenarios before deciding on the one that the group will use. (You may want to have one or two conflict scenarios in mind in case the group is unable to decide on a situation that they want to use.)

Or, here is one possible conflict:

Maria, Sarah, and Janice work at an ad agency. They are the team that is responsible for coming up with new ideas for campaigns. The three of them have agreed that each week they will send their written proposals to each other the day before the staff meeting so that they have time to discuss what they will recommend to the larger group. Sarah never gets her proposal in on time. Maria and Janice are becoming quite upset about this because it affects the team's productivity. Maria and Janice have decided to have a conversation with Sarah. Either Maria or Janice can be the main actress, the person who will use the CARA process.

After the group has agreed on a conflict scenario, set up a chair for the participant who comes forward. Make sure that the main actress can see the four steps on the easel paper on the wall. Invite the person to share the scenario briefly with the rest of the group and to give enough information so that the other participants can play the other roles.

As the main actress shares the conflict situation, identify the other actors and actresses involved in the situation. Set up chairs for each of those people. Then ask:

Who would like to play one of the other roles?

Invite them up to take the other seats.

Then say:

> The main actress will play herself and will try to use the four steps. The other actors or actresses have not heard of the four steps, so they will not use them. The role of those remaining in the circle is to be observers. Their task is to think of other ways to use the four steps. If at any time during the real-play you have a suggestion of how to play the main role, tag-in—take the main actress' place, when you are moved to do so. Now, everyone take a minute to get into your roles. Ready, begin.

Let the real-play last for awhile, giving the main actress, and possibly others who tag-in, enough time to practice the steps. Then sound the bell and invite the participants to return to their seats in the large group and debrief.

Go through each step of the CARA process by asking the group the following questions:

- Which steps did the main actress do well?
- How did she center herself?
- How did she articulate her truth?
- How did she receive the truth of the other person?
- What, if any, agreement was reached?
- Which steps could be improved?

Then ask the group:

- What did you learn in this real-play?
- How can you apply what you learned to your life?

Write the responses on easel paper.

During the debrief it may be helpful to bring out some of the following points:

> For longer, ongoing conflicts (for example, with those in our family), it is better not to dwell on past differences, but to build on the truths that we can bring together. Be future-oriented instead of past-oriented.

> In some cases, the other person's truth or behavior may cross your boundaries. If the other is unwilling to change her words or behavior, you can take action to protect yourself (in other words, using the Two Hands of Nonviolence, place your hand in the stop position), while at the same time being open to the continued dialogue and relationship (the outstretched hand). You set both the negative and positive consequence of the other person's behavior at the same time. Setting limits takes the following format:

• If…, then…

For example, if someone keeps meeting you for dinner later than your agreed-to time, and the steps have not been effective in finding a resolution that leads to agreement, you might say in a very neutral tone:

> "If you do not arrive by 6 pm, I will go to dinner by myself. If you arrive by 6 pm, I will be happy to go to dinner with you."

This way, you are setting limits with the other and protecting yourself in the process. You are also offering the positive alternative. This statement is not done in a punitive way, but is put forward as a natural consequence. See Sharon Ellison's work for more details about setting limits.

To close this exercise, share:

> I hope this exercise has given you the opportunity to apply what you have   learned about communicating nonviolently by practicing it in a real-life situation.

CARA is based on a four-part process developed by the late Bill Moyer, and is used with permission. Elements used in Steps Two through Four are drawn from Sharon Ellison's process called Powerful, Non-Defensive Communication. See her book, *Taking the War Out of Our Words: The Art of Powerful, Non-Defensive Communication.* Source: Adapted from Slattery, Butigan, Pelicaric, and Preston-Pile, *Engage: Exploring Nonviolent Living.*

Closing — 10 min

Share the following:

> Let us end our time together by taking a few deep breaths and releasing them, or if we need to, by shaking the conflict we just experienced out of our bodies.

Ring the bell.

> Imagine the person you are experiencing conflict with. Bring her or him silently into the circle. Remembering the practice of LovingKindness, we will go around the circle and complete these sentences. "I desire_____for myself. I desire the same for my opponent."

Let us again say together:

May we all be well, happy, and peaceful. May no harm come to us. May we all be kind, understanding, and courageous in meeting the difficulties life offers. May our actions in the world be motivated by love. May we all be free from suffering.

Ring the bell.

Looking Ahead — *3 min*

In preparation for the next session, remind participants to do the Life Practice, journal topics and questions, and the next session's readings, found at the end of this session.

Life Practice

Think of a person with whom you are currently experiencing a conflict. If you feel ready, have a conversation with him or her, using the CARA four-step process. You can prepare ahead of time by practicing the real-play with a friend or group member.

My Story
By Darlene Thomas

I was in between paychecks, staying in a motel, and I couldn't pay the bill. No one, no agencies, would help me—until I called St. Mary's Center. I was crying so much. The case-worker told me to calm down and to come on over. That very same day, I started staying at the shelter.

I was afraid. I didn't know what to expect. It was the first time I had ever been homeless.

While I stayed in the shelter, I attended a class in nonviolence. I wanted to see what nonviolence was. I wanted to learn how to be nonviolent.

The class really helped me. I used to be very verbal. I'd react pretty angrily. In this class, I learned how to talk to people better. I was able to talk to folks in the shelter calmly, even if some of them acted crazy.

I also learned a lot about patience. I had to wait awhile to get housing, but I learned how to wait patiently. And, I talked to others and helped them hang in there. I talked one woman into returning to the shelter—she left because it took so long to find housing. After she returned, she finally got housing.

And, I joined the Senior Advocates for Hope and Justice at St. Mary's Center. I went to talk to the Oakland City Council and to the California state senators in Sacramento. The class helped me learn how to talk to politicians who didn't agree with us about what low-income housing is. We mean housing for really poor people, homeless people! Because I learned about nonviolence, I was able to communicate with them much more effectively, instead of just yelling at them. Hopefully, they heard what we had to say!

Source: This story was told to Cindy Preston-Pile for *Traveling with the Turtle*.

Journal Topics and Questions

1) Were you encouraged or discouraged to be creative as a child? How was this experience for you?

2) In your life now, how do you create? What do you create?

Readings for Session 8

Our Creative Power
By Julia Occhiogrosso

I had spoken from the heart that evening to the Holy One. After months of confusion and fears around bringing a new life into a painful world, I asked the Spirit to send wisdom and guidance. Should I try to have a baby? In sleep that night the images came to answer. Out of the dark an explosion shook the earth. Sea waters touched the skies, tossing sea creatures into the night air. Soldiers with guns and gas masks came walking out of the night ocean. It was the end of the world.

Within seconds of having this perception a new image came into view. Bright sunlight filled the garden as I mused on healthy rows of full leaf mustard greens lined adjacent to healthy rows of colorful pansy flowers.

Even as we face the fear and despair of "end of the world" scenarios there is a garden somewhere, on the earth, in our souls, someplace unknown perhaps, where life in all its fullness will always be ready to break forth in full color.

Life breaking forth is *creative power*. It is infinite possibility and it is true hope.

Our True Self, our divine self, is the home of our creative power. When we are in our most authentic selves we can access this power. Creative power flows freely from this dwelling. As much as we reside in this dwelling, we will become Co-creators with the Spirit; fostering peace, integrity, compassion, beauty, justice and healing.

Days after having this dream I became pregnant. My husband and I were filled with the excitement and longing to become parents. We were filled with the anticipation of having another to share our love with. I was so convinced of the rightness of this path, that I was dismayed and deeply saddened when the pregnancy ended abruptly with a miscarriage. What about the dream? What did this all mean?

After a period of grieving my thoughts came back to the dream. It still spoke the message of hope for me. It was still there providing the wisdom and guidance I needed once again. I was ready to look for the life breaking forth even in the midst of the "end of my world."

Our creative power is an inexhaustible resource available for us to return to. It is always ready to offer us a new way, a new idea, a different path in the journey toward fulfilling our dreams, our purpose, our vision.

The power of the dream image was still unfolding within me. The decision to parent born out of the dream was still present. It was inviting us to create life in a different way. We were to create new life through adoption.

Creative power requires enormous trust. It requires trust to create a great painting or a loving relationship. Creative expression is possible when we can let go of the results just long enough to lose ourselves deeply in the Great Mystery of the process itself. Abundant and un-expected beauty often emerges when we make the choice to give willingly into the unknown, without being completely sure of what may prevail. When we take risks of any degree, we are opening a space for the creative power within us to take form in the world. Two years after having the dream my husband and I adopted two toddlers. We became parents.

Our story is not unique. There are thousands of people who have adopted children. Indeed, ordinary people every day make countless decisions large and small that are creative and life giving. I draw inspiration from the many different stories that I have heard of people who sacrifice themselves to care for an infirm family member. Single parents who have to hold full-time jobs and raise children. People who come out of very oppressive living environments and manage to be forgiving and generous. They are for me examples of people accessing creative power to build a more peaceful world.

To use our creative power to promote peace, we need to make a distinction between what the market culture defines and encourages as creative and what a peace maker hopes to create. All too often creative power is associated with the ingenuity of creating a new product, gadget or invention. These products may even have seemingly important social benefits. They may seem to make mundane tasks easier. Like a dish washer, washing machine, or cell phone. And while they may seem to enhance our quality of life their benefits are short lived and limited. These products were created to play a role in the market economy. Here creative power is aligned with the demands and principles of market culture. It is sustained by the myth of progress. All that is created in this arena is experienced as moving us higher on the ladder toward human fulfill-ment. Yet frequently what is "created" is produced by exploited labor, has a negative impact on the environment and does little to humanize the planet.

Naming this distinction we begin to see that for peacemakers creative power needs to be claimed and shared in a way that honors life-giving principles. The two most significant of these principles are that all life is sacred and that all human life is in relationship with one another and the earth. What harms one harms all. What heals one heals all.

Guided by these principles peacemakers seek to meet the daily moments of their lives with compassion and integrity. Whether they are tending gardens or tending children, whether they are waiting tables or cleaning hotel rooms, whether they are organizing a peace protest or facilitating peace workshops they must always ask the question: how is my approach in keeping with these principles?

At this time in my life, I find my creative peacemaking is centered around mothering our now 10 and 11 year old sons. Each day holds new challenges. How do I respond as peacemaker when a child is acting out in anger? What can we do to help heal the wounds of loss and grief? How do I offer effective alternatives to my sons on how to respond to conflict and violence in their lives? How do I create a home environment that awakens the unique expression of their creative peacemaker?

Indeed, in just voicing the questions we are transported into a place of transformation. A place where dreams and the unconscious potential are discovered, embodied and brought to life. A place where the seed of our creative power takes root and refuses to die. Reminding us that even in our darkest moments the dream of peace can become reality by conscious creative acts.

Source: Julia Occhiogrosso, written for *Traveling with the Turtle*.

A Spirituality of Naturalness
By Sue Monk Kidd

One particular way we can embody Sacred Feminine experience in our daily lives is to embrace a spirituality of naturalness. Like springwater, this spirituality arises out of our nature, our feminine nature. It's native to us, not artificial or manufactured or piped in from some other place. Very simply; this spirituality is true to who we are as women; it comes from within us and flows out....

Sacred Feminine consciousness seizes us by the shoulders, looks in our eyes, and tells us with passion and simplicity: If you don't get anything else, get this. This is your life, right now, on this changing earth, in this impermanent body, among these excruciatingly ordinary things. This is it. You will not find it anywhere else.

A natural (and feminine) spirituality tends to incorporate three very organic, basic, but overlooked things into our sacred experience: the earthly, the now, and the ordinary.

THE EARTHLY I live only a few hours from the ocean, and I try to get there as often as possible. The last time I was there, on a September morning, I took my scarf, a wild purple thing with gold fringe that I'd bought in a used clothing store in New Mexico, and I went down to the shore with my flashlight just before the sun came up, when no one was around, not even the crabbers. I took my scarf and danced in my bare feet in the breaking light, on and on along the waves that had by then all turned to harps. The wind whipped my scarf, whipped through me. I was living out my freedom. I was paying my respects to Herself, rejuvenating my connection, pulling myself like a thread through the shoreline. On that morning I felt that I was one of the ten thousand broken shells tumbling in the surf or one of the pelicans, with her belly skimming the ocean, open-billed, gulping in the mystery firsthand. I told myself: This is my spirituality.

To dance with waves, sand, birds, and shells, to immerse ourselves in these earthly things, whether in jubilation at the earth's beauty or sadness over her ruin, or to simply participate in earth's small, unceasing, familiar rhythms is to embody a spirituality of naturalness. When we do these things, we are stitching ourselves into the tattered fabric of the earth. We are learning, as the Lakota Sioux say, "to live well in the natural world."

Cut off from nature, we get sick inside. We lose our sense of belonging to the earth. This belonging fuels the core of energy inside us that sustains our activism. And when we lose that, we lose drive and power. We are not able to be the tree that holds the leaning. The more we draw the earthly into our spirituality, the more responsive we become, and our responsiveness calls forth the responsiveness of others.

The afternoon after my early morning dance, I walked along the beach, picking up trash. Soon Sandy came to help, then two people, perfect strangers, joined us. Further down the beach a few children came to help. Before it was over I'd handed out half a box of garbage bags. Sandy joked that I was the pied piper of beach trash. That evening I realized that what had happened in the afternoon was not at all separate from the connection I'd felt to the earth early that morning as I pirouetted along the waves.

THE NOW A spirituality of feminine naturalness not only teaches us that the earth is our true home but that this moment is our true home. "You cannot step twice into the same river," wrote Heraclitus, "for other waters are continually flowing on." This river is your life, and it is different every moment. The important thing (the sacred, empowering, natural thing) is to step deeply into it every single moment and be there as fully as you can, seeing as clearly as you can.

Being fully in the now implies a certain acceptance of what is....When we do this, we start to come home to the now. We accept where we are standing in the river right now, and we enter the immediacy of it, even when it's painful, because by doing so we are being present to our lives. We are attending to them, living them with awareness. If you think about it, how else can we be fully alive?

As we become alive and awake to the present moment, we start to "look deeply into things and see how we can change ourselves and how we can transform our situation."[17] And gradually, as we change, things around us change. We may not realize it, but by being present and looking deeply, we are becoming activists. We start to see that the roots of injustice, the oppression of the feminine, and the planetary crisis are after all linked to how we shop and dispose of our garbage and react to the morning news and ignore our bodies and teach our children and swallow our anger at our mates....

THE ORDINARY The really important question is, What does the Sacred Feminine have to do with how we go through an ordinary day? In a way all sacred experience and all journeys of soul lead us to the smallest moment of the most ordinary day.

Yesterday I woke too early and lay there listening to the dogs snoring beneath the bed. I watched Sandy's unshaven face lying on the pillowcase, the same face I have waked to for twenty-six years. And the same light as always was expanding across the room, falling in like bright water, making me want to stay there and watch how it flowed over us, illuminating a continent of small things—my glasses beside the bed, my journal, piles of books. There were the children's pictures framed on the dresser—babies then, gone away now....I felt my flesh pressed against the sheet; pressed upon this moment. From the bathroom I heard the faucet dripping, then the murmur of my breath moving in and out of my nostrils, and behind it all the pendulum clock in the distance, clicking like a metronome atop a piano, creating the domestic cadence against

which this morning and all other mornings played.

I rose to make the coffee. I walked to the door and paused. When I looked back, I saw my life shining within every ordinary thing. And I was seized by the same feeling I get whenever I see the ocean—the feeling that it is all too much to behold, too beautiful, too much to bear—and I was filled with an aching love for it.

In the next instant the moment was gone, and I was climbing down the stairs, walking into the kitchen, into a day of small, humble, distracting things, and somehow nothing seemed more holy to me than just being there, naturally myself, in the midst of it.

Such moments are not as common for me as I might wish. But when they come, they leave me with a willingness to relate to my ordinary space—my work and family and friends and all the mundane duties—more authentically. I want to be in my feminine center in the midst of those plain places and to tell the truth and be the truth.

I heard a story about a man who went about the countryside asking people how they would spend their last day on earth. He came upon a woman who was out hoeing her garden, surrounded by her children and neighbor women. He decided he might as well ask her, too, even though he didn't expect much of an answer. "Woman," he asked, "if this were your last day on earth, if tomorrow it was certain you would die, what would you do today?"

"Oh," she said, "I would go on hoeing my garden and taking care of my children and talking to my neighbors."

The woman knew that there is nothing more important than being fully where we are, in the plain, ordinary events, day in and day out...

I think women understand that we create change as we live out the experiences of our souls in the common acts of life.

[17] Thich Nhat Hanh, *Peace is Every Step: The Path of Mindfulness in Everyday Life* (New York: Bantam Books, 1991), p. 112.

Source: Sue Monk Kidd, *The Dance of the Dissident Daughter.*

Bulgarian Tile Projects Have Roots in Berkeley
By Matthew Artz

Sally Hindman has made a name for herself in Berkeley as the homeless advocate who co-founded *Street Spirit*. But if all goes according to plan, her biggest legacy could be in Varna, Bulgaria.

Hindman first traveled to the Black Sea port town two years ago to adopt an orphaned Roma ("Gypsy") child, but in the finest tradition of Berkeley do-gooders she threw her arms around the entire town.

While spending nearly five months in Varna waiting for officials to process the adoption of her now 3-year-old daughter Sylvia, Hindman followed through on her planned tile wall art project for local Roma youth, assisted the local Jewish community win international grants to rebuild its synagogue left in disrepair since World War II and immersed herself in the city's history, including its role as a chief point of departure to Palestine for European Jews fleeing Nazi persecution.

Now, armed with a grant from the U.S. embassy in Bulgaria...Hindman is planning a return trip early next year to oversee construction of a second tile wall she hopes can honor the city's Jewish past and create a better future for all its residents. "I want it to facilitate healing around the past and put forth a vision for creating a tolerant community," she said.

The centerpiece of the wall will be a memorial to the victims of the Ship Salvador, which on Dec. 4, 1940 departed Varna for Palestine with 321 refugees and sank in the Marmara Sea off the coast of Turkey. Two hundred and one passengers drowned, 66 of whom are believed to have been orphans.

"Every time I visited that little gypsy child, I kept imagining the boatload of people escaping in the middle of winter. Especially since my husband was a little Jewish child," she said.

When it comes to treatment of Jews, Bulgaria scores fairly well for an eastern European country. Nearly all of the country's estimated 50,000 Jews avoided concentration camps, thanks largely to energetic support of Bulgarian society against the Nazi's puppet regime.

But like nearly all countries in Eastern Europe, Bulgaria's Roma minority, which a 1992 census placed at 312,000, suffers from ingrained prejudice and has seen its standard of living drop...since the country emerged from Soviet domination.

"In Bulgaria, Roma never gets a fair chance for jobs or education," said Sani Rifati, president of Voice of Roma, a charitable organization based in Sebastopol, California....Inevitably, he added, many Roma women decide they can't care for their babies and give them to orphanages, the fate Sylvia suffered prior to her adoption by Hindman. Hindman said she witnessed local disdain for both minority groups during her first stint in Bulgaria. She watched a police officer beat a Roma man on a train and she tore down posters of hook-nosed Jews that served as an advertisement for a joke book about Jews.

Even before her journey to Varna, though, she had drawn parallels between the two groups, which contributed to her and her husband's decision to adopt a Roma.

"We wanted to reconnect with Eastern Europe and with my husband's roots there," she said. "We thought we might have something to offer a Roma child."

Sylvia knows who her "mommy" is. The rambunctious girl, who competed gamely for Hindman's attention during a recent interview, will accompany her mother in Varna and attend nursery school in her home town.

While Sylvia enjoys a homecoming, Hindman will be hard at work pulling off the tile project. She hopes the wall will be both a work of art and a vehicle for Roma, Jewish and ethnic Bulgarian children to learn about each other and move beyond centuries-old prejudices.

Before she begins the project, Hindman is working to raise…donations to pay for Roma youth facilitators to lead tolerance workshops where Roma and Jewish youth will discuss the discrimination they face.

Each of the Jewish children participating in the project will design a tile with the name of a victim of the Ship Salvador. Hindman tracked down all the names by searching archives at Yad Vashem, the holocaust museum in Jerusalem….

Hindman's last tile wall was built by 250 Roma youth, many of whom were orphans…. The young artists painted tiles demonstrating their future dreams and the final work now stands on permanent exhibit at the Varna Children's Museum.

The future location of the proposed project rests with the Varna City Council, said Hindman, who said she would lobby for high-visibility space.

"This wall is a pledge for a tolerant city," she said. "It's a statement that this is our past but it's never going to happen again."

Source: Matthew Artz, "Bulgarian Tile Projects Have Roots in Berkeley," *Berkeley Daily Planet.*

Session 8

*Creative Power: Expanding Our
Vision of Peacemaking*

Session 8
Creative Power: Expanding Our Vision of Peacemaking

In this Session We Will:
- Claim our creative power
- Consider what it means to create
- Reflect on the obstacles that keep us from acknowledging and using our creative power
- Share ways that we create or make peace in our everyday lives

Agenda
Introduction — *2 min*
Reflections from the Last Session — *10 min*
Opening Ritual — *15 min*
What Does it Mean to Create? — *20 min*
What Keeps Me From Claiming My Creative Power? — *15 min*
Creating Peace in Our Everyday Lives — *40 min*
Closing — *15 min*
Looking Ahead — *3 min*
       Life Practice
       Journal Topics and Questions
       Readings

Materials Needed
- ☐ Shared Agreements
- ☐ Prayer table
- ☐ A cloth
- ☐ A colorful candle
- ☐ Matches
- ☐ An 8 ½ x 11 sheet of white paper for each person in the group
- ☐ Pens
- ☐ Several more 8 ½ x 11 sheets of white paper cut into smaller pieces. Each member of the group will need several pieces to write on for "What Keeps Me From Claiming My Creative Power?"
- ☐ A bowl
- ☐ Compact disk or audio tape player (if desired)
- ☐ Recorded music (if desired)

Facilitator Notes
Session preparation — A week before
• Review the entire session. Practice reading any visualizations or meditations, and role-play or practice setting up and facilitating exercises beforehand. Whenever possible, put material into your own words. Feel free to make notes on 3x5 cards or in the book next to the written instructions.
• Cut some of the 8 ½ x 11 sheets of paper into smaller pieces so that each woman will have several to write on for the "What Keeps Me From Claiming My Creative Power?" exercise.

Session preparation— The day of
• Arrange the chairs, including your own, in a circle, with a small table in the center. Place the cloth, candle, and matches on the table.
• Tape the Shared Agreements to the wall.
• Play some background music as people arrive, if desired.

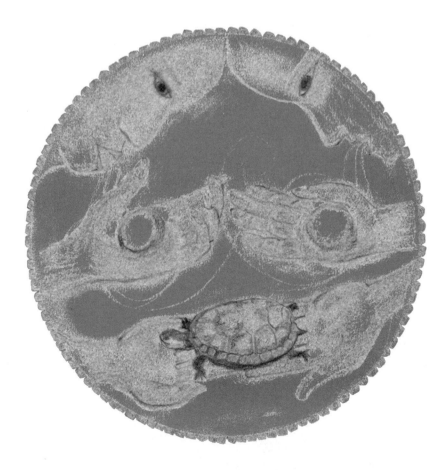

Session 8
Creative Power: Expanding Our Vision of Peacemaking

Introduction — *2 min*

Convey the following in your own words:

> Welcome to Session 8. In Session 7 we practiced peaceful ways of responding to conflict. As we gather this time, we will claim the creative power that we possess by considering what it means to create and reflect on the obstacles that keep us from acknowledging and using this power. We will recognize, release, and celebrate this awesome power by sharing ways that we create peace, justice, healing, and compassion in our everyday lives.

Reflections from the Last Session — *10 min*

Share the following:

> Find a partner and share with her any insights that came up or experiences you had between sessions, or reflections you had on the Life Practice, journal questions, or readings.

Opening Ritual — *15 min*

Light the candle to begin this ritual. Say the group mantra together: We are good, beautiful, strong, and holy. We are women of spirit. We are women of peace. We seek healing and wholeness for ourselves and our world.

Then read the following meditation slowly for the group, inviting members to participate at whatever level they are able when they are asked to move their hands and arms.

Hand Meditation

> Let us begin.
>
> Close your eyes and sit as erect as possible, your feet flat on the ground, and your hands on your lap, palms up, without touching each other....
>
> Begin to be aware of your breathing. Tune into the sensations of your whole body breathing. Let your breathing relax all of you.

Check the tension points. Relax your calves, your thighs, your buttocks, your stomach, your back, your shoulders, your arms. Press your eyes tightly for a few seconds, and release immediately. This will free your forehead of its intensity. Let your head tip forward in slow motion so that the tension muscles of your neck can relax. Let your jaw loosen and let it take a gentle yawn.

Begin to experience your whole body smiling. Feel how good it is to be here, now, and have nothing to do but be. Be aware of the mystery of your own breath. *(Pause)*

Become aware of the air at your fingertips, between your fingers, on the palm of your hands. Experience the fullness, strength, and maturity of your hands. Think of your hands, think of the most unforgettable hands you have known. Remember the oldest hands that have rested in your hands. Think of the hands of a newborn child...your baby...your nephew or niece—of the incredible beauty, perfection, and delicacy in the hands of a child. Once upon a time your hands were the same size. *(Pause)*

Think of all that your hands have done since then. Almost all that you have learned has been through your hands, turning yourself over, crawling, creeping, walking and balancing yourself, learning to hold something for the first time, feeding yourself, washing and bathing, and dressing yourself. At one time your greatest accomplishment was tying your own shoes. *(Pause)*

Think of all the learning your hands have done and how many activities they have mastered, the things they have made. Remember the day you could write your own name. *(Pause)*

Hands are not just for ourselves but for others. How often they were given to help another. Remember all the kinds of work they have done, the tiredness and aching they have known, the cold and the heat, the soreness, and the bruises. Remember the tears they have wiped away, our own or another's, the blood they have bled, the healing they have experienced. How much hurt, anger, and even violence they have expressed, and how much gentleness, tenderness, and love they have given. *(Pause)*

Now call to mind those hands that have helped and guided you—your spouse, a loved one, a teacher. *(Pause)*

Now raise your hand and place it on your heart. Press gently and feel the heartbeat learned in your mother's womb.

Slowly lower your hand to your lap as though you carry your heart. In actuality, your hand is a heartbeat.

Think of all the places that carry your heartbeat.

Reach out on either side and take a hand…don't just hold the hand, explore the history of that hand…whose hand is that? It could be anyone's hand…it could be… the Holy One's…hand. It is the Holy One's…hand…because the only hands that… [She]…has are our hands…our hands that build a nonviolent community.

Source: Quoted and adapted from Sister Mary Mattias Ward, *Hand Meditation*, unpublished.

Continue by saying:

Let go of each others' hands and hold your own hands out toward the middle of the circle that we might bless them and the potential they have to bring life and healing to another. Let us bless their creative power.

Read the following blessing, one line at a time, and have the group respond:

Facilitator:	Blessed be the works of your hands, O Holy One.
Group:	*Blessed be the works of your hands, O Holy One*
	Blessed be these hands that have touched life…
	Blessed be these hands that have touched life.
	that have nurtured creativity…
	that have nurtured creativity.
	that have held pain…
	that have held pain
	that have embraced with passion…
	that have embraced with passion
	that have tended gardens…
	that have tended gardens
	that have closed in anger…
	that have closed in anger
	that have planted new seeds…
	that have planted new seeds
	that have harvested ripe fields…
	that have harvested ripe fields
	that have cleaned, washed, mopped, scrubbed…

that have cleaned, washed, mopped, scrubbed
that are wrinkled and scarred from doing justice…
that are wrinkled and scarred from doing justice
that have reached out and been received…
that have reached out and been received
that hold the promise of the future…
that hold the promise of the future.
Blessed be the works of your hands, O Holy One.
Blessed be the works of your hands, O Holy One.

Source: Adapted from a prayer by Diann Neu, "A Hand Blessing," from *WATERwheel.*

What Does it Mean to Create? — *20 min*

Explain the following in your own words:

We have blessed our hands, hands that have nurtured creativity. As we ponder further this incredible gift that we have been given, the ability to create, let us first consider: What does it mean to create? We are going to spend some time reflecting on this question. How would you describe the process, the act of creating? What does it feel like, look like, taste like, sound like, smell like? We will each write a variation of haiku, a Japanese form of poetry, about what it means to create.

Give everyone a sheet of paper and a pen. As you read these instructions, leave time between each direction for the women to write:

- Draw four lines on the sheet of paper. On the first line, write the word "creating."
- On the second line write two words that describe creating.
- On the third line write one sentence of five or fewer words about what creating means.
- On the fourth line write a synonym (another word) for creating.

After everyone is finished writing, say:

Let us go around the circle and read our poems. (You may want to begin this process.)

Poetry Alive Tribe

Feeling humble & building upon
A foundation of love tenderness & grace
Reflection being the key to the soul
Soul & spirit bonded together as one
Which carries me closer to my creator
Praying for the sureness to become
a <u>complete woman</u>
I feel, I write what I feel, and not what I see
When I read it back, it sounds like me
I then can face life with peace of mind
& balance that brings forth completeness
Peace is a state of mind, everyone wants to achieve.
It's a freedom mentally & spiritually
Unspoken child, words mild, spirit Wild
Let me cast a spell to dream endless possibilities the whole while
To live life to its fullest, so when I leave
I leave with a blaze of glory
I will then know, I lived it the way I understand
For I am small, yet I walk tall, with confidence & faithfully showing it.
We are grateful for this experience, POETRY CLASS.

Source: Written by women in the Options Program at Riverside Correctional Facility in Philadelphia, who participated in a poetry workshop organized by the American Friends Service Committee National Criminal Justice Program. Tonya McClary, "Poetry as Healing," in *The Vision*, Fall 2005, page 4.

What Keeps Me From Claiming My Creative Power? — *15 min*

Share the following in your own words:

We have described what it means to create. We all possess the ability to create—this power, this prodding, this potential that dwells within us and yet we are not always able to claim this gift for ourselves and express it in the world. Perhaps we associate creating with those who are professionals—professional painters, ballet dancers, or musicians. This narrow view of creating can keep us from bringing "something into existence"

(*New Oxford American Dictionary* definition of create), something that only we can give birth to—a project, a baby, the story that is within us to tell.

Give each woman several pieces of paper and a pen and say:

> On the pieces of paper that you hold in your hands, I invite you to write or draw a few of the obstacles that keep you from acknowledging, naming, and using your creative power. What do you need to let go of in order to say "Yes, I am a creative person"?

Place the bowl on the prayer table. When group members are finished writing or drawing these obstacles, invite them to come forward, one at a time, and read them aloud if they so desire, tear them up, and then place them in the bowl. Or, everyone might prefer to tear up her obstacles at the same time and then place them in the bowl.

Hold the bowl up and conclude by saying in your own words:

> Freed of these obstacles that keep us from embracing fully this glorious, divine gift of creative power, let us now explore ways that we are already being creative—and creating peace—in our daily lives.

Set the bowl aside.

Creating Peace in Our Everyday Lives — *40 min*

How Do I Create? — *10 min*

Say:

> Let us first reflect briefly on the journal questions. Find a partner and respond to these questions:

> *Life breaking forth is creative power. It is infinite possibility and it is true hope.*
>
> Julia Occhiogrosso

> • How do you create?
> • Or, how do you use this power?

You may want to let the pairs know when five minutes has passed so the other woman has the opportunity to share. Invite everyone back to the large group at the end of ten minutes.

Reflection — *5 min*

Read the following or share in your own words:

> As women, we all have the potential to bring new life into this world through our

bodies, hearts, and souls. In her reflection, Julia Occhiogrosso writes that, "Life breaking forth is *creative power*." Creative power sings of newness, endless possibilities, a different path taken—adopting a child when we thought we would give birth to one, working less so we can care for an older parent, forgiving someone who hurt us decades ago.

Creative power speaks of imagining and establishing new relationships that are filled with compassion, care, and healing. In the sidebar, "From War, I Dance," Celia Trang Le, who lived through the Vietnam War, says that she dances "to create new images of my neighbors. I dance to touch the hearts of others who are in every way different from me." Similarly, Sally Hindman describes how she sought to facilitate healing and create a more tolerant community by bringing together Roma, Jewish, and ethnic Bulgarian children to work together on a tile wall art project. We make peace with each other as we discover new ways of being together.

Using our creative power in our relationships with others expands our vision of what it means to make peace. The power of creativity is that it opens an infinite number of ways to be a peacemaker. How do you use your creative power to make peace in your ordinary, everyday life? How do you create peace, make peace, live peace, be peace?

Large Group Sharing — *25 min*

Ask the group to respond to the following question:

- How are you creating peace in your family, with friends, at work, or in your community? For example, how are you facilitating healing or building and nurturing relationships?

Closing — 15 min

Dance to Create Peace

Form a circle away from the chairs. Set the bowl filled with obstacles that keep each woman from using her creative power in the middle of the circle. Then introduce this dance by giving the following directions in your own words:

> Let us now celebrate the creative spirit that is moving among us by embodying our creative power, by dancing a dance on behalf of the many ways that we create peace.

> I invite you to first of all scatter our obstacles to claiming our creativity, that are in this bowl, on the ground that we might transform them through our dance. (*You will be dancing on the pieces of paper.*)

> Now join hands. We will first take two steps to the right—move your right foot and then place your left foot next to your right foot. Do that again. Now, we will take two steps to the left—move your left foot and then place your right foot next to your left foot. Repeat.

> Then we all take four steps forward into the circle beginning with the right foot and raising our held hands and then take four steps back to the place where we were standing, lowering our arms.

> We will first say the following words together as we dance. Then as we continue, the dance, see if the words become a tune or a chant:

> Creative Spirit flow through me (step right twice)

> Creative Spirit flow through me (step left twice)

> Repeat

> Bringing peace and harmony (take four steps into the circle)

> Bringing peace and harmony (take four steps back out)

Call out, and then invite the group to add other adjectives that describe Spirit—Loving, Joyful, Playful, Peaceful, etc. Again, create your own melody or chant. You can also do other simple movements to the music or chant.

From War, I Dance
By Cecilia Trang Le

Cecilia Trang Le and her family escaped Vietnam by boat on their ninth attempt to leave their homeland. After becoming a U.S. citizen, working with children with AIDS, joining a religious community, and earning two degrees, she still longed for happiness.

Not too long ago, I knew nothing of peace and too little of joy. Born during the war in Vietnam, I was fed daily by the anguishes and fears of my people. For the first 16 years of my life, my movements were taught to hide; silence was my home language. Spirit was held hostage and my body carried sorrows of three generations. I understood nothing of peace.

Now living in the land of "Life, Liberty, and the Pursuit of Happiness," I have begun to dance my way to embrace new life, new freedom; and to entertain myself with possibilities. Yet the more I dance, the more I remember. I remember how poverty and war destroy life and dignity of being. I remember how painful it is to witness my father in chains and beaten by another human. I remember how fearful it is to live in the shooting zone, and how hopeless to go to bed each night knowing that I might wake up in the bloodshed of my mother or sisters.

With memories of war, I am now consciously breathing for peace, and I dance because I can't afford to forget my ancient connections. I dance to remember who I was and who I have become. I dance to ask questions that my ancestors couldn't ask. I dance because tragedies and miracles of life are simply too much for me to comprehend rationally. I dance to face my own hatred and to practice self-forgiving. I dance in memory of, on behalf of, and instead of. Each dance makes visible a new space in me for compassionate relationships. Weaving through memories of violence and grief, I dance to embrace my own limitations and truth. I dance to create new images of my neighbors. I dance to touch the hearts of others who are in every way different from me. I dance to the common language of breathing bodies, to the universal emotions and desires.

And I will continue to be a beginner of dance. I dance at the speed of my body, and stay connected to my heart, in order to be truthful. I dance attentively to each joint and bone that holds my body together. In order to learn compassion, I dance celebrating my breathing cells and muscles, in their joys and pains, in order to honor the harmony of our whole earth. Each day I dance a new story, and the story unfolds a new dance in me. In the community of awakening bodies, our human stories of birthing and dying, of love and fear, of joys and sorrows, of darkness and light, of void and fulfillment, all become one whirling resonance—the Dance of the Eternal Universe.

Source: Cynthia Winton-Henry, with Phil Porter, *What the Body Wants.*

Looking Ahead — 3 min

Life Practice

1) Nurture your creativity. Clear a space in your life—an emotional or physical space, time in your schedule—to allow your creative power to grow. See what happens.

2) Or, create something new, something that wasn't there before, in one of your relationships.

Journal Topics and Questions

1) What are some ways that you have created community throughout your life? Has this been an important part of your life journey? If so, why? If not, why not?

2) In your experience, what characteristics, dynamics, or agreements are necessary for the formation of a good, nurturing community?

Readings for Session 9

How To Change the World:
The Millionth Circle
By Jean Shinoda Bolen

"THE HUNDREDTH MONKEY" is a story that inspired antinuclear activists to keep on keeping on, when the common sense view was that the nuclear arms race could not be stopped. The story and its moral was taken to heart as an allegorical tale based upon theoretical biologist Rupert Sheldrake's Morphic Field Theory: namely, that a change in the behavior of a species occurs when a critical mass—the exact number needed—is reached. When that happens, the behavior or habits of the entire species changes. The most widely read version of the tale was written by Ken Keyes, Jr., which I retell as follows:

Off the shore of Japan, scientists had been studying monkey colonies on many separate islands for over thirty years. In order to keep track of the monkeys, they would lure them out of the trees by dropping sweet potatoes on the beach. The monkeys came to enjoy this free lunch, and were in plain sight where they could be observed. One day, an eighteen-month-old female monkey named Imo started to wash her sweet potato in the sea before eating it. I imagine that it tasted better without the grit and sand or pesticides, or maybe it even was slightly salty and that was good. Imo showed her playmates and her mother how to do this, her friends showed their mothers, and gradually more and more monkeys began to wash their sweet potatoes instead of eating them grit and all. At first, only the female adults who imitated their children learned, but gradually others did also.

One day, the scientists observed that all the monkeys on that particular island washed their sweet potatoes before eating them. Although this was significant, what was even more fascinating was that this change in monkey behavior did not take place only on this one island. Suddenly, the monkeys on all the other islands were now washing their sweet potatoes as well—despite the fact that monkey colonies on the different islands had no direct contact with each other.

"The hundredth monkey" was the hypothesized anonymous monkey that tipped the scales for the species: the one whose change in behavior meant that all monkeys would from then on wash their sweet potatoes before eating them. As an allegory, The Hundredth Monkey holds the promise that when a critical number of people change their attitude or behavior, culture at large will change. What used to be unthinkable is done by some, and then many; once a critical number of people make that shift, it becomes what we do and how we are as human beings. Someone has to be a thirty-seventh monkey, and a sixty-third, and a ninety-ninth, before there is the hundredth monkey—and no one knows how close we are or how far away that hundredth monkey is until suddenly, we are there.

If you have ever walked a labyrinth, the journey is like this. You walk and walk, following a path that turns and changes directions over and over. You have no way of knowing how far it is to the center, until suddenly you are there. Once at the center—a symbolic place

of insight and wisdom—you stay as long as you wish. Then it is time to take that knowledge or experience out into the world. And once again, you walk and walk the labyrinthine path, not knowing how close or far you are from the place you will emerge. Until you take that one last turn, and suddenly, you are out.

Like Imo and Her Friends

For human culture to change—for there to be a hundredth monkey—there has to be a human equivalent of Imo and her friends. For patriarchy to become balanced by the discerning wisdom and compassion that are associated with the feminine aspects of humanity, and by the indigenous wisdom and relatedness to all living things and to the planet, that shift will come in this hundredth-monkey way. I believe that this will happen when there are a critical number of women's circles: for patriarchy to change, there has to be *a millionth circle*. That's because what the world needs now is an infusion of the kind of wisdom women have and the form of the circle itself is an embodiment of that wisdom. Marshall McLuhan's famous expression, "The medium is the message," greatly applies to women's circles: a circle is nonhierarchical—this is what equality is like. This is how a culture behaves when it listens and learns from everyone in it.

In more ways than one, women talk in circles: conversation takes a spiral shape in its subjective exploration of every subject. Listening, witnessing, role modeling, reacting, deepening, mirroring, laughing, crying, grieving, drawing upon experience, and sharing the wisdom of experience, women in circles support each other and discover themselves, through talk. Circles of women supporting each other, healing circles, wisdom circles, soul sister circles, circles of wise women, of clan mothers, of grandmothers. Circles of crones, circles of pre-crones, lifetime circles and ad hoc circles, even circles of women in cyberspace and the business place, circles are forming everywhere. It's "Imo and her friends" getting together in circles, and learning how to be in one.

The more circles there are, the easier it is for new circles to form; this is how morphic fields work. Each circle is a regeneration of the archetypal shape and form that draws from every woman's circle that ever was, and each circle in turn adds to the field of archetypal energy that will make it easier for the next circle. Morphic fields and archetypes behave as if they have an invisible pre-existence outside of space and time, become instantly accessible to us when we align ourselves with that form, and are expressed in our thoughts, feelings, dreams, and actions. The circle is much more than the experience of this generation, a sacred circle especially.

See One, Do One, Teach One

See one, do one, teach one. When I was in medical school, this was the medical student mantra. This is how doctors learned procedures, an apprenticeship model of hands-on experience. Circle experiences are much the same, though it may be that the first circle you see is in your mind's eye and imagination. Then you might join a woman's circle or form one. Being in a circle is a learning and growing experience that draws upon the wisdom and experience, commitment, and courage of each one in it. Circles go through stages and changes, flourish or flounder, heal or hurt its members, and may be a transient experience or a lifetime one. Just as relationship skills carry over into circles, there is a vice versa; the circle experience can have a radically positive effect on relationships outside the circle, because it can provide a model—a place to practice honest and caring communication, until this is what you do and expect from others in your life. In this way, it can lead you to change the patriarchal structure of your relationships. As we begin to change our personal relationships, that change spreads. It's like throwing pebbles in a pond; each one has an impact and an effect, with concentric rings of change rippling out and affecting other relationships.

Changing Yourself and Your Share of the Patriarchy

If you suppress or put a lid on how you feel, minimize or deny what you see, or don't say what you want, and nobody in your life seems to notice, a circle is an egalitarian learning place. Just by being there. A circle that is trustworthy has a spiritual center and a respect for boundaries. It is a powerful transformer of the women in it. Circles also function as support groups; if you want to change something in your life or in yourself, it's a home base from which to go out and try. In a patriarchal climate, a circle of equals can be like an island of free speech and laughter. It makes us conscious of the contrast, through which we become aware of what we do to perpetuate the status quo, and how we might change it.

Every important relationship is a universe of two. Even though there are only two people in it, you are either in a circle or a hierarchy. If there is an unspoken assumption that you will defer or be subordinate and accept the other's judgment or choices in place of your own—you are living in a patriarchy of two. It is your particular share of the patriarchy, which can change if you do.

From One Circle To the Millionth Circle

Being in one circle leads to being in others. In the same way that colonists in ancient Greece took coals from the fire in the center of the round hearth, from the home temple, with which to light the fire in the new temple, and a new bride took fire from her mother's hearth to light the fire in her new home, anyone who has been in a sacred circle can take that spirit—and that archetype and morphic field—into a new circle, or another part of her life.

You might move and form a new circle. Or not move, and start a second circle. You might speak of your circle to a friend, and be the inspiration for her to start a women's circle.

Or you may read this book, and decide that you want a circle to be in. The propagation of circles can, in this way, resemble the spread of strawberry plants: they throw out runners that put down roots and become new plants, until there is a field of them.

Women's circles form one at a time. Each circle expands the experience of being in one to more women. Each woman in every circle who is changed by it takes this experience into her world of relationships. Until, on one fine day, a new circle will form, and it will be *the millionth circle*—the one that tips the scales—and brings us into the post-patriarchal human era.

Source: Jean Shinoda Bolen, *The Millionth Circle: How to Change Ourselves and The World.*

Karuna Counseling: Transitions Within a Collective
By Linda F. Weiskoff

"Karuna Counseling for Women and their Friends," located in Atlanta, Georgia, is one of the oldest counseling collectives in the United States, existing since the early 1970s. Karuna's history includes the evolution from an all-white to a bi-racial organization. What follows are the reminiscences of some of the past and present Karuna members who met during the spring of 1991 for a series of discussions and interviews about Karuna's history with respect to racial integration [as] well as my own summary and interpretations.

EARLY DAYS OF THE COLLECTIVE

The early 1970s in Atlanta was a time of tension and anticipation, both in the general public and in the women's community. The old white power structure running the city was about to give way to a new city government run by African-Americans....

Racism became increasingly discussed and debated within the white women's community....However, activism was focused on self-empowerment. Lesbians began claiming their power in the face of devaluation by established women's advocacy groups....It was out of the interest in self-empowerment that Karuna was born in 1974....

At its inception, the collective was composed of nine white women, one-third of whom were lesbian, two-thirds heterosexual. Some of the group members identified themselves as social activists while others were more strongly identified as mental health professionals. The women were unified in their support of feminist values and the rights of lesbians. Much of the group's energy was devoted to fighting homophobia...racial diversity was not addressed.

In 1977, Beverly Jones, an African-American applicant, was turned down for membership with the explanation that, in spite of her experience as a therapist, she did not meet Karuna's criteria because she did not have a degree. To some, this reasoning deflected the racial issue. It also clearly showed the group's inclination toward professionalism, to the discomfort of the social activists.

Beverly's reaction to the rejection was disappointment which then turned to anger."... My experience, not just with Karuna, but with other feminist groups, was that feminism was for white women....It felt exclusionary."

Marlene Johnson, an African-American woman who later joined Karuna, shared her feelings about the women's movement...in the 1970s by saying, "As a black lesbian, I saw a lot of the movement as being for white women, and I saw it for white straight women who not only didn't accept black women, but weren't terribly accepting of lesbians. So I had two shots against me. Having experience with the black movement, which didn't give women power, and certainly gave nothing to lesbians, and then having watched the feminists, I really didn't have high hopes for Karuna doing something, or really making a change, or for being heard.

FACTORS CAUSING A SHIFT TOWARD INTEGRATION

Within the next few years, Karuna's composition changed. Racial diversity continued to surface as an issue. Some members believed that rejecting Beverly had been a big ethical mistake....Some of the newer members wished to racially integrate the organization.

Another factor in the movement toward racial diversity was the high value Karuna placed on processing feelings and ideas. Personal experiences and differences were respected, and openness was encouraged. All decisions were made through a lengthy process of reaching consensus.... Each woman was encouraged to have her own voice and take responsibility for herself. Karuna had become a place where lesbian and heterosexual women got to know each other intimately. Karuna's history of honoring and processing differences promoted racial diversity....

The collective felt empowered enough to take a look at itself with respect to racism and racial diversity. Phyllis Glass recalled: "When I first came in, soon after Beverly had been rejected, it felt like the ghosts that got talked about were homophobia and the issue of needing a degree. People were concerned with getting accepted into the mental health community and dealing with sexual orientation....Once we got strong enough in those pieces of our identity, we had the energy to look at this part."

Beverly's tenacity was another important factor in Karuna's movement toward integration. Beverly believed Karuna reflected something important in her. While other African-American women in her life talked about being stuck in ways that despaired of change, Karuna represented the experience of meeting with a group of women, getting power, and moving toward change. As a result, after Karuna's initial rejection, she

decided not to abandon the issue. She developed a workshop on racism and, in 1980, offered it to Karuna. Members were receptive to the invitation.

Phyllis: "I remember feeling excited, relieved, and scared to death."

Beverly presented her racism workshop….The experience heightened the group's sensitivity and helped…members acknowledge the degree to which racism was institutionalized within the organization. The group invited Beverly to join. Beverly stated that she wouldn't feel safe as the only woman of color in the group, and the invitation was extended to Marlene. Although Marlene had an appropriate degree, she lacked direct clinical experience which had been an important selection criterion….Her acceptance was a clear statement of social activism, rattling those members whose priority was professionalism.

BEGINNING THE INTEGRATION

The period that followed was characterized by struggle and suspicion. The collective dealt with conflicts in values and definitions and underlying mistrust on both sides. Marlene, unlike Beverly, was skeptical that the organization could overcome…white elitist attitudes….Due to her lack of counseling experience, the collective required her to attend a course in feminist therapy….This unique requirement fed into Marlene's distrust and concerns about tokenism in the group.

In part, Marlene's cynicism came from her disappointment with Atlanta's lesbian community. "I had hopes they'd be different from the general community, but they were just as racist. I felt burned by the lesbian community and was cynical about any organization talking about wanting to deal with racism." Marlene decided to join the collective but felt "I was part of a quota system and not seen as myself. Feedback was—I wasn't viewed as a therapist."

Ilene Schroeder: "I think that was partly right, but not so much 'Oh, this will fill our quota.' It was more out of wanting to be politically correct."…

The classes in feminist therapy were a requirement for Marlene and also for Eleanor, a new and differently abled white member. Eleanor, like Marlene, lacked the credentials to satisfy Karuna's "professionalism." Both felt resentful and believed that the group did not acknowledge their individual expertise. They questioned whether or not the group considered them truly equal collective members.

In current discussions, their questioning has been validated. Judith: "This whole question of how to shift from an all-white organization to a bi-racial one—I think we were struggling with that, as well as with education and class. We were scared, so we said, 'Okay, we'll give them some special training, these people who aren't like us.' And it didn't work. Thank god y'all persisted."…

DEEPER LEVELS OF INTEGRATION

At this point, several things helped to alleviate tension and increase group cohesiveness. Karuna decided to hold a meeting specifically about racism, in which everyone talked very personally about her experiences with race and integration. This was helpful and hopeful. As Eleanor remembers, "I was scared before it happened and relieved afterwards. It felt like the air had been cleared. Somehow we demonstrated a willingness to listen, be open and talk." Eventually one source of resentment was removed when the person who taught the feminist therapy classes left Karuna and they were discontinued.

In 1984, another African-American woman, Linda Grays, joined the collective. This balanced the racial composition. Beverly felt for the first time that Karuna had a genuine commitment to diversity. Linda G. remembers: "There was an acceptance and a valuing of my blackness—not as a token, and not as, 'Well, let's pretend that it's not really there,' but from the standpoint of, 'This is who you are and we want to get to know you better.'"...

We risked and learned from each other and we no longer felt as threatened as we had earlier. The feminists no longer tried to "educate" Marlene, and Marlene and Beverly no longer educated the group about racism. We found a way to be respectfully vocal about our differences. We became more empathic with one another. As we got to know each other more personally, strong friendships were formed. Comfort replaced tension.

Marlene: "Part of what I liked about Karuna was when [the African-American women] stopped being an experience, like going to parties and being the 'black' friend, and started being a part of Karuna. Then it was okay."

As Karuna became bi-racial on a deeper, more intimate level, white members experienced the impact that integration had on themselves and their practices. They became more aware of the narrowness of their upbringings.

Beth-Ann Buitekant: "Being brought up in the dominant culture you're never taught about other cultures. It's almost impossible to know another person's experience [unless you have some interface with the culture]." Nicki Scofield: "With Karuna being bi-racial, we've been able to help each other fill in some of the class, race and culture gaps which prevent us from knowing our clients more intimately."

Karuna's diversity has helped deepen white members' respect for difference, allowing them to become acquainted with a spectrum of ways to be with clients, and challenging them to give up the notion that there is only one right way. It has allowed the group to do therapy in an atmosphere which encourages addressing prejudice in an open manner. Racial diversification has actualized some members' beliefs.

Isabelle: "It really validated something within me. Some of the good feminist values that I have weren't fully acted on until I was able to be in a place that had racial diversity." Linda Weiskoff: "In a very personal way the experience has helped me to clarify my definition of what a woman is. I bring this with me to every client I see."...

CONCLUSION

Several themes emerge from Karuna's experience which are important considerations for women interested in developing multi-racial feminist organizations. As the examination of

Karuna's process illustrates, simply taking steps to include women of color in an organization does not address the complexity and depth of the integration process. Developing into a bi-racial collective has been quite difficult for Karuna. In making the choice to become bi-racial, an all-white organization went through a painful process of introspection....

In light of Karuna's experience, women interested in developing multi-racial organizations in the 1990s might consider bringing together women of different races at an organization's inception. This would not circumvent the struggle to achieve true integration. However, it would provide a positive context for dialogue and would allow for greater diversity in a group's approach to issues, problems, and solutions.

Source: "Karuna Counselling: Transitions Within a Collective," in Jeanne Adleman and Gloria Enguidanos, eds., *Racism in the Lives of Women.*

Mandorla Denied
By Marta Donayre

As any individual, I have many aspects to my persona. I am a Latina, an immigrant, a lesbian, an artist, a writer, an activist, etc. The way I see it, each aspect is an archetype, and it is the intersection of these archetypes that give birth to the individual. In my particular case, when the immigrant archetype meets the lesbian archetype we have an immigrant lesbian, AKA me. If we were to imagine each archetype represented in a mandala, I would live in the football-shaped intersection: the mandorla. Or would I?

Ideally, living in a mandorla world would lead one to believe in the belonging to both of the mandalas that define it. Personally, I should feel welcome in both the immigrant and the LGBT communities. But my experience leads me to believe this may not be the case after all.

From Sept. 27 until Oct. 3, 2003, I joined around 800 other people in the Immigrant Workers Freedom Ride. Buses left 12 American cities and crossed the nation advocating for workers rights, a path to citizenship, family reunification and civil rights and civil liberties for all. I joined the ride to advocate for immigration rights for same-sex binational couples, and was the only participant in the country to represent a non-union LGBT group. After the rides were over, I knew that I had made great friends and allies along the way. Even a vocal opponent to my participation is now an advocate for same-sex partners' immigration and marriage equality.

A few months later, I attended a meeting in Washington, D.C. to talk about priorities for the coalition formed during the rides. I spoke on behalf of the Uniting American Families Act (at the time called Permanent Partners Immigration Act, PPIA), and asked for a commitment from organizers. In a sea of smiles and supporters, I was told that the coalition was indeed committed. As a matter of fact UNITE HERE International Union, the lead sponsor of the rides is on board with UAFA. Yet, I was also told that issues would be chosen in a strategic manner. It took me a while to understand my emotions. I was confused by both the support and the slap on the face. Political strategy aside, I felt as if I was told that my issue was not important enough, that my suffering and the suffering of countless binational couples is not part of the immigration agenda. Not really knowing what to do with this information at the time, I left it at that.

On a separate occasion, I met with LGBT immigration activists at the 2004 Annual Immigration Equality conference in Los Angeles. The year 2004 was tumultuous. The strategy for UAFA was always to create distance from marriage. "Oh no!" We would tell Congress people. "We are not interested in marriage, only in this one out of 1,049 federal rights, benefits and responsibilities."*

The San Francisco marriages of 2004, the Federal Marriage Amendment and the marriages taking place in Massachusetts changed all that. It became impossible to separate the two, and the FMA would make a bill such as UAFA a moot point. UAFA and anything related to immigration for lesbian, gay, bisexual, transgender and queer people took the back seat. Marriage, and only marriage, came to our front burner. We had a tremendous threat in the form of the amendment, a magnificent opportunity due to public discourse, and in the process we lost our message.

Panelists came to the conference from across the country to talk about the state of LGBT and immigration politics. During a panel, the issue of marriage was naturally brought up. I must admit that when I heard the question about using immigration as a marriage-messaging tool, I thought *oh puh-leeze! It is obvious that immigration is the perfect messaging tool.* Incredulous, I heard an East Coast marriage activist saying, "We are actually shying away from the immigration theme because it is too controversial."

Huh? Last I checked Congress wasn't debating a xenophobic constitutional amendment, it was a homophobic one. How could he think that immigration could be more controversial than marriage? I was delighted to see California marriage advocates jump to the fray and say that in the Golden State the nexus is very clear. Sadly, the bitter brew had already invaded my mouth. I found out what other activist across the country thought about me.

Looking back at both events I no longer see myself *in* two communities, but instead *outside*. No matter which community I turn to the answer seems to be "yes, but not now." The "not now" part is drenched in prejudice, making me feel like an untouchable. When it comes to immigration groups, I cannot help but think that homophobia is at heart. I am not talking about flagrant homophobia where people are adamant about it. It is more subdued, where people are unable to see their own biases and deeply inside they believe they are LGBT friendly, even when their actions *dejan mucho que desear*.**

Likewise, the comment that immigration is too controversial to be included in the national marriage debate smacks of xenophobia. Absolutely everyone in the LGBT community would agree that equality is a must, and most are likely to sympathize with the cause of binational couples. But similarly to the immigration community, people in the LGBT community only see their culturally-motivated biases, even when they think they are being fair, honest, and an ally. All they are able to see is their own xenophobic views.

As a matter of fact, the marriage movement has usurped immigration and binational couples as a talking point, while neglecting them. Any effort to support UAFA has dwindled, and marriage is now seen as the only solution for these couples. Instead of pushing forward with UAFA, we are told to wait for the state-by-state marriage strategy, which at some point in the distant future would allow for a successful lawsuit against the Defense of Marriage Act. Binational couples are being actively pushed aside by the marriage movement that is carefully weeding them out from even becoming plaintiffs in legal marriage challenges such as the ones in New York, Massachusetts and California.

At the end of the day, I come home to a family that may face separation.*** I look back to the two groups that I supposedly belong to and feel betrayed by both. At the end of the day I understand a little bit better how pervasive and corrosive discrimination is. People who are supposed to be *mi familia* see me as a liability. At the end of the day, my safe and comfy looking mandorla no longer exists. I am left behind, in between two circles that never really intersected. At the end of the day I am community-less.

* *The U.S. General Accounting Office (GAO) did a study in 1996 that revealed that there were 1,049 federal rights, benefits and responsibilities associated with marriage. In 2003 the GAO conducted a new survey and found out that the number is actually 1,138. I am using the original figure to reflect the argument used at the time.*

** *Leave much to be desired.*

*** *Since writing this article, the author obtained her permanent residency in the United States and her family no longer faces separation. Yet she remains active in the LGBTQ immigrant rights movement.*

Source: Marta Donayre, "Mandorla Denied," written for *Traveling with the Turtle*.

PART THREE

COMMUNITY POWER

Session 9

Powerful Communities:
Creating Circles of Equality

Session 9
Powerful Communities:
Creating Circles of Equality

In this Session We Will:
- Call to mind the communities of women we are, or have been, a part of
- Reflect on the support and power we have felt within them
- Explore how diversity makes our communities powerful by considering when we have created inclusive circles and when we have excluded others

Agenda
Introduction — *2 min*
Opening Ritual — *15 min*
Community Mosaic — *15 min*
Reflection on the Power of Community — *15 min*
The Importance of Diversity — *60 min*
Closing — *10 min*
Looking Ahead — *3 min*
       Life Practice
       Journal Topics and Questions
       Readings

Materials Needed
- ☐ Shared Agreements
- ☐ Small prayer table
- ☐ A colorful cloth
- ☐ A candle
- ☐ Matches
- ☐ Different colored pieces of construction paper cut into various shapes—circles, triangles, squares—several for each group member for the Community Mosaic
- ☐ Colored pencils, markers and/or crayons
- ☐ Flipchart
- ☐ Easel paper
- ☐ Markers
- ☐ Masking tape
- ☐ Compact disk or audiotape player
- ☐ Recorded music

Facilitator Notes

Session preparation — The week before

- Review the entire session. Practice reading any visualizations or meditations, and role-play or practice setting up and facilitating exercises beforehand. Whenever possible, put material into your own words. Feel free to make notes on 3x5 cards or in the book next to the written instructions.
- Cut different colored pieces of construction paper into various shapes—circles, triangles, squares—several for each group member for the Community Mosaic

Session preparation — The day of

- Arrange the chairs, including your own, in a circle, with a small table in the center. Place the cloth, candle, and matches on the table.
- Tape the Shared Agreements to the wall.
- Play some background music as people arrive, if desired.

Session 9
Powerful Communities:
Creating Circles of Equality

Introduction — 2 min

Convey the following in your own words:

Welcome to Session 9. In Session 8 we reflected on the ability we possess to create, including the many ways that we make peace in our everyday lives. In this session, and the next one, we will explore the power of community—with each other and with the natural world.

Community power comes from creating what Jean Shinoda Bolen calls a "circle of equals," an inclusive community where we listen to and learn from each other. Each woman's sense of self and her worldview are broadened and her life changes as she encounters the diverse life experiences that the other members bring to the group.

In this session, recognizing the necessity of community, we will call to mind the communities of women we are, or have been a part of, and reflect on the support and power we have felt within them. We will then explore how diversity makes our communities more powerful by considering when we have created inclusive circles and when we have excluded others.

Reflections from the Last Session

Share the following in your own words:

During this session we have much to share with each other. Some of what we choose to share may stretch both us and other members of our group, so we need as much time and space as possible. For that reason, we will not share our reflections from the last session.

Opening Ritual — 15 min

Begin by inviting the women to relax, to breathe, to shake off the anxieties and responsibilities that were part of their day. Then invite them to say the group mantra together: "We are good, beautiful, strong, and holy. We are women of spirit. We are women of peace. We seek healing and wholeness for ourselves and our world."

Ask two women to read the following dialogue. Introduce the ritual by sharing the following in your own words:

Let us listen to a conversation between a Chilean woman and a woman from the United States. On September 11, 1973, in Santiago, Chile, the presidential palace was bombed and Chile's democratically elected government was overthrown. President Salvador Allende died in the coup and dictator Augusto Pinochet began a reign of terror, arresting, torturing, assassinating, or jailing many college students, professors, artists, and musicians. He was able to gain power with the support of covert operations of the U.S. military.

On September 11, 2001, the Twin Towers in New York City and the Pentagon were attacked.

Remembering September 11, A Dialogue

American. I was an ordinary woman.
Chilean. I was an ordinary woman.
A. Who lived a normal life.
C. Who lived a normal life.
A. My husband carpooled to work. I shopped at the mall.
C. My husband rode the bus to work. I made my own clothes.
A. I waited in long lines at the check out counter in the grocery store.
C. I waited in long lines at the bakery for the daily rationing.
A. I took my children to baseball games, movies, and amusement parks.
C. I watched my children play with a rag ball in the street.
A. Then one morning.
C. Then one morning.
A. I heard a plane fly by very low overhead.
C. I heard the planes take off from the military base.
A. And watched with horror as it crashed into a building downtown.
C. And suddenly heard explosions downtown.
A. I ran inside and turned on the TV.
C. I ran inside and turned on the radio.
A. Panic immobilized me as another plane crashed into the second tower.
C. My heart stopped as our president spoke his last words before the transmission went dead.
A. Fire engulfed the towers as they collapsed in a cloud of dust that burst over the city.
C. Gunfire erupted as the troops began to search and scourge through the city.
A. Somehow I know my man will never come home.

C. Little did I know my man would never come home.

A. With my cell phone in my hand, I waited. My flicker of hope faded with the sunset.

C. I waited more than 25 years with hope at each sunrise.

A. He disappeared with so many others in the flames and the rubble.

C. He disappeared with so many others who were herded into the stadium.

A. Why do they hate us?

C. Who are our enemies?

A. Faceless ghosts flitting in and out and leaving terror in their wake.

C. What did we do to them that they should do this to us?

A. They lived in our towns, went to our schools, hijacked our planes, and killed our people.

C. They bought out our newspapers, infiltrated our military, flew the planes they sold us, and incited the killing.

A. How dare they attack the heart of our country and destroy our symbols of freedom, economic stability, and democracy?

C. How dare they attack the heart of our country and destroy the presidential palace, symbol of freedom, popular suffrage, and democracy?

A. Our military leaders [were] brought to their knees by violence at the door of their stronghold.

C. Our military leaders [knelt] before them as their ships lay waiting off our coast.

A. And my man never came home.

C. And my man never came home.

A. And I know fear as a weight settling in the pit of my stomach.

C. And fear became a pit I struggled to climb out of.

A. I dared not open the mail, afraid of death in an envelope.

C. I dared not open the door, afraid of death in plainclothes.

A. I dared not send my children to summer camp, afraid of airplanes and airports.

C. I dared not let my children play outside, afraid of tanks, tear gas, random shootings.

A. Deep inside I barely survive, alone and afraid.

C. Deep inside, for many years, I barely survived, alone and afraid.

A. Hate is one step behind fear.

C. Hate was one step behind fear.

A. Today, I want them to hurt as badly as I did.

C. Twenty-eight years later, I watched them hurt as badly as I did. *(She looks over at the other woman.)*

A. I think I could never forgive them *(Crumples to the ground.)*

C. I thought I could never forgive them. *(Touches the back of the other woman, who looks up at her, then extends her hand to help her to her feet.)*

A. I am an American woman *(lights a match)*.

C. I am a Chilean woman *(lights a match)*.

A. And my life changed on September 11, 2001.

C. And my life changed on September 11, 1973.

Source: Elena Huegel, "Remembering September 11, A Dialogue," in *United Church News*.

Have both women light the candle together.

Invite the group to pass the lit candle around the circle, offering silent prayers for healing, reconciliation, and peace.

Community Mosaic — 15 min

Tell the group in your own words:

> We will begin our exploration of community by creating a mosaic. A mosaic combines diverse elements to form a more or less coherent whole.

> We just heard the stories of two women with very different life experiences, who at the same time shared something in common—the tragic loss of their husbands, the experience of death. We, too, will now bring together our various life experiences, the different communities of women to which we each belong, or have belonged, and make a group mosaic of them. What communities of women have been important in our lives? How do we gather as women?

Hand each woman several pieces of the construction paper that are cut into different shapes, and colored pencils or crayons.

> Write the name of one group on each piece of paper—or draw an image to represent that group. Use as many pieces of paper as you like.

When the women are finished, say:

> We will place on the floor the names and images of the different circles that we have belonged to, creating a community mosaic of many shapes and colors. Take a few minutes to gaze upon the numerous circles of women that have touched our lives. *(Leave the mosaic on the floor.)*

Reflection on the Power of Community — 15 min

Then say:

These groups of women that we just named are, or were, an important part of our lives. Perhaps there have been other communities not represented in our mosaic that have also influenced us in significant ways—communities that we were a part of at different stages of our lives, either for a short or long period of time. Find a partner and consider the following questions:

- When have you experienced the power of community with women most deeply?
- When have you felt that common strength, encouragement, and sense of belonging?

A Circle of Equals
By Jean Shinoda Bolen

The circle is a principle as well as a shape. It goes counter to the social order, pecking order, superior/inferior, ranking order that compares each individual woman to others. Sitting in a circle, each woman has a physical position that is equal to every other woman in the circle. She takes her turn and the circle turns, she speaks up and is heard. Still old habits prevail, until the practice of equality makes equality the expected norm.

Creating a Circle of Equals is a Work in Process

The idea of a circle of equals is held as a common intention. Each woman is committed to developing and maintaining it, for herself and for the circle. Every woman in the circle matters to herself and to the circle. Every woman contributes to the circle by her presence, and when she speaks, by what she discerns and shares. Once the circle is formed, any significant decision needs to be made by a process of consensus. This only works if there is honesty. If one fears to be truthful, lest feelings be hurt or punishment follows, there is codependency. Codependency and equality are incompatible. Silence is consent.

If one woman dominates the circle and takes up "all the air in the room," it is not she alone, but she and everyone else who are equally responsible. Each woman speaks only for herself and not as if for the others in the circle. Each woman has a responsibility to the circle to pay attention to what is going on in herself and in the circle, and to speak up. In any circle, some are more verbal, faster to react, and quicker to arrive at a conclusion than others. Balance comes from hearing from everyone.

Practicing Equality: Check In and Go Around

Each in turn speaks to the questions, How are you, really? What concerns you most now? Depending on the situation, on the woman, and on the circle, it may be health, relationships, work, creativity, spiritual life, or politics. In this way, over time, we are witnesses to each other's lives. We know what is truly important and the nature of each one's personal journey. We feel the pain, celebrate with joy, and are kin. Sometimes we have ideas and suggestions, as an equal to an equal, which is not doing therapy nor infantilizing.

Source: Jean Shinoda Bolen, *The Millionth Circle: How to Change Ourselves and The World.*

The Importance of Diversity — *60 min*

Invite everyone to return to the large group and share the following in your own words:

> We shared with each other experiences of community where we were encouraged, welcomed, and included, where we felt the power of community. Such an experience is deepened as we include others from diverse backgrounds or who look at the world in a different way, or celebrate the diversity that is already present in our group. We benefit from the different perspectives, gifts, strengths, and ideas that are contributed to the community.
>
> During the next hour, we will spend some time reflecting on ways that communities we have been a part of, or this community, have been inclusive, recognizing the diverse gifts that everyone brings. And we will reflect on times that we have either excluded others from our circle or not supported the diverse gifts that all members bring.

Here are several sets of questions that the group can reflect on. Choose one set for the group to explore, either ahead of time or during the session.

1) *If group members have known each other for awhile or a high level of trust has been built up, the group may want to reflect on its own experience as a community.*

   a) What different gifts, strengths, and life experiences do members bring that enhanced our group? How is our group more powerful because of this diversity?

   b) Do we ever exclude anyone's gifts, contributions, or ways of being? Is everyone fully equal in our group? How does exclusion affect our power as a group?

   Or, What is missing from our group that would make it more powerful? Who is not here in this room? What different social locations, religious or cultural traditions, perspectives or values, etc., would make our community more powerful?

2) *Or, the group can reflect on other community experiences they have had. Invite them to again think of a community that they are now or have been a part of.*

   a) What different gifts, strengths, and life experiences did members bring that enhanced this community and your own life journey? How was this community more powerful because of such diversity?

   b) When have you or someone else been excluded from a community you are a part of? How did this affect the group and its power as a community?

   Or, What is missing from this group that would make it more powerful? Who is not a part of this community? What different social locations, religious or cultural traditions, perspectives or values, etc. would make this community more powerful?

Thank everyone for their willingness to share their experience of community.

Woman of All Nations
By Ines Maria Talamantez

Deep within
I am wild in my sorrow
I am a woman
      a working woman
      a good Apache woman
      a gathering woman
      a Red World woman
      a brown Chicana woman
      a mother woman
      a loving woman
      a blue woman
      a eucalyptus woman
      a soft woman
      a loud woman
      a resisting woman
      a trouble making woman
      a hunting woman
      a moving woman
      a quiet woman
      a dancing woman
      a singing woman
      a spirit woman
      a desert woman
      a mountain woman
      an ocean woman
      a White World woman
      a trail making woman
      a changing woman
      Look around you.
      Look around you.
What do you see. What do you see.
What will you do. What will you do.
When will we walk together.
When will we walk together.

Source: Diane Bell and Renate Klein, eds.,
Radically Speaking: Feminism Reclaimed.

Closing — *10 min*

Share the following in your own words:

> We seek to create powerful communities. We want to affirm and nurture the diverse gifts and life experiences present in our own group and other communities of which we have been a part. And we want to welcome into our circles those who are different from us in some ways.

> Form a circle around the mosaic, and listen to some music. As we listen together, we will first motion with our bodies how we sometimes exclude others from our circles. Then we will move in a way that shows how we welcome people into these groups. (*Play music.*)

Close by holding hands as you stand around the mosaic.

Looking Ahead — *3 min*

In preparation for the next session, remind participants to do the Life Practice, journal topics and questions, and the next session's readings, found at the end of this session.

Life Practice

1) Take the time to listen to a woman who is not ordinarily part of one of your circles or communities. How did you feel during this interaction? What did you learn?

2) For the next session, bring an object from nature that is special to you that you found either while you were outside or in your home. You will have an opportunity to share this object with the group.

Journal Topics and Questions

1) Reflect on what being around nature does for your spirit and sense of self. Do you feel connected or disconnected to the natural world?

2) What is your favorite place to visit in nature—in person or in your mind? Why?

Readings for Session 10

The Indigenous Women's Network: Our Future, Our Responsibility
By Winona LaDuke

I am from the Mississippi Band of Anishinabeg of the White Earth Reservation in northern Minnesota....Aniin indinawaymugnitok. Me gweich Chi-iwewag, Megwetch Ogitchi taikwewag. Nindizhinikaz, Beenaysayikwe, Makwa nin dodaem. Megwetch indinawaymugunitok.

I am greeting you in my language and thanking you, my sisters, for the honor of speaking with you today about the challenges facing women as we approach the 21st century.

A primary and central challenge impacting women...will be the distance we collectively as women and societies have artificially placed ourselves from our Mother the Earth, and the inherent environmental, social, health and psychological consequences of colonialism, and subsequently rapid industrialization of our bodies, and our nations....

The situation of Indigenous women, as a part of Indigenous peoples, we believe is a magnified version of the critical juncture we find ourselves in as peoples, and the problems facing all women and our future generations as we struggle for a better world. Security, militarism, the globalization of the economy, the further marginalization of women, increasing intolerance....

The Earth is our Mother. From her we get our life...and our ability to live. It is our responsibility to care for our Mother, and in caring for our Mother, we care for ourselves. Women, all females, are the manifestation of Mother Earth in human form. We are her daughters and in my cultural instructions...we are to care for her. I am taught to live in respect for Mother Earth. One hundred years ago, one of our Great Leaders—Chief Seattle stated, "What befalls the Earth, befalls the People of the Earth." And that is the reality of today, and the situation of the status of women, and the status of Indigenous women and Indigenous peoples.

While I am from one nation of Indigenous peoples, there are millions of Indigenous people worldwide. An estimated 500 million people are in the world today. We are in the Cordillera, the Maori of New Zealand, we are in East Timor, we are the Wara Wara of Australia, the Lakota, the Tibetans, the peoples of Hawai'i, New Caledonia and many other nations of Indigenous peoples. Indigenous peoples. We are not populations, not minority groups, we are peoples. We are nations of peoples. Under international law we meet the criteria of nation states, having a common economic system, language, territory, history, culture and governing institutions. Despite this fact, Indigenous Nations are not allowed to participate at the United Nations....

[T]here would likely be little argument in this room, that most decisions made in the world today are actually made by some of the 47 transnational corporations...whose annual income is larger than the gross national product for many countries of the world.

This is a centerpiece of the problem. Decision-making is not made by those who are affected by those decisions, people who live on the land, but corporations, with an interest which is entirely different than that of the land, and the people, or the women of the land. This brings forth a fundamental question: What gives these corporations like CONOCO, SHELL, EXXON, DIASHAWA, ITT, RIO TINTO ZINC, and the WORLD BANK, a right which…is superior to my human right to live on my land, or that of my family, my community, my nation, our nations, and to us as women? The origins of this problem lie with the predator-prey relationship industrial society has developed with the Earth, and subsequently, the people of the Earth. This same relationship exists vis-à-vis women. We collectively find that we are often in the role of the prey to a predator society, whether for sexual discrimination, exploitation, sterilization, absence of control over our bodies, or being the subjects of repressive laws and legislation in which we have no voice. This occurs not only on an individual level, but, equally, and more significantly on a societal level. It is also critical to point out at this time that most matrilineal societies, societies in which governance and decision-making are largely controlled by women, have been obliterated from the face of the Earth by colonialism, and subsequently industrialism. The only matrilineal societies which exist in the world today are those of Indigenous nations. We are the remaining matriliineal societies. Yet we also face obliteration….

Almost all atomic weapons which have been detonated in the world are…detonated on the lands or waters of Indigenous people. This situation is mimicked in the North American context. Today, over 50% of our remaining lands are forested, and both Canada and the United States continue aggressive clearcutting policies on our land. Over two thirds of the uranium resources in the United States, and similar figures for Canada, are on Indigenous lands….We have huge oil reserves on our reservations, and we have the dubious honor of being the most highly bombed nation in the world, in this case, the Western Shoshone Nation, on which over 650 atomic weapons have been detonated….We also have two separate accelerated proposals to dump nuclear waste in our reservation lands, and similarly over 100 separate proposals to dump toxic waste on our reservation lands…

We…understand clearly the relationship between the environmental impacts of types of development on our lands, and the environmental and subsequent health impacts in our bodies as women.

Uranium mining in northern Canada has left over 120 million tons of radioactive waste. This amount represents enough material to cover the Trans-Canada Highway two meters deep across the country….Since 1975, hospitalization for cancer, birth defects and circulatory illnesses in that area have increased dramatically—between 123 and 600 percent in that region. In other areas impacted by uranium mining, cancers and birth defects have increased to, in some cases, eight times the national average. The subsequent increases in radiation exposure to both the local and to the larger north American population are also evidenced in broader incidences of cancer, such as breast cancer in North American women, which is significantly on the rise. There is no distinction in this problem caused by radiation, whether it is in the Dine of northern Canada, the Laguna Pueblo people of New Mexico, or the people of Namibia.

The rapid increase in dioxin, organichlorides, and PCBs (polychlorinated byphenots) chemicals in the world…has a devastating impact on Indigenous peoples, Indigenous women, and other women. Each year, the world's paper industry discharges from 600 to 3200 grams of dioxin equivalents into water, sludge and paper products according to United States Environmental Protection Agency statistics. This quantity is equal to the amount which would cause 58,000 to 294,000 cases of cancer every year.…According to a number of recent studies, this has significantly increased the risk of breast cancer in women. Similarly, heavy metals and PCBs contamination of Inuit women of the Hudson Bay region of the Arctic indicates that they have the highest levels of breast milk contamination in the world.…In summary, I have presented these arguments for a purpose. To illustrate that that these are very common issues for women, not only for Indigenous women, but for all women. What befalls our mother Earth, befalls her daughters—the women who are the mothers of our nations. Simply stated, if we can no longer nurse our children, if we can no longer bear children, and if our bodies themselves are wracked with poisons, we will have accomplished little in the way of determining our destiny, or improving our conditions. And, these problems, reflected in our health and well being, are also inherently resulting in a decline of the status of women, and are the result of a long set of historical processes. Processes which we, as women will need to challenge if we will ultimately be in charge of our own destinies, our own self-determination, and the future of our Earth our Mother.

Source: Winona LaDuke, United Nations Fourth World Conference on Women, Beijing, China, 1995.

WAGES Trains Women For Eco-Friendly Cleaning Co-Op
By Sharon Abercrombie

Claudia Zamora is one of the many professional house cleaners who used to suffer with headaches, allergies and "feeling really tired, really bad all around."

Her health took a holistic turn for the better three years ago when she and a group of other women started their own cleaning cooperative, Natural Home Cleaning.

Now the Oakland woman is "really happy" with her work.

Natural Home Cleaning teams use baking soda, vinegar, and other environmentally friendly, biodegradable nontoxic cleaning products. Instead of paper towels and disposable wipes and mops, the women work with durable tools—old cotton T-shirts, putty knives, razor blades and screw drivers for whisking away stubborn household grime. They also use vacuum cleaners equipped with HEPA filters.

Natural Home Cleaning is the newest and one of three Bay Area eco-friendly housecleaning cooperatives operating in Oakland, Redwood City, and Morgan Hill/San Jose, [California].

To make it happen, Zamora and her friends linked up with WAGES (Women's Action to Gain Economic Security), a local non-profit organization that helps set up housecleaning and other types of worker-owned cooperatives.

WAGES provides these co-ops with education, leadership training, management support, conflict resolution, constructive communication, financial literacy, computer training and tax assistance. For example, co-op members learn to read and interpret financial statements during their five- to 10-hour a week classes, which extend over several months. They study without fretting about child-care because WAGES staff provides this service as well.

WAGES provides the educational base, but each cooperative is its own boss, setting its own wage scales, job descriptions and schedules.

Each member pays a small membership fee to join the cooperative—$400 over time. And each cooperative takes out a small business loan—typically $15,000-$25,000—from Lenders for Community Development, a consortium of community development banks in San Jose. WAGES encourages cooperatives to raise funds from garage and food sales to decrease the size of their start-up loans.

WAGES supports itself through foundation grants and individual contributions.

Three women community activists started WAGES 10 years ago to help low-income immigrant women move out of minimum-wage jobs into better positions with financial stability, explained Hilary Abell, executive director.

The first year, WAGES trained three groups of women—(two in Spanish and one in English) in cooperative business planning. In 1997, the groups started a party supply and non-toxic professional housekeeping business.

By the next year, however, they realized that the service side of their business was more viable than the retail one, so in 2000 they created Emma's Eco-Clean in Redwood City. In 2001 a second cooperative, Eco-Care Professional Housecleaning, opened in Morgan Hill. It has since expanded into the greater San Jose area.

In 2003, Natural Home cleaning professionals started their business, opening an office... on Oakland's International Boulevard.

Clients pay $25 an hour to each house cleaner. Half of that pays for transport costs, health care insurance and other benefits, administrative costs, supplies and vacuums, said Abell.

Graciela Berkovich, general manager of Natural Home Cleaning and a member of St. Barnabas Parish in Alameda, grew up around toxic chemicals because her mother cleaned houses in Los Angeles for 30 years. In contrast to those cleaning agents, the products used by the cooperative "are great," she said. "Our business has a lot of integrity because it protects women's health."

Berkovich schedules cleaning jobs, trains newcomers to the co-op and provides phone support for Spanish-speaking staff who might need assistance in communicating with their English-speaking clients.

Berkovich is busy. Her office has 130 regular clients in the East Bay, scattered between Richmond and San Leandro. Last year, the total number of both regular and one-time customers was 900.

On the work side, Natural Home has 16 cleaners. The cooperative would like to increase its staff by another dozen in order to keep pace with the increasingly high volume of customer demand.

Haven Bourque, Vice President of Straus Communications, an environmental public relations firm in San Francisco, was Natural Home Cleaning's first client. She has since become a regular customer, explaining that she "feels great" about being part of a movement that empowers Latina women to own and operate their own business.

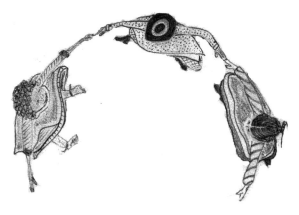

"I think their philosophy of using natural cleaning materials is entirely appropriate for a co-op that is concerned about health—the health of our communities and the health of the natural environment."

Being a green company has not hurt sales either. Hilary Abell said that collectively, in 2005, Natural Home Cleaning and its two sisters in Redwood City and San Jose generated $1 million. Abell added that several local mid-wives are now recommending Natural Home Cleaning services to their pregnant clients, to help keep moms and their babies healthier.

Last fall, the three cooperatives helped WAGES celebrate its 10th anniversary with a party at an Oakland church. The guest speaker was Julia Butterfly Hill, the young environmentalist who lived for two years in the branches of an old-growth redwood tree to protect it from loggers' saws in the late 1990s.

That night, Hill called WAGES "a phenomenal organization. You can't have human dignity without planetary health and you can't have planetary health without human dignity. They go hand in hand."

Source: Sharon Abercrombie, "WAGES Trains Women for Eco-Friendly Cleaning Co-op," in *The Oakland Catholic Voice.*

Nobel Redefines What it Means to be a Peacemaker
By Abraham McLaughlin

JOHANNESBURG, SOUTH AFRICA—Kenyan environmentalist Wangari Maathai—this year's Nobel Peace Prize winner—has been called many things during her decades of activism. Her supporters call her brave, outspoken, and "the green militant." Her enemies have called her crazy, stubborn, and brash—especially when doing things like leading a group of women to strip off their clothes during one protest.

But she's never been called a peacemaker—until now. In fact, ever since the Nobel committee chose her last week, some have grumbled that a person best known for planting trees isn't quite worthy of the prestigious award. Yet the choice, observers say, symbolizes a broadening notion of what constitutes a peacemaker in today's world—and a widening definition of peace itself. Indeed, the elite Nobel club is gradually expanding beyond politicians like Mikhail Gorbachev or Nelson Mandela to include people like Ms. Maathai and Iranian rights activist Shirin Ebadi. It highlights a growing recognition that women, civil society, and issues like human rights and the environment are crucial to creating peace, observers say.

The committee and others "are starting to address the issue of peace at its roots," says Sanam Naraghi Anderlini of Women Waging Peace, a group based in Washington. And, she points out, the committee has increasingly recognized civil society as key. Six of the last 10 awards have gone to nongovernmental organizations or people—including Jimmy Carter for his post-presidential efforts; Jody Williams, who campaigned against land mines; and Doctors Without Borders for providing healthcare in crisis areas.

In announcing this year's award, committee chairman Ole Danbolt Mjoes said: "We have expanded the peace concept to include environmental issues because we believe that a good quality of life on Earth is necessary to promote lasting peace."

It's the first time the prize has gone to an environmentalist. And it sparked some criticism. "You don't give the Nobel chemistry prize to a professor in economics," says Carl Hagen, a politician in Norway. "A peace prize should honor peace, not the environment."

But people-powered movements like Maathai's may be some of the few places where peace is actually being forged these days, some observers say. Much of the world is focused on the war on terror and Iraq. And there's an absence of any major peace efforts in the Israeli-Palestinian conflict or other major hot spots. "So much of the discourse since 9/11 has been, "We're going to bomb you and shoot you," Ms. Anderlini observes. But by choosing Maathai, Anderlini says the Nobel committee seems to be saying, "Peace comes through constructive engagement on the grass-roots level."

For three decades, Maathai has led the Green Belt Movement, which claims to have planted some 30 million trees in 15 countries in Africa. Amid deforestation and desertification, many African women spend more time walking to and from wells each day. In East Africa, the time spent getting water has doubled since 1990, according to the U.N. Trees help slow desertification, not to mention providing shade and firewood.

And there's growing focus on the link between conflict and environmental issues. A recent U.N. report mapped areas in Africa with two or three overlapping environmental issues and found a strong correlation with conflict. Hot spots included Burundi, Rwanda, eastern Congo, and Zimbabwe—all areas with current or recent conflicts.

There's also an awareness of how women are key to conservation—and thus to preventing conflict. In China, groups mobilized by women have planted willow and poplar trees to halt advancing deserts and create good land for growing vegetables. And in Thailand they have boosted biodiversity by saving 230 vegetables and other species from neighboring forests before they were clear-cut.

Besides the growing focus on conflict's root causes, the concept of peace is expanding beyond an absence of war, into the idea of "human security," where quality of life is good enough to avoid sparking conflict. Consequently, peacemaking has "broadened to include dealing with things that undermine the normal fulfillment of human life," says Chadwick Alger, who's on the editorial board of *The International Journal of Peace Studies*, published by George Mason University in Fairfax, VA. This includes environmental problems and "all kinds of things that lead to a shorter life for people."

Source: Abraham McLaughlin, "Nobel Redefines What it Means to be a Peacemaker," *The Christian Science Monitor.*

Session 10

The Earth is Our Mother: Our Connection to Creation

Session 10
The Earth is Our Mother:
Our Connection to Creation

In this Session We Will:
- Experience our connection to, and our relationship with, creation
- Hear about violence perpetrated against nature and its relationship to violence done to women and impoverished people
- See that the gifts we have within us can bring healing to our Earth, our sisters, and all who are oppressed

Agenda
Introduction — *2 min*
Reflections from the Last Session — *10 min*
Opening Ritual — *15 min*
Preparation for the Councils — *15 min*
The Council of All Beings — *25 min*
The Council of Women from Around the World — *25 min*
Large Group Reflection — *15 min*
Closing — *10 min*
Looking Ahead — *3 min*
      Life Practice
      Journal Topics and Questions
      Readings

Materials Needed
- ☐ Shared Agreements
- ☐ Small prayer table
- ☐ A colorful cloth
- ☐ A candle
- ☐ Matches
- ☐ A bowl of dirt
- ☐ Natural objects that each woman brings to place on the altar
- ☐ 8 ½ x 11 sheets of paper—1 for each participant
- ☐ Pens
- ☐ Easel paper
- ☐ Markers
- ☐ Flipchart or masking tape to tape questions for both Councils on the wall
- ☐ Compact disk or audiotape player
- ☐ Recorded music of natural sounds

Facilitator Notes
Session preparation — The week before
- Review the entire session. Practice reading any visualizations or meditations, and role-play or practice setting up and facilitating exercises beforehand. Whenever possible, put material into your own words. Feel free to make notes on 3x5 cards or in the book next to the written instructions.
- Write Council of All Beings and the questions for that Council on one sheet of easel paper and Council of Women from Around the World and the questions for that Council on another sheet. Feel free to shorten the questions. Tape both lists to the wall in different areas of the room.

Session preparation — The day of
- Arrange the chairs, including your own, in a circle, with a small table in the center. Place the cloth, candle, matches, and the bowl of dirt on the table.
- As the women arrive, invite them to place their objects from nature on the prayer table.
- Tape the Shared Agreements on the wall.
- Play some background music, perhaps of natural sounds, as people enter.

Session 10
The Earth Is Our Mother: Our Connection To Creation

Introduction — *2 min*

Welcome to Session 10. In Session 9, we considered the power that we possess when we gather as community. In this session we will experience our connection to creation, exploring another important value of women's spirituality: reverence for Earth. We will hear the pleas of Earth's creatures and its peoples, including women from around the world, to stop the devastation of our planet. And, we will see that the gifts we have within us can bring healing to our Earth, our sisters and all who are oppressed.

Reflections from the Last Session — *10 min*

Share the following:

Find a partner and share with her any insights that came up or experiences you had between sessions, or reflections you had on the Life Practice, journal questions or readings.

Opening Ritual — *15 min*

Play the CD of natural sounds in the background, light the candle, then say in your own words:

Let us take a moment to arrive in this space. Take a few deep breaths. Let us say our group mantra together: "We are good, strong, beautiful and holy. We are women of spirit. We are women of peace. We seek healing and wholeness for ourselves and our world."

Now listen to the sounds of nature that are all around us. (*Pause for awhile*)

When you are ready, I invite you, one at a time, to indicate which item from nature you brought with you and tell us why it is special to you. (*You might need to turn down the music for this part.*)

When everyone is finished sharing, say:

Let us take one last moment together to gaze upon the wonder and beauty of creation, and to breathe in the peace and serenity that it offers us.

Preparation for the Councils — 15 min

Convey the following in your own words:

> To deepen our experience of interconnectedness with all beings, heal our separation from the natural world and find in the web of life the power that will help us act in its self-defense, we will first convene what is called the Council of All Beings. This communal ritual allows us to step aside from our human identity and speak on behalf of other life-forms, bringing a fresh appreciation for the damage that we have inflicted on Earth and all of its creatures.

> After the Council of All Beings, we will convene the Council of Women from Around the World. We will hear the voices of different women who have suffered because of the ways we, as humans, have harmed our Earth.

> Half of the group will be life-forms that are not human. Half of the group will be women from around the world. Who would like to be a life-form? Who would like to be a woman? (*Assist the group in dividing into two groups, each with approximately the same number of members.*)

Then say:

> We will spend the next period of time in two separate groups. As part of the preparation for these Councils, each of you will spend time reflecting on what life-form or what woman you choose to be. To assist you in this process, I will lead the life-forms through a simple visualization process. At the same time my co-facilitator will lead the women through a similar process. (*If there is no co-facilitator, ask the group if someone would lead this visualization. After identifying the woman, show her where the Visualization for the Countil of Women from Around the World is on pages 199-200.*) Then give everyone a piece of paper and a pen and let them know that they can write down their reflections if they want.

Show each group where to gather, near the list of questions for their Council.

Group 1: Visualization for The Council of All Beings

Slowly share the following in your own words:

> Life-forms that are not human seek to be heard at the Council that we will soon convene. They want to communicate through you. Close your eyes and take several deep breaths. Take a few moments to relax deeply so that a being can choose you. Stay with your first impulse. Allow yourself to be surprised. It is fine if you are chosen by a life-form that

you do not know very much about. It may be an animal, a plant, or ecological feature, such as a creek or a mountain. (*Pause*)

Visualize this being, how it looks, the way it moves. (*Pause*) Request this being's permission to enter it so you can imaginatively sense its body from within. (*Pause*)

During The Council of All Beings, you will share part of your story. You may speak for several minutes. During your turn, talk about the following:

1) Describe what it's like to be this life-form, the powers and perspectives you are given.

2) Describe the...difficulties you may be experiencing now, due to loss of habitat, pollution, toxic dumping, drift nets, clearcutting, factory farming, etc.

3) Since humans are causing these difficulties and abuses, and only they can correct them, consider what strengths of yours you can offer to the humans to help them make the changes necessary to your survival—and the survival of life on Earth.

If the group needs an example, here is a brief one:

River might say: I am River—beautiful, coursing with power, strong. I offer you peace, serenity, and refreshment on a hot summer day. Come and swim in my depths. Ride my currents. "Oh humans, as River I was a bearer of life. Look at what I bear now that you've poured your wastes and poisons into me. I am ashamed and want to stop flowing, because I have become a carrier of sickness and death." (p.163) And yet, I offer you my strength and power. Use it to carry on, to stop the destruction. Save me. Save yourselves.

Take time now to reflect on these three areas in silence and to consider what you would like to say at the Council of All Beings.

Source: Excerpted and adapted from Joanna Macy and Molly Young Brown, *Coming Back to Life: Practices to Reconnect Our Lives, Our World.*

Group 2: Visualization for The Council of Women from Around the World

Slowly share the following in your own words:

We are going to hold a Council of Women from Around the World. One woman, in particular, wants to communicate through you. She may be a woman from anywhere in the world—from another country or this country, or your own neighborhood. Her life is greatly affected by the harm we are doing to Mother Earth. Try to let her speak through you rather than seeking to become her, since we recognize that we can never fully understand another's experience.

Close your eyes and take several deep breaths. Take a few moments to relax deeply so that a woman can choose you. Stay with your first impulse. Allow yourself to be surprised. (*Pause*)

Visualize this woman, where she lives, how she looks, the way she moves. (*Pause*) Then request her permission to enter her so you can imaginatively sense her body from within. (*Pause*)

During The Council of Women From Around the World, you will share part of your story. You may speak for several minutes. During your turn, talk about the following:

1)   Describe what it's like to be this woman, the powers and perspectives you are given.

2)   Describe the…difficulties you may be experiencing now, due to…pollution, toxic dumping…clearcutting, factory farming, etc.

3)   Consider what strengths of yours you can offer to the humans to help them make the changes necessary to your survival—and the survival of life on Earth.

If the group needs an example, here is a brief one:

My name is Sylvia. I am a woman who lives in Utah, a wife, mother, librarian. I am also a downwinder, as are many members of my family and many of my friends. When the government tested nuclear bombs at the Nevada Test Site, the toxic wind swept down our way. I now have only one breast—I lost the other to cancer. But I am a survivor. I survived the radiation from those bombs and I survived chemotherapy. I offer you my resilience. We must stop making and testing nuclear bombs. They affect us all. We are all downwinders.

Take time now to reflect on these three areas in silence and consider what you would like to say at the Council of Women from Around the World.

The Council of All Beings — *25 min*

When members of both groups are finished writing their reflections, invite them back to the circle and share the following:

We will begin with the Council of All Beings. I invite the women who will speak at the Council of Women from Around the World to sit quietly and listen to the various life-forms that will share their stories during this Council.

Let the Council of All Beings begin. You life-forms who are not human, please speak to us.

When everyone has spoken, say:

Thank you, life-forms, for spending time with us. Because of the web of life, the gifts that each of you gave us are already present within us. We are grateful for these gifts that can bring healing to our planet and to our lives as women.

Before these life-forms depart, is there a word or phrase of thanksgiving, acknowledgement, or apology, that you women would like to say to them?

After the women have spoken to the life-forms, convey the following in your own words:

Let us conclude by helping these life-forms return to their home: Earth. Take a moment to thank your life-forms for the privilege of speaking for them. Then release them—either by brushing your bodies, gently breathing your life-form outward, placing your hands on the ground or by some other gesture that feels appropriate.

The Council of Women from Around the World— 25 min

Open this Council by saying:

We will now hold the Council of Women from Around the World. I invite the women who were life-forms but are now human again to sit quietly and listen to the women who will share their stories during this Council.

Let the Council of Women from Around the World begin. Women attending this Council, speak to us.

> *The soul of the world and our own souls intertwine and influence one another. There is one Great Being who enlivens the dance of our beautiful planet and everything that exists.*
>
> **Joyce Rupp**

When everyone has spoken, say:

Thank you, women, for spending time with us. Because of the web of life, the gifts that each of you gave us are already present within us. We are grateful for these gifts that can bring healing to our planet and to our lives as women.

Before these women depart, is there a word or phrase—of thanksgiving, acknowledgement, or apology that the rest of you would like to say to them?

After these women have spoken to the other women at the Council, convey the following in your own words:

Let us conclude by helping these women return to their dwellings. Take a moment to thank the women who chose you for the privilege of speaking for them. Then release them—either by brushing your bodies, gently breathing her back to the universe, or by some other gesture that feels appropriate.

Large Group Reflection — *15 min*

Conclude these Councils by asking:

We have heard from both life-forms and women who are greatly affected by the harmful way that we treat Mother Earth. How was this experience for you?

Closing — *10 min*

Say:

Let us close by standing in a circle, our hearts joined in gratitude for our connection with creation. I will pass this bowl of dirt around. As this small portion of Earth comes to you, let the soil run through your fingers and, if you feel moved to, share a hope or prayer for healing for our Earth, its creatures and its people. As the bowl makes its way around the circle, feel free to touch the objects that we all brought as well.

Looking Ahead — *3 min*

In preparation for the next session, remind participants to do the Life Practice, journal topics and questions, and the next session's readings, found at the end of this session.

Life Practice

1) Spend some time in nature, slowly walking around, touching trees, listening to the sound of running water, inhaling the intoxicating scent of flowering vines or digging soil, planting seeds, and watching them grow. Let your senses come alive.

2) If you would like to learn more about global warming, see the movie "An Inconvenient Truth." Then, decide on an action, no matter how small, that you can do to slow down this destructive phenomenon.

The Cosmic Dance
By Joyce Rupp

I lean back in memory and catch a hint of what I knew long ago when I was a small child living on a farm in rural Iowa. It is the melody of the cosmic dance playing in my soul since those early days, a song that has never stopped singing in me.

As I grew older I lost some of my awareness of the cosmic dance for awhile.... But eventually I made some startling discoveries—three of them—and they have changed my life forever. The first of these is the amazing revelation that I am made of stardust, that every part and parcel of who I am materially was once a piece of a star shining in the heavens. The second discovery is that the air I breathe is the air that has circled the globe and been drawn in and out by people, creatures and vegetation in lands and seas far away. But the most astounding discovery that both awakened and affirmed my early childhood awareness is the fact that I am part of a vast and marvelous dance that goes on unceasingly at every moment in the most minute particles of the universe.

I picture these invisible particles that compose every piece of existence as having little dancing feet. Something as sturdy as a boulder does its own boulder dance but it also weaves in and out of the dance of the soil, the dance of the worm, the dance of the wolf. The stone, the soil, the worm, the wolf, cannot be contained. They dance with everything else that "is." What a marvel, to think that each cell of my body is part of an intricate interweaving of the dynamic life of creation!...

No one person has been able to fully communicate this amazing dance of life to me, but Thomas Merton comes close with his description in *New Seeds of Contemplation*. Merton's use of the phrase "cosmic dance" set my heart singing. When I read it, I felt my early childhood experience of the inner dance being echoed and affirmed:

When we are alone on a starlit night; when by chance we see the migrating birds in autumn descending on a grove of junipers to rest and eat; when we see children in a moment when they are really children; when we know love in our own hearts; or when, like the Japanese poet Basho, we hear an old frog land in a quiet pond with a solitary splash—at such times the awakening, the turning inside out of all values, the "newness," the emptiness and the purity of vision that make themselves evident, provide a glimpse of the cosmic dance.[1]

[1] Thomas Merton. *New Seeds of Contemplation* (New York: New Directions Books, 1961), pp. 296-297.

Source: Joyce Rupp, *The Cosmic Dance: An Invitation to Experience Our Oneness.*

Journal Topics and Questions

Reflect on one of the first times that you participated in some type of action for peace, justice, and social change. What drew you to this cause? What did you do and why did you act in this manner? Whom did you act with? How did this experience affect your life? If you have not participated in such an action, reflect on a person, community, or movement whose actions for peace have inspired you.

Readings for Session 11

Using Right Means
By Michael Nagler

Almost everyone today is familiar with the principle that right ends cannot be brought about by wrong means. It is this recognition that differentiates a nonviolence-based effort, which is a mutual learning process for change, from an ordinary power struggle. "Means are ends in the making," Gandhi explained. While some would say means are just means, to the nonviolent actor they are, he said, "everything." In the case of a revolutionary struggle, for example, he held that "violent revolution will bring violent *swaraj* [independence]."

What exactly are the right means in nonviolent struggle? Of course, the basic criterion for right means is that they be non-injurious, not harming the legitimate interests of our opponent (or anyone else). But this is only the negative aspect of right means, and history shows that there is much more to consider.

There are two common mistakes often made by movements for social change. One is to place too much weight on symbolic techniques—a march, a demonstration, a set of ribbons. The other is to be too reactive to wrongs without seeing or seeking to elicit right behavior from our opponents. We must not only "non-cooperate with evil," as Martin Luther King put it, but be willing also to "cooperate with good." Many fledgling movements get stuck in the protest mode, and this can worsen relationships with the opponent, hardening his resistance. In nonviolence, courage often means taking the initiative to go that extra step in trust; wisdom often means pro-actively building a better system.

Once we grasp that nonviolence is an active force, it should follow that active, concrete measures are the most appropriate and likely to be the most effective. Many a budding movement has fought for the right to wave a flag or march down a street, while the regime they opposed waited out of harm's way for a more favorable time to crack down.

Perhaps the most tragic example of a symbol gone wrong in modern nonviolent history is the disaster of Tiananmen Square. Students, workers and many supporters gathered in vast numbers to demonstrate their solidarity and make their feelings known. However, they had no clear idea of what to do next. The square became a symbol of their disobedience. We all know the results.

In hindsight we can see that if the resisters had instead gone back to their universities and villages to educate the people and take concrete, achievable steps for change, the democracy movement in China—and the brave people who embodied it—might still be alive. Their attachment to the symbolic square caused the movement to waste its opportunity to build on the popularity gained by their great courage.

In the famous Salt March of 1930, Gandhi showed master showmanship and control of symbolic expression, walking over two hundred miles to the sea to break the unjust salt laws by the simplest possible act of picking up a pinch of salt: But it is often forgotten that he was going to the real sea to collect real salt—an act that was constructive, concrete and in this case, "illegal." Similarly, when he had led the Great March in South Africa fifteen years earlier, he was not just protesting, he was moving three thousand striking miners and their families to his ashram, or spiritual community. Again, it was technically against the law for them to enter the Transvaal at that time. Neither of these "marches," in other words, was merely symbolic. *Symbols can enhance or grow out of concrete actions, but they should never take the place of concrete actions.*

Generally speaking, concrete nonviolent measures can be either constructive or obstructive—one can "cooperate with good" *and* " non-cooperate with evil." The Montgomery bus boycott, for example, was not designed to "put the bus company out of business, but to put justice in business," King explained. In actual fact, constructive mechanisms are usually much more effective, though much less dramatic.

So, in practice, we should be constructive wherever possible and obstructive when necessary. That is the sign of a strong movement that has the potential to go beyond battles to a final victory. The *satyagrahi* tries first to dialogue, build institutions, build bridges, and take care of basic needs not met by the controlling power. When necessary, however, resisters must be prepared to stand in the way of what they regard as evil; either actively in the form of entering a forbidden zone…or in the form of strikes and other kinds of non-cooperation.

We could say that it is *best* to make salt or spin cotton (or start your own schools and clinics and newspapers, as the Poles did in responding to martial law in 1981); *second best* to block an evil from happening (the way the Filipino people protected with their own bodies a military camp that had defected from the Marcos regime and the Russian people surrounded their parliament building to protect it from a coup in 1991); and *third best* to not cooperate with it when it has already happened (the way the Czechs disobeyed curfew and other orders of the occupying Soviet troops in 1968-69).

Symbols can serve to rally people together for support, but that support will be empty if the resisters are not moving forward with concrete goals. Oppressive regimes may not be bothered by posters; they can always wait for a march or demonstration to go away. But they cannot survive a cottage industry when they are trying to exploit a people or a free school when they are trying to indoctrinate them.

Periodically during Gandhi's long struggle, the British felt they had the upper hand, did not need to listen to him, and could ignore whatever protests he could mount. Far from being defeated, Gandhi and his co-workers would throw themselves into a "Constructive Program:" village uplift, communal unity, cottage industry, new education, and eradication of substance abuse. All these efforts indirectly eroded colonial power and gave the *satyagrahis* much greater solidarity, confidence and legitimacy when the next crisis came.…

A constructive program can be carried on throughout our protest and non-cooperation campaign. Since a constructive program does not depend on the opponent—it's entirely "proactive"—it can go on constantly. In between times of confrontation, it can become the main focus.

Just to clarify these stages, we can mention some modern examples that have been used with good effect at the appropriate times. Constructive programs, or "acting out the future" have included building solar panels and windmills, volunteering in disadvantaged schools, and forms of neighborhood-building. Preventing wrongs from happening is a defensive approach, the next most valuable approach, especially appropriate as a short-term strategy. Examples include monitoring domestic or international conflicts, or actually intervening to prevent them as the Michigan Faith and Resistance peacemakers interpose themselves between Ku Klux Klan marchers and counter-demonstrators or Christian Peacemaker Teams intervene in Hebron, Central America, and elsewhere. Noncooperation and other forms of "obstructive program" when wrongs *are* happening include the recent trespassing campaign at the School of the Americas at Fort Benning, Georgia, where many Latin American human rights violators have been trained, and war-tax refusal. The courageous refusal of Burma's democratic opposition leader, Aung San Suu Kyi, to go along with many hindrances the military regime has imposed on her, is another example. Thanks to Aung San Suu Kyi's strong Buddhist background, she has not only been able to persevere courageously in her resistance but to avoid expressions of resentment or vengeance toward the individuals who have cruelly suppressed her and her people.

Reconciliation seeks to heal the wounds of violence and prevent further violence by promoting justice and diffusing hatred. If everyone eschewed vengeance and reached out for compassion when they were victimized, the way Eileen Egan did; if more activists practiced compassion like Sister Helen Prejean does; if there were more efforts like the Victim Offender Reconciliation Program (VORP), there would be far less crime in the U.S. and elsewhere.

Source: Michael Nagler, "The Steps of Nonviolence," *Fellowship Publications.*

Constructive Program—Reflections
By Janet Chisholm

"Can't peace and justice activists be *for* something, instead of always being so negative, always organizing against this or that, always tearing down, confronting, criticizing, rebelling and protesting?" we are asked. "Yes," is our answer. "Together we can create a new culture of peace." *Fellowship Magazine*, Jan-Feb 2005.

Constructive Program was Gandhi's main hope for India. It meant confronting Indians' own acceptance of their dependency, powerlessness and exploitation under British rule. Helping them envision and implement instead a just society of their own creation. Reweaving the strands of Indian culture and restoring relationships between Muslims and Hindus and the Hindu castes. In the campaign for Indian independence, these were his priorities. This was his vision. It is a historically neglected side of Gandhi's work, perhaps because it seems less dramatic and powerful than organized public resistance. Yet Gandhi himself considered Constructive Program far more important, more foundational, more sustaining and deserving a greater share of time and energy than resistance.

Constructive Program in India clearly benefited from Gandhi's ability to articulate an overarching vision for cultural change that could link a variety of efforts and from his promotion of a unifying symbol and action. The spinning wheel was already a cultural symbol of creative life energy, but under Gandhi came to represent the work involved in Constructive Program: developing economic independence through meaningful local work, providing basic necessities like clothing for everyone, building solidarity with the poor, and "simple living so that all might simply live." The mere act of spinning cotton offered a concrete way for every person, no matter the circumstances, to contribute on a daily basis and feel united with others in the struggle. It signified the reward of persistence and provided an almost spiritual, meditative discipline. As a powerful declaration of self-help and of independence already-in-the-making, spinning confronted the lie of Indian dependence with actions of Truth.

Peace scholar and activist Michael Nagler, Ken Preston-Pile from Pace e Bene, and I from the FOR [Fellowship of Reconciliation] have all spent time reflecting on what the lessons of Gandhi's Constructive Program may be for us today. By nature it is preventive, designed to reintegrate into the community those who are marginalized or rejected. As a result, it helps a movement gain and sustain momentum and unity, positively influences others, contributes to the intended new social order, reduces the sense of powerlessness and increases self-reliance. Near the conclusion of a resistance campaign, when the crisis is past and activists tend to fall away, Constructive Program carries on to solidify and implement changes. Nagler cautions that we should not be fooled into thinking Constructive Program is less effective than a campaign of resistance. It is a valuable complement to and preparatory training for a confrontational struggle involving resistance and direct action.

Constructive Program should not be confused with soup kitchens, shelters, prisons and other efforts that are like bandages patching up an unjust society. It is not about charity. It does not try to perpetuate the status quo. On the contrary, Constructive Program challenges systemic and structural violence by finding and applying solutions. Some of Gandhi's projects addressed needs related to job creation, land reform, health services, sanitation, substance abuse, education, the role of women, and discrimination.

Personal transformation is required, as well as social transformation. Participants are expected to evaluate and work to correct their own weaknesses, particularly passive acceptance of exploitation. The community, too, must identify and make improvements where there is tension, disunity or injustice. Through spiritual practices and purification, personal discipline, education and training, and community building, individuals are encouraged to seize the power which they already control over their own behavior and to achieve "self-rule." According to

Gandhi, the energy of nonviolence had to fill individuals first in order to bring about positive social change.

What would Constructive Program look like today? There are many existing constructive projects that represent personal and social transformation, that present alternatives to the status quo and are likely building blocks for a new culture. Participants in FOR training have planned community bicycling, counter recruitment/job counseling, Spanish books for Spanish-speaking families, a food co-op, a nonviolence resource center, nonviolence training, and a U.S. Department of Peace. Other constructive projects include fair trade goods, joint Israeli-Palestinian youth camps, co-op housing and preschools, restorative justice, Emily's list to elect women to Congress, desert landscaping, creating pocket parks and community playgrounds, Habitat for Humanity, organic gardening, complementary medicine, sister cities projects, independent media and bookstores, consensus decision-making and shared leadership, water and energy conservation, community arts and events, community meals, block watch, spiritual practice and meditation, peace education and training in conflict transformation.

The overarching vision for a Constructive Program that could link these projects is less obvious. Can we articulate a broad vision that incorporates our shared values and helps us feel that we are all working for the same end, even if not on the same projects or in the same location? Are there symbols that might call us to common daily actions that would create a sense of solidarity? Or do we already have these and we just need to raise them up? Any suggestions?

Source: Janet Chisholm, "Constructive Program—Reflections," *Fellowship Magazine*.

A Place Where Women Rule:
All-Female Village in Kenya is Indication of
Burgeoning Feminism Across Africa
By Emily Wax

UMJOA, KENYA—Seated cross-legged on tan sisal mats in the shade, Rebecca Lolosoli, matriarch of a village for women only, took the hand of a frightened, 13-year-old girl. The child was expected to wed a man nearly three times her age, and Lolosoli told her she didn't have to.

The man was Lolosoli's brother, but that didn't matter. This is a patch of Africa where women rule.

"You are a small girl. He is an old man," said Lolosoli, who gives haven to young girls running from forced marriages. "Women don't have to put up with this nonsense anymore."

Ten years ago, a group of women established the village of Umjoa, which means unity in Swahili, on an unwanted field of dry grasslands. The women said they had been raped and, as a result, abandoned by their husbands, who claimed they had shamed their community.

Stung by the treatment, Lolosoli, a charismatic and self-assured woman with a crown of puffy dark hair, decided no men would be allowed to live in their circular village of mud- and-dung huts.

In an act of spite, the men of her tribe started their own village across the way, often monitoring activities in Umjoa and spying on their female counterparts.

What started as a group of homeless women looking for a place of their own became a successful and happy village. About three-dozen women live here, and run a cultural center and camping site for tourists visiting the adjacent Samburu National Reserve. Umjoa has flourished, eventually attracting so many women seeking help that they even hired men to haul firewood, traditionally women's work.

The men in the rival village also attempted to build a tourist and cultural center, but were not very successful.

But the women felt empowered with the revenue from the camping site and their cultural center, where they sell crafts. They were able to send their children to school for the first time, eat well and reject male demands for their daughters' circumcision and marriage.

They became so respected that troubled women, some beaten, some trying to get divorced, started showing up in this little village in northern Kenya. Lolosoli was even invited by the United Nations to attend a recent world conference on gender empowerment in New York.

"That's when the very ugly jealous behaviors started," Lolosoli said, adding that her life was threatened by local men right before her trip to New York. "They just said, frankly, that they wanted to kill me," Lolosoli said, laughing because she thought the idea sounded overly dramatic.

Sebastian Lesinik, the chief of the male village, also laughed, describing the clear division he saw between men and women. "The man is the head," he said. "The lady is the neck. A man cannot take, let's call it advice, from his neck."

"She's questioning our very culture," Lesinik said in an interview at a bar on a sweltering afternoon. "This seems to be the thing in these modern times. Trouble-making ladies like Rebecca."

In a mix of African women's gumption and the trickling in of influences from the outside world, a version of feminism has grown progressively alongside extreme levels of sexual violence, the battle against HIV-AIDS, and the aftermath of African wars, all of which have changed the role of women in surprising ways.

A package of new laws has been presented to Kenya's parliament, intended to give women unprecedented rights to refuse marriage proposals, fight sexual harassment in the workplace, reject genital mutilation and to prosecute rape, an act so frequent that Kenyan leaders call it the nation's biggest human rights issue. The most severe penalty, known as the "chemical castration bill," would castrate repeatedly convicted rapists and send them to prison for life.

In neighboring Uganda, thousands of women are rallying this month for the Domestic

Relations Bill, which would give them specific legal rights if their husbands take a second wife, in part because of fear of HIV infection.

Eleven years after the Rwandan genocide, in which an estimated 800,000 people were killed, women in the country hold 49 percent of the seats in the lower house of parliament. Many of them are war widows who have said that they felt compelled to rise up in protest after male leaders presided over the 1994 slaughter of Tutsi tribal members by the Hutu majority....

"We are at the start of something important for African women," said Margaret Auma Odhiambo, a leader of western Kenya's largest group for widows. The members are women whose husbands have died from AIDS complications.

Lolosoli's effort to speak out for change in her patch of the continent shows the difficulties of changing the rhythm and power structure of village life. Before Lolosoli even went to the U.N. conference, she was going house to house in the nearby town of Archer's Post, telling women they had rights, such as to refuse to have sex with their husbands if they were being beaten or ill-treated.

"A woman is nothing in our community," she said, referring to the members of her tribe, including the men in the village across the road.

"You aren't able to answer men or speak in front of them whether you are right or wrong," she said. "That has to change. Women have to demand rights and then respect will come. But if you remain silent, no one thinks you have anything to say. Then again, I was not popular for what I was saying."

At the U.N. conference in New York, Lolosoli said she and other women from around the world bonded as they watched an episode of Oprah that focused on women, verbal abuse and cheating husbands.

"You just cry and cry," sighed Lolosoli, who said many men in her tribe still take several wives. "Then again, I was really inspired to know that a lot of women face challenges of this nature and make it."

When she came back to Kenya, armed with ideas and empowerment training workbooks, she stood her ground even when some of the men filed a court case against her, seeking to shut down the village.

"I would just ignore the men when they threw stones at me and ask, 'Are you okay, are your children okay, are your cows okay?'" she said. Her tactic and calm reaction was disarming, she recalled. "After everything, they weren't going to stop us."

Lolosoli is still battling her brother over his attempt to marry the 13-year-old.

But lately, the residents of the men's village have been admitting defeat. They are no longer trying to attract tourists. Some have moved elsewhere. Others have had trouble getting married, because some women in the area are taking Lolosoli's example to heart.

"She has been successful, it's true." sighed Lesinik, who said maybe he is a little bit jealous. He then shrugged and said, "Maybe we can learn from our necks. Maybe just a little bit."

Source: Emily Wax, "A Place Where Women Rule...," Washington Post Foreign Service.

PART FOUR

SISTERHOOD

Session 11

Sisterhood is Still Powerful: Women and Social Change

Session 11
Sisterhood is Still Powerful:
Women and Social Change

In this Session We Will:

- Become aware of social change movements and actions throughout history that have been led by women
- Familiarize ourselves with different approaches to working for peace as part of an organization or movement
- Prepare ourselves for an action that we will plan in Session 12 by reflecting on the ways that each of us has chosen to work for peace

Agenda

Introduction — *2 min*
Reflections from the Last Session — *10 min*
Opening Ritual — *10 min*
Nonviolent Social Change Movements and Actions Led by Women — *40 min*
How Do We Make Peace? — *50 min*
Closing — *5 min*
Looking Ahead — *3 min*
       Life Practice
       Journal Topics and Questions
       Readings

Materials Needed

- ☐ Shared Agreements
- ☐ Prayer table
- ☐ A colorful cloth
- ☐ A candle
- ☐ Matches
- ☐ Bell
- ☐ Flipchart
- ☐ Easel paper
- ☐ Masking Tape
- ☐ Markers
- ☐ Posters of women involved in social change movements, campaigns, or actions to put up on the walls (if desired)
- ☐ Compact disk or audiotape player (if desired)
- ☐ Recorded music (if desired)

Facilitator Notes
Session preparation — The week before
- Review the entire session. Practice reading any visualizations or meditations, and role-play or practice setting up and facilitating exercises beforehand. Whenever possible, put material into your own words. Feel free to make notes on 3x5 cards or in the book next to the written instructions.
- Tape several pieces of easel paper or 8 ½ x 11 sheets strung together and make the Time-line for Nonviolent Social Change Movements and Actions Led by Women with the dates, names of women or groups and descriptions of their actions found later in the session. Feel free to make your own additions.

Session preparation — The day of
- Arrange the chairs, including your own, in a circle, with a small table in the center. Place the cloth, candle, and matches on the table.
- Tape the Shared Agreements to the wall.
- Play some background music as people arrive, if desired.

Session 11
Sisterhood is Still Powerful:
Women and Social Change

Introduction — *2 min*

Convey the following in your own words:

> Welcome to Session 11. In Session 10, we experienced the deep relationship we have with creation and affirmed the responsibility we have to care for Earth and all Her peoples and creatures.
>
> Rooted in such interconnectedness, we can now move forward with our efforts to end violence and injustice. As we come together as communities of women, we become a force that must be reckoned with: sisters. Sisterhood is powerful when we join with women around the world to recreate our society according to the values and practices of women's spirituality.
>
> This time as we gather, we will first experience the power of sisterhood by becoming more aware of social change movements and actions throughout history that have been led by women. We will then familiarize ourselves with different approaches to working for peace as part of an organization or movement. We will conclude by preparing ourselves for an action that we will plan in Session 12 by reflecting on the ways that each of us has chosen to work for peace, social justice, and environmental harmony.

Reflections from the Last Session — *10 min*

Share the following:

> Find a partner and share with her any insights that came up or experiences you had between sessions, or reflections you had on the Life Practice, journal questions, or the readings.

Opening Ritual — *10 min*

Light the candle and invite the group to begin the ritual by saying together the group mantra "We are good, beautiful, strong, and holy. We are women of spirit. We are women of peace. We seek healing and wholeness for ourselves and our world."

Then say:

Let us now honor the women we know who have come before us, women of spirit, women of peace, who have lead the way as they have worked for justice and peace. Let us together read the following:

Refrain:
Standing before us, making us strong
Lending their wisdom to help us along
Sharing a vision, sharing a dream
Touching our hearts, touching our lives
Like a deep, flowing stream.

Read these verses:

These are the women who throughout the decades
Have led us and helped us to know
Where we have come from and where we are going
The women who've helped us to grow.

These are the women who joined in the struggle
Angry and gentle and wise
These are the women who called us to action
Who called us to open our eyes.

Then say:

Call out the names of women you know—family members or friends who have helped you to grow, and played an important role in your peacemaking journey.

Repeat the refrain together:

Refrain:
Standing before us, making us strong
Lending their wisdom to help us along
Sharing a vision, sharing a dream
Touching our hearts, touching our lives
Like a deep, flowing stream.

Read these verses:

> These are the women who nurtured our spirits
> The ones on whom we could depend
> These are the women who gave us our courage
> Our mentors, our sisters, our friends.
>
> These are a few of the women who led us
> We know there have been many more
> We name but a few, yet we honor them all
> As women who went on before.

Then say:

> Please call out names of well-known women who have given you courage and nurtured your spirit as women of peace.

End by saying the refrain together:

> **Refrain**
> Standing before us, making us strong
> Lending their wisdom to help us along
> Sharing a vision, sharing a dream
> Touching our hearts, touching our lives
> Like a deep, flowing stream.

Source: Carole Etzler, *Standing Before Us.*

Nonviolent Social Change Movements and Actions Led by Women — *40 min*

Timeline

1300 BCE	**Egypt:** Hebrew midwives refuse to kill male babies
1818	**Venezuela:** hospital laundresses strike to demand back pay
1892	**China:** Unbound Feet Society formed
1909	**New York:** "The Uprising of 20,000"— Garment workers from 500+ shops strike
1920	**USA:** Women get the right to vote
1943	**Germany:** Non-Jewish German women secure release of Jewish husbands

1955	**Indonesia**: 500,000 women demonstrate for women rights, International Women's Day
1962	**USA**: Fannie Lou Hamer organizes Blacks to register to vote
1962	**USA**: Dolores Huerta joins Cesar Chavez to form first Farmworkers' Union
1970s	**Europe**: Take Back the Night begins
1977	**Argentina**: Mothers of the Plaza de Mayo march on behalf of their disappeared family members
1977	**India**: Women in Chipko movement save trees
1979	**Canada**: Native women of Tobique Reserve walk 100 miles to protest
1979	**Iran**: 15,000 women march, protest lack of freedom whether or not to wear a veil
1987	**Israel**: Women in Black movement begins
1987	**Spain**: Madrid lesbian "kiss-in"
1989	**Zimbabwe**: First counseling service for rape survivors opens
1990	**Australia**: "Family Secrets" art exhibit (by incest and domestic violence survivors)
1996	**Northern Ireland**: Women's Coalition wins two seats at negotiating table
2000	**Burundi**: Women's groups hold "cry-in" during peace talks
2005	**USA**: Cindy Sheehan vigil sparks 1400 peace vigils to end war in Iraq

Sources: Adapted from Pam McAllister, *This River of Courage: Generations of Women's Resistance and Action* and *You Can't Kill the Spirit: Stories of Women and Nonviolent Action*; Aruna Gnanadason, Musimbi Kanyoro and Lucia Ann McSpadden, eds., *Women, Violence and Nonviolent Change*; Lisa Schirch, ed., *Women in Peacebuilding: Resource and Training Manual*.

Place the timeline on the table in the center of the circle or on the floor. Share the following in your own words:

> This timeline lists a few of the social change movements and actions for peace and justice that women have initiated. These women are here with us now, standing before us. I invite you to spend some time in silence reading these names, reflecting on all of these women from across the globe who have struggled to make our world a better place.

After a little while, say:

> There are so many other women who have acted for peace. What other names do we want to add to this list? (*Take turns writing their names on the timeline.*)

Then ask the group to respond to the following:

- Which woman on this timeline has been most influential in your life?
- What role did this woman, and the action she undertook, or the movement she started, play in your peacemaking journey?

Close by saying:

These women have shown us different ways of working for peace as part of a larger group, community, or movement. We will continue our exploration of nonviolent social change movements by considering what *our* approach to peacemaking is as part of these larger bodies.

> *Radical groups of women continue our commitment to building sisterhood, of making feminist political solidarity between women an ongoing reality. We continue the work of bonding across race and class....And we have the good fortune to know every day of our lives that sisterhood is concretely possible, that sisterhood is still powerful.*
>
> **bell hooks**

How Do We Make Peace? — *50 min*

Overview of Constructive and Obstructive Program — *5 min*

Summarize the following points in your own words or invite the group to read them silently or out loud:

- Michael Nagler states that, "Concrete nonviolent measures can be either constructive or obstructive—one can 'cooperate with good' and 'non-cooperate with evil.' He believes that "we should be constructive wherever possible and obstructive when necessary."
- Obstructive program is resistance to evil. Throughout history, women have resisted when necessary. They have organized boycotts, or "girlcotts," avoiding a certain activity until demands are met. They have refused to shop at certain stores, have sex with their partner, or cook meals. Women have gone on strike. They have raised public awareness through marches, candlelight vigils, as well as by gathering signatures for petitions to be sent to government or corporate officials.
- Constructive Program (CP) means being *for* something, not just being against something, while at the same time challenging the status quo. CP encourages us to envision and create the type of society or church we want to be a part of. CP is a less familiar approach to peacemaking because it seems less dramatic than some of the actions described above. Yet CP is powerful—it moves people beyond a sense of helplessness and despair by empowering them to take action independently of the

oppressor. CP is proactive rather than reactive, concrete, rather than symbolic. It can effect lasting change.

- Some contemporary examples of Constructive Program are: the Fair Trade Movement where those who grow coffee and cocoa are paid just wages; building solar panels and windmills as alternative sources of energy; offering childcare in the workplace; growing organic, community gardens.
- Many successful social change movements have integrated both of these elements. The timeline offers several examples of both approaches.

Constructive Program Brainstorm — *10 min*

Say:

> Since Constructive Program is a less well-known way of acting for peace, let us spend a few moments brainstorming further examples of Constructive Program, some in which you may have participated.

Record the group's responses on flipchart paper.

Small Group Sharing — *15 min*

Convey the following in your own words:

> Now we will take some time to share with each other some of the ways that we, personally, have chosen to work for social change. Find a partner and reflect on these questions:
>
> 1) How have you "been for something" by participating in some form of Constructive Program?
> 2) Or, how have you resisted violence and injustice by participating in some form of Obstructive Program?

You may wish to sound the bell halfway into the sharing, to make sure each person has a chance to share.

Large Group Reflection — *20 min*

Invite everyone to return to the large group. Ask members to respond to the following:

1) What did you learn about constructive and obstructive programs by listening to each others' stories?

2) How does what you learned prepare you for the next session's action planning?

Iraq: "The Invasion Has Brought Us Poverty"
Economic Nonviolence Empowers Women
By Peggy Gish

Along the entrance to the Women's Will organization, Maxine Nash and I saw banners saying, "The Occupation Kills Your Sons, Don't Buy from the Occupiers," "Boycott the Invaders," and "Iraqi Mothers United Against Sectarian Fighting." Inside the meeting room another more colorful banner said, "No Peace Without Justice."

We walked into a teach-in already in progress. Hana Ibrahim, coordinator of Women's Will and Dr. Balkiss, member of the board (two middle-aged Muslim women), alternatively spoke to about eighteen women and five men about one way Iraqis could resist the U.S. occupation.

"We would silently defeat the occupation, not by killing, but by refusing to cooperate economically with America," said Dr. Balkiss. "America is trying to make this a free market for itself and treating Iraq like another state. We should have our own sovereignty. Even before the tanks came in, the media war succeeded in promoting American products. Iraqis have been buying the cheaper American products, and this has undermined our economy. The invasion has brought us poverty."

Hana went on to say that there are many things women can do. "Any mother can refuse to buy Coca Cola and other U.S. products. We know how to manage our lives here. We have our own meats, fruits and vegetables. Iran and Syria don't deal with the U.S. economically and they do all right." She referred to Gandhi's urging the Indian people to spin their own thread and weave their own cloth.

During the discussion, one woman told the group about her relative's wedding, where the family served American soft drinks, but the people refused to drink them. When the family brought in Iraqi soft drinks, the guests drank them. Another woman said that she knew how to make her own shampoo out of natural products. "If they put in a McDonalds in Baghdad, we will boycott it," added another. Hana concluded the meeting, "Women should work through civil society. Working nonviolently can strengthen peaceful structures. Small actions, such as putting up posters, and large actions, like demonstrations, all add up and make a difference. Whatever it takes, we will win."

Source: Christian Peacemaker Teams, CPTNET.

The Women's Path of Peace

During a regional security council meeting in late 1996, a nun revealed that 95 percent of the women in one community of Uraba had been raped. This ignited something deep within a few women activists in the city of Medellin. They called for an act of solidarity: a thousand Colombian women from women's groups around the country to go to Uraba and put their arms around those who had suffered the humiliation of war.

Across Colombia, busloads of women departed for Uraba. Many traveled for several days. Some left their communities for the first time. Many did not have permission from their husbands or fathers, but went anyway. And when fifteen hundred Colombian women arrived in Uraba on November 25—the International Day for the Elimination of Violence against Women—they hugged their sisters. Thus was born La Ruta Pacifica de las Mujeres....

La Ruta Pacifica de las Mujeres simply called Ruta (Path) is a movement that seeks to strengthen nonivolent action against war....After the first mobilization, women set out for other regions that were under the assault of war. They launched nationwide marches to Bolivar, Cartagena, Barrancabermeja, and Bogota and regional marches to many other areas....

On November 25, 2003, Ruta led three thousand women in a caravan of a 100 buses to the Southern jungle department of Putumayo. Putumayo is at the heart of joint U.S.-Colombian drug-eradication efforts that include the aerial fumigation of coca fields....Over 300 women's groups from across Colombia endorsed Ruta's statement against the "militarist policy of the current government, which favors the use of weapons and force to treat problems that are rooted in and generate poverty."...They demanded that the "women and men of Putumayo be allowed to influence the decisions that affect their lives and health and those of their children, and the land which sustains them."

During the Putumayo mobilization, the U.S. Ambassador to Colombia spoke against Ruta's declaration. Ruta leaders consider the attention significant. "The Ambassador wouldn't say anything unless he felt our movement had political weight," said Marina Gallega of Ruta. "And we have influence outside of Colombia because our peaceful opposition to war and violence appeals to women everywhere."

The United Nations Development Fund for Women (UNIFEM) and the British organization International Alert agreed. In 2001, they awarded the Millennium Peace Prize to La Ruta Pacifica de las Mujeres....Ruta accepted the award with following words: "we have told the warring men that we do not deliver children for war, and that we will not allow our hands and wombs to contribute to war. Our bodies will not serve as war booty....We demand that the arms race supported by the developed countries stop....We demand that not one more dollar be spent on war."...

It is Ruta's unique solidarity—indeed sisterhood—that gives women the strength to march in the face of war and violence and authoritarianism....And it is their efforts to be coherent in word and action from a feminist perspective that makes Ruta an unconventional movement so full of hope.

Source: Excerpted from American Friends Service Committee and Fellowship of Reconciliation, *Building from the Inside Out: Peace Initiatives in War-Torn Colombia.*

Closing — *5 min*

Close by gathering in a circle and calling out names of people and places that need peace.

Remind everyone that during the next session your group will plan a nonviolent action for peace. (See journal topics and questions.) You may need longer than two hours to do so. See if the group would be willing to stay a half hour or an hour longer if necessary.

Looking Ahead — *3 min*

In preparation for the next session, remind participants to do the Life Practice, journal topics and questions, and the next session's readings, found at the end of this session.

Life Practice — *3 min*

Learn more about Constructive Program by either visiting a group that is involved in CP such as an alternative school, a housing cooperative or co-housing community, a house church, a community radio station or a group that uses art for healing and social change. You could also talk to someone who has been involved in a local branch of peacemaking efforts through such organizations as Nonviolence Peaceforce or Peace Brigades International. Or, read an article about one such effort.

Journal Topics and Questions

1) During the next session, the group will plan an action for peace that it will then carry out before the final session. In preparation for this action, think of a social justice issue that is important to you that you would like the group to address. It may be an issue dear to your heart that perhaps you are already responding to in some way—or one that you would like to address. Or it could be a social problem that is the focus of the work of an organization that another group member belongs to. The violence or injustice that you choose may affect primarily or exclusively women or all people.

2) Then, decide what form you would like the group's response to take. Will the group undertake Constructive Program by creating a solution to the identified problem? For instance, develop a one-time "listening project" or a longer term "sister relationship" with an organization comprised of women from backgrounds different from your own, participate in counter-recruitment activities that offer youth alternatives to joining the armed forces, or help to create a community garden.

Or, will the group resist this violence in some way—through planning a prayerful vigil, a sing-in, a boycott, civil disobedience, or by collecting petitions or joining a gathering that others have planned? The possibilities are endless!

Readings for Session 12

Interview of Dolores Huerta
By Monica Elizondo

Dolores Huerta is a firm believer that everyone, especially women and young people, should be involved in trying to create positive social change. Children should not be used as an excuse for getting involved. Huerta is the mother of eleven children and look at all that she has accomplished. She believes parents should involve their children and bring them along in their activist pursuits. Monica asked to interview Dolores Huerta for a fifth grade biography report. Dolores enthusiastically answered her questions.

1. *What was your life like in Elementary? What did you do as a young girl?* It was nice in Elementary School. There was lots of diversity and different types of kids. We had potluck parties where we ate each other's food. We used chopsticks to eat Chinese food. We made African American corn cakes, which were like little tortillas. We ate Philippine food. It was wonderful. I learned how to relate to different types of people and that has helped me as an adult in the work that I do and when I have to negotiate contracts. The teachers were strict then, we had to try hard. The good teachers didn't play favorites.

2. *Cesar Chavez's mother taught him to fight conflicts with his mind and by speaking up rather than using his fists. What did your parents teach you about when you were young?* I grew up in a single parent home. My mother was very gentle, she didn't believe in violence. She was devoted to St. Francis and she said the prayer of St. Francis all the time. Do you know it? "Make me an instrument of peace; where there is hatred let me sow love..." She also admired St. Clare and the work she did for the poor. My mother tried to help the poor. She taught me many things: Do things for others. Don't wait to be asked— help them. Don't expect appreciation for the good things you do. Don't take advantage of people. Don't be hostile to people who take advantage of you. Don't gossip or talk bad about other people. Gossip is a form of violence.

3. *Can you tell me about the first time you met Cesar Chavez?*
    Oh yes, we met here in Oakland. It was at a dinner dance for the CSO (Community Service Organization). We were volunteers....I wanted to meet Cesar because he was a good organizer.

4. *What was it like to be a woman in the United Farm Workers Union?*
    There were and are many women organizers. They encouraged women to get involved. Women were in charge and were active in strikes and protests. There were women who took care of the labor contracts.

5. *Was it hard being a woman in the United Farm Workers Union?*
    One thing that makes it hard for women is that some women hold themselves back.

They don't have confidence in themselves; they are too concerned about making mistakes. Men just do things. Women need to believe they can do it. It is best when women encourage each other to get involved and take leadership positions. Cesar Chavez also put women in leadership positions.

6. *What did it feel like to be on the protest march from Delano to Sacramento?*
   We were tired, hungry; we wanted clean socks and a place to take a bath. I imagine that is what the homeless feel like everyday. People gave us food and we had places to sleep and take a shower. We made sacrifices for advances of the farm workers.

7. *How did you feel when you went to jail for helping people?*
   Jail is not pleasant but when you go to jail for a good cause, you sacrifice your freedom to help other people get their freedom. Jail is humiliating. You feel like a prisoner, but again, you have to make sacrifices when working for people's rights.

8. *What can I do to make a difference for migrant workers or help the world?*
   Write letters to Senators, Congresspersons. Tell them to pass laws for migrant workers' rights and to get residence here in the U.S. Get other kids to write letters with you. Learn about lobbying with your friends.

9. *Any final thing you want to say?*
   It is so important to be an advocate for peace and get others involved too.

Source: First Annual Pace e Bene Nonviolence Award Ceremony, October 22, 2005.

We Refuse to Be Enemies
By Sumaya Farhat-Naser and Gila Svirsky

Dr. Sumaya Farhat-Naser, a Palestinian woman, is the cofounder and former director of the Jerusalem Center for Women, a Palestinian organization committed to Middle East peace based on justice, human rights, and women's rights. Gila Svirsky is a Jewish Israeli peace activist. She was the head of the peace groups Bat Shalom and B'Tselem and a cofounder of the Coalition of Women for Peace.

Although the news has not yet reached the international media, we would like the world to know that women in Israel and Palestine are ready to make peace.

For the past 13 years, women have been the most vibrant, daring, and progressive part of the peace movement on both sides of our divide. Palestinian and Israeli women have been meeting and negotiating with each other for years, even when the very act of speaking to each other was illegal in Israel and prohibited in Palestine.

These negotiations began in secret years ago in local homes and churches. Then we felt safer meeting in Basel, Berlin, Brussels, Bologna, and other European cities. Today, we meet openly when we can, often in symbolic venues, such as the Notre Dame Center on the border between Palestinian and Israeli Jerusalem.

While there have been dissension and debate, and while we have often held these discussions in painful circumstances, we have always held aloft the common vision of peace. Were it left to us, we would long ago have reached a peace agreement that settles the difficult issues between us.

We women advocate an end to the situation of occupier and occupied. We want to see Israel and Palestine as two separate states, side by side, with Jerusalem the shared capital of both. We desire a just solution to end the suffering of the refugees. We believe that each nation has an equal right to statehood, independence, freedom, security, development, and a life of dignity.

And, in a crucial point of agreement, we condemn all forms of brutality, violence, and terrorism—whether by individuals, political groups, governments, or the military. We have had enough of the killing, on both sides. Too many Palestinian and Israeli children are now dead or orphaned or maimed for life. And too many of our own sons, fathers, and brothers have done that killing—for war not only victimizes the innocent but also brutalizes the perpetrators.

As Israeli and Palestinian women, we have tried to educate our own peoples about the validity of both claims to this territory; we've worked against our societies' efforts to demonize the other side. We have promoted dialogue between women, paid mutual condolence calls to the families of victims on both sides, been arrested for protesting actions that violate our national consensus, and spoken out in a clear voice to demand a just solution.

And, apart from our public organizational activity, we women also operate as secret agents. We are not just the mothers, teachers, nurses, and social workers of our societies. We also serve up politics with dinner and teach the lessons of nonviolence to every child in our classrooms, every patient in our care, every client we advise, every son and daughter we love. We plant subversive ideas of peace in the minds of the young before the agents of war have even noticed. This is a long process whose results are not visible overnight, but we believe in its ultimate success.

The women's peace movement in Palestine and in Israel believes that the time has come to end the bloodshed, to lay down our weapons and our fears. We refuse to accept more warfare in our lives, our communities, our nations. We refuse to go along with the fear. We refuse to give in to the violence. We refuse to be enemies.

Source: Exerpted from Medea Benjamin and Jodie Eraus, eds., *Stop the Next War Now: Effective Responses to Violence and Terrorism.*

Statement to the Vatican of Community Support for Sister Joan Chittister
By Sister Christine Vladimiroff

For the past three months I have been in deliberations with Vatican officials regarding Sister Joan Chittister's participation in the Women's Ordination Worldwide Conference, June 29 to 30, Dublin, Ireland. The Vatican believed her participation to be in opposition to its decree...that priestly ordination will never be conferred on women in the Roman Catholic Church and must therefore not be discussed. The Vatican ordered me to prohibit Sister Joan from attending the conference where she is a main speaker.

I spent many hours discussing the issue with Sister Joan and traveled to Rome to dialogue about it with Vatican officials. I sought the advice of bishops, religious leaders, canonists, other prioresses, and most importantly with my religious community, the Benedictine Sisters of Erie [PA]. I spent many hours in communal and personal prayer on this matter.

After much deliberation and prayer, I concluded that I would decline the request of the Vatican. It is out of the Benedictine, or monastic, tradition of obedience that I formed my decision. There is a fundamental difference in the understanding of obedience in the monastic tradition and that which is being used by the Vatican to exert power and control and prompt a false sense of unity inspired by fear. Benedictine authority and obedience are achieved through dialogue between a community member and her prioress in a spirit of co-responsibility. The role of the prioress in a Benedictine community is to be a *guide in the seeking of* God. While lived in community, it is the individual member who does the seeking.

Sister Joan Chittister, who has lived the monastic life with faith and fidelity for fifty years, must make her own decision based on her sense of Church, her monastic profession and her own personal integrity. I cannot be used by the Vatican to deliver an order of silencing.

I do not see her participation in this conference as a "source of scandal to the faithful" as the Vatican alleges. I think the faithful can be scandalized when honest attempts to discuss questions of import to the church are forbidden.

I presented my decision to the community and read the letter that I was sending to the Vatican. 127 members of the 128 eligible members of the Benedictine Sisters of Erie freely supported this decision by signing her name to that letter. Sister Joan addressed the Dublin conference with the blessing of the Benedictine Sisters of Erie.

My decision should in no way indicate a lack of communion with the Church. I am trying to remain faithful to the role of the 1500-year-old monastic tradition within the larger Church. We trace our tradition to the early Desert Fathers and Mothers of the 4th century who lived on the margin of society in order to be a prayerful and questioning presence to both church and society. Benedictine communities of men and women were never intended to be part of the hierarchical or clerical status of the Church, but to stand apart from this structure and offer a different voice. Only if we do this can we live the gift that we are for the Church. Only in this way can we be faithful to the gift that women have within the Church.

[Note: *Some of the nuns who signed the letter did so from wheelchairs. And, 35 of the younger nuns signed a statement asking that any punishment given by the Vatican to Chittister be given to them, as well.*]

Source: Sister Christine Vladimiroff, "Statement to the Vatican of Community Support for Sister Joan Chittister," press release issued by Sisters of St. Benedict of Erie, PA.

Session 12

Acting for Peace

Session 12
Acting for Peace

In this Session We Will:
- Choose an issue of violence and injustice that is important for the group to respond to
- Decide on a nonviolent action that reflects the values and practices of women's spirituality that the group will do together.
- Plan this action and then carry it out

Agenda
Introduction — *2 min*
Opening Ritual — *10 min*
Gathering of Issues Close to Our Hearts — *20 min*
How Will We Respond? — *25 min*
Nonviolent Action Preparation — *60 min*
Closing — *3 min*

Materials Needed
☐ Shared Agreements
☐ Small prayer table
☐ A colorful cloth
☐ A candle
☐ Matches
☐ Bell for Opening Ritual
☐ Flipchart
☐ Easel paper
☐ Markers
☐ Compact disk or audiotape player (if desired)
☐ Recorded music (if desired)

Facilitator Notes
Session preparation – The week before
- Review the entire session. Practice reading any visualizations or meditations, and role-play or practice setting up and facilitating exercises beforehand. Whenever possible, put material into your own words. Feel free to make notes on 3x5 cards or in the book next to the written instructions.

Session preparation — *The day of*

- Arrange the chairs, including your own, in a circle, with a small table in the center. Place the cloth, candle, and matches on the table.
- Tape the Shared Agreements to the wall.
- Play some background music as people arrive, if desired.

Session 12
Acting For Peace

Introduction — 2 min

Convey the following in your own words:

> Welcome to Session 12. In Session 11, we lifted up women who have worked for social change and reflected on different ways that we have done the same. As we gather this time, we will sit in silence and look deep into our hearts to see what unjust situation we would like to respond to as a group. We will then plan a nonviolent action that reflects the values and practices of women's spirituality to carry out together. In acting for peace, we seek the transformation of ourselves and our societies.

If the group agreed to stay for an additional amount of time, remind them.

Reflections from the Last Session

Share the following in your own words:

> During this session we have much work to do, and we need as much time as possible, so we will not share our reflections from the last session.

Opening Ritual — 10 min

Light a candle and invite everyone to say the group mantra: "We are good, beautiful, strong, and holy. We are women of spirit. We are women of peace. We seek healing and wholeness for ourselves and our world."

Then, prepare to enter into a period of "Quaker silence:"

> Let us be quiet together for awhile, as our Quaker sisters and brothers do when they gather. Let us wait for the Spirit to speak to us individually and communally about this nonviolent act for peace and justice that we will plan during this session, and then carry out sometime in the near future. Let us join our hearts and minds together during this time of silence that much fruit may be born during our conversation. I will ring a bell to mark the beginning and end of this time, about eight minutes. We will then share what has been revealed to us during this silence and through our journaling.

Ring the bell to begin the time of silence and then to close it.

Gathering of Issues Close to Our Hearts — *20 min*

Share the following in your own words:

> The time that we have together to plan a nonviolent action is brief and yet, we hope, sufficient. We want to plan something that we all can be engaged in and we want it to be a doable, small, simple step. As Clarissa Pinkola Estes writes, we want it to help mend "the parts of the world that are 'within your [*or our*] reach.'"

> In order to do this, we first of all need to choose an issue or problem that we believe is in need of change, and on which we will focus. We also need to consider what our goal will be—whom we would like to influence or interact with and what we would like them to do.

> Again, to keep our action doable, let us keep in mind that someone in our group might already be working on an issue that is important to us as well.

> Out of the time we just spent in silence, then, let us consider these questions:

- What issue is your heart most drawn to?
- Whose faces did you see—the people who are suffering? Did you also see the faces of those who are contributing to these peoples' suffering?
- Who are the people you would like to affect on this issue or problem, and what would you like them to do?

Record the responses on flipchart paper. Look for commonalities. After several ideas have been generated, see if the group can agree on an issue.

Then ask:

> Would someone like to propose a goal that would help improve this situation or solve this problem?

> Once the group has agreed on the issue to be addressed and the specific goal, you can move to the next step of deciding what action to take.

> Source: Adapted from Slattery, Butigan, Pelicaric, and Preston-Pile, *Engage: Exploring Nonviolent Living.*

How Will We Respond? — *25 min*

State the following in your own words:

> We want to design our action with our goal in mind. Of course, usually we do not achieve our goal with only one action, but each action contributes to this eventual possibility.

How would we like to respond to this issue or problem—by creating an alternative solution (Constructive Program) or through resistance?

Again, let us ask ourselves: .

- Do we want to join in an action that is already planned, or initiate one ourselves? Is anyone else already working on this issue—either a member of this group or an organization that we know?
- Let us also keep in mind some of the tools we have learned during our time together, such as the CARA process and the Two Hands of Nonviolence. They may assist us both in planning and carrying out our action.

If the group needs some examples of actions that a small group can take, a few ideas are listed below or you may want to offer some examples of your own. If the group already has enough ideas, begin brainstorming possible actions that the group could take that would respond to the chosen issue and draw members closer to their goal. Ask the group to reflect on how these suggested actions reflect the values and practices of women's spirituality. (Refer to the description of women's spirituality from Session 1 that is reprinted on the next page)

Record the group's responses on flipchart paper. Decide on an action.

Possible Actions

- If the issue is lack of understanding and interaction between people of various faith and cultural traditions and the goal is to bring together women from these different traditions for dialogue, a group could organize a meal and a panel discussion followed by small group discussion for these women. Or, you could visit www.peacexpeace.org and consider establishing an ongoing relationship with a circle of women in a different country.
- If the issue is war, to influence local citizens to become more aware of the human costs of a current war and write letters or join the antiwar movement in some way, a small group could organize the reading of names of people killed on both sides of a war at an appropriate site.
- To inform church members or neighbors of an issue (a local issue that the community is struggling with or needs to be aware of—health care, women's inequality, immigration, etc.) and encourage them to get involved, an action could be setting up an information table on the issue in a setting where people have many different views on these issues. The action might include developing printed materials (information fliers, etc.) and handing them out.

- If your group would like to respond to the isolation that women in prison experience, members could write letters to incarcerated women, or offer a version of this group process to them.

Source: Adapted from Slattery, Butigan, Pelicaric, and Preston-Pile, *Engage: Exploring Nonviolent Living.*

Women's Spirituality is: a worldwide awakening of womanpower whose vision is the transformation of our selves and our societies. The ancient spiritual voice of woman now speaks its long-hidden wisdom....

This emerging voice speaks of:
- a deepening appreciation of the Feminine Divine in whose image we are
- the empowerment of ourselves as women
- the possibility for both women and men to become whole human beings
- the loving of our bodies, emotions, and minds
- the importance of stories of our lived experience that are gateways to self-knowledge, wisdom, and self-validation
- the awareness that everything and everyone is sacred, especially ourselves
- the recognition and release of our creative power, individually and communally
- the necessity of community
- reverence for the Earth, celebration of Her seasons and cycles, and those of our lives
- the recognition that all life is interconnected
- the creation of world peace, social justice, and environmental harmony

Source: Quoted and paraphrased from *Woman of Power.*

Nonviolent Action Preparation — 55 min (or longer)

Share the following: (Use the checklist to plan the action if it is helpful for your group. Some of the questions are geared more towards organizing a protest or an action of resistance.)

We now need to develop the different dimensions of our action. We can use the following checklist to guide us if we find it helpful. This checklist is long, not to overwhelm us, but to give us an idea of some of our options. We don't have to do everything on it.

Plan the specifics of the action, taking either 55 minutes or that plus the extra amount of time the group agreed to extend the meeting. For each of the areas that need attention, ask for volunteers (one person or a small committee) to take responsibility for the following task areas.

Source: Adapted from Slattery, Butigan, Pelicaric, and Preston-Pile, *Engage: Exploring Non-violent Living.*

The Nonviolent Action Checklist

Framework

- What is the goal (i.e., whom are we trying to influence, and what do we want them to do)?
- What is the action or event? Are we creating our own or joining an existing action or group?
- How does this event communicate the goals and principles of women's spirituality before, during, and after the event?
- What will the scenario be (including place and time)?
- What person or small group will provide overall coordination of the event?

Outreach

- Will the group be trying to work with other groups or communities? If so, who will make the contacts?
- Will the group have a leaflet or a flyer to pass out, explaining to the public what it is doing? If so, who will prepare it?
- Will the group do publicity? Will you try to reach other people to join you? If so, who will do it?
- What kind of media work will you do? Will you send out a press release ahead of time?
- Will there be spokespeople during the event, ready to talk to the press? Will they have a series of "talking points"?
- Do we need to contact authorities ahead of time? If so, who will do this?

Logistics and Miscellaneous Tasks

- Will the group need props and other materials? If so, who will make or get them?
- Will the group need peacekeepers (a group of volunteers who will try to ensure that the event remains nonviolent)?
- Will the group need legal observers (people who will track and support anyone who might get arrested—purposely or by accident)? Who will organize these?

- Does the group need to raise money? For what? How much? How will it do this?
- Will the group need a stage? A sound system? A truck to transport materials?
- What about transportation?
- Who will clean up after the event?

Source: Adapted from Slattery, Butigan, Pelicaric, Preston-Pile, *Engage: Exploring Nonviolent Living.*

Finalize plans. Group members will probably find it necessary to communicate with each other, either in person or by e-mail, in preparation for the action. Either plan another time to meet or make sure that everyone has exchanged contact information.

If, at the end of this session, the group is either unable to reach consensus regarding a specific action and cannot meet again, or it is too logistically challenging to carry out any type of action, spend a few moments reflecting on what the group members learned from this process of trying to plan a nonviolent action.

Potluck Possibility

As part of the final gathering, Session 13, ask if the group wants to gather earlier for a potluck meal.

Closing — *5 min*

Invite the group to ask that its action be guided by compassion and courage. Bring into the circle those who are suffering because of this injustice, and those who you hope will change their actions. Ask if there are any other hopes or concerns that members want to express before you undertake this public witness together.

Looking Ahead — *3 min*

In preparation for the next session, remind participants to do the Life Practice.

Life Practice

1) Complete your assigned tasks in preparation for the group action.

2) As you light your candle during your reflection time, hold your group members and your upcoming action up to the Light. Please bring your candle to the final session.

Session 13

Celebrating Our Power as Women!

Session 13
Celebrating Our Power as Women!

In this Session We Will:
• Evaluate the group action
• Evaluate the *Traveling with the Turtle* process
• Send each other forth to be peacemakers in our world

Agenda
Potluck (if desired)
Introduction — *2 min*
Opening Ritual — *10 min*
Action Evaluation — *25 min*
Next Steps — *25 min*
Program Evaluation — *25 min*
Sending Forth — *30 min*

Materials Needed
☐ Small prayer table
☐ A colorful cloth
☐ Compact disk or audiotape player
☐ Recorded music
☐ Copies of the Final Evaluation form
☐ Flipchart
☐ Easel paper
☐ Markers
☐ Masking tape
☐ Candles each woman received during Session 1 (they bring them)
☐ One slightly larger candle
☐ Matches
☐ Bell

Facilitator Notes
Session preparation — The week before
• Review the entire session. Practice reading any visualizations or meditations, and role-play or practice setting up and facilitating exercises beforehand. Whenever possible, put material into your own words. Feel free to make notes on 3x5 cards or in the book next to the written instructions.

- Make copies of the evaluation form for participants.
- Write the following questions for the Action Evaluation on easel paper:
  - How did you feel during the action?
  - Did we achieve our goals?
  - What values and practices of women's spirituality did you see at work during our action?
  - What most inspired or moved you about the action?
  - What challenged and stretched you?

  - Divide another sheet of flipchart paper in half vertically. On the left side, at the top of the paper, write: Liked or Worked. On the right side, write: Could Be Improved.
  - Remind participants to bring the candles they received at Session 1.

Session preparation — *The day of*
- Arrange the chairs, including your own, in a circle. Place the cloth, all of the candles with the larger one in the middle, and matches on the table.
- Tape the Shared Agreements to the wall.
- Play some background music as people arrive, if desired.

Session 13
Celebrating Our Power As Women!

Gather for a Potluck [optional]

Introduction — 2 min

Convey the following in your own words:

> Welcome to our final session. This session marks the end or our *Traveling with the Turtle* journey. We have done much together. We have explored different aspects of women's spirituality—our image of the Divine, our power-within, ways that we can express our anger constructively, respond to conflict nonviolently, and create peace in our everyday lives. We have formed community in this circle and explored ways to widen our circles by entering into relationship with both people whose life experience has been different from our own and all of Earth's creatures. And we have acted for peace together. During this final session we will reflect on our action, this process, and close by blessing each other on our journeys as peacemakers.

Opening Ritual — 10 min

Introduce this opening ritual in your own words:

> As part of our life's journey as women birthing peace in our lives, and during our experience of *Traveling with the Turtle*, sometimes we have walked. At times we have moved steadily forward, sure of ourselves and our place in the universe. Other times we have walked crookedly, backwards, or we have stopped, because of an obstacle in our path, or because we have chosen stillness. There also have been times when we ran, flew and soared, borne upward by the gift of grace. In this exercise—Walking, Stopping, and Running—we will experience, celebrate, and play with these different moments in our lives.

Play music of your choice and then give the following instructions, pausing after each one:

> Walk in any direction.
> Change direction.
> Find the edges of the space as well as the center.
> Walk in an unusual path.

Walk backward.
If you run into someone say "thank you!"
Walk forward again.
Stop.
Run.
Stop.
Walk.
Play with walking, stopping and running on your own time.
Ready, go.

Play for the duration of one song.

Source: Adapted from Phil Porter and Cynthia Winton-Henry, *Leading Your Own Life: The InterPlay Leadership Program. Secrets of InterPlay I.*

Action Evaluation — *25 min*

Say the following in your own words:

Spend some time reflecting on the nonviolent action we just did together. This was a time when we walked or ran together. We also stopped together—to listen and learn. What did we see and hear? What did we learn?

It is important that we take time to evaluate our action and share how we have been changed by this interaction.

Respond to some of the following questions (*Turn to the sheet of paper on which the questions are written.*):

1) How did you feel during the action?
2) Did we achieve our goal(s)?
3) What values or practices of women's spirituality did you see at work during our action?
4) What about this action most inspired or challenged you?

Record people's responses on flipchart paper. Let us know about your action by filling out that portion of the evaluation form during your evaluation of the Traveling with the Turtle process.

Next Steps — *25 min*

Then say:

> We have planned and carried out one action together. What, if any will be our next steps?
>
> Do all or some of us want to continue to meet as a group? If so, what would we like to do?

Have the group read the Sidebar "Next Steps" and explore what the group, or individuals in the group, would like to do next.

If you are unable to reach consensus during this time, you may need to leave more time at the end of the session in order to reach a decision or to agree on the next meeting date and time. Either affirm the decision the group has made, or continue exploring possibilities after the sending forth.

Next Steps

Form an Affinity Group or Peacemaking Circle

- Some or all of the members of the current group may wish to continue as a group to offer one another support, to deepen your study of women's spirituality and peacemaking, and take nonviolent action together.
- Variously called small groups, affinity groups, or base communities, these Peacemaking Circles create an environment to support our work, to explore the depths of nonviolence and peacemaking, to take action, and to reflect on the meaning of the process of personal and social transformation.
- We suggest that you set a date for your first meeting and decide what you'd like to do. Many of the things listed below could be part of the activity of the group.
- Even if only a few people want to start a group, that's fine—talk with other friends and colleagues about forming a group. If you have many new people in the group, you might want to lead the *Traveling with the Turtle* process for those who haven't gone through it yet.
- Whatever group emerges, we suggest two things. First, choose a name for your group. Second, let us know about your group.

Start a Women's Spirituality and Peacemaking Book Club

- Drawing from the resource list or other suggested books, participants might read and discuss significant books on women's spirituality and peacemaking once a month for a year.

Offer the *Traveling with the Turtle* Process to Other Women

- Start a new *Traveling with the Turtle* group with friends in your religious or spiritual community, at work, or school. Consider taking this process into prisons or working with other marginalized women. If you would like more information on the Pace e Bene Prison Project, contact us.

Create a Women's Ritual Circle

- Come together regularly to create rituals that mark important moments in our lives as women. Each member could a take turn leading the group.

Practice Active Listening and Conflict Resolution Skills

- Start a group that practices active listening and using conflict resolution skills such as the CARA process or Powerful Non-Defensive Communication (www.pndc.org) as a way of addressing real-life situations in members' lives.

Connect with Other Women Throughout the World

- Partner with a Sister Circle in another country. Visit www.peacexpeace.org to see how your group can connect with groups of women throughout the world via the Internet. Establish friendships, learn more about the plight of women in the country you choose to connect with and ways that you can accompany them as they seek to improve their lives. Or consider creating a similar circle with a group of women in the U.S.

Source: Adapted from Slattery, Butigan, Pelicaric, Preston-Pile, *Engage: Exploring Nonviolent Living.*

Program Evaluation — 25 min

Share the following in your own words:

We have evaluated our action and decided on our next steps. Now we will spend some time evaluating the *Traveling with the Turtle* process. We will do a group verbal evaluation and then individual written evaluations.

Verbal Evaluation — *10 min*

Then say:

> To help us evaluate this process I'm going to read aloud the Table of Contents so that we will remember all of the sessions we have completed.

Table of Contents

Session 1 Women's Spirituality: A Force for Nonviolent Peacemaking
Session 2 Empowering Images of the Divine

PART ONE: Power-Within
Session 3 Unleashing Our Power-Within
Session 4 What Gets in the Way?
Session 5 Our Movement Toward Healing

PART TWO: Power-With
Session 6 Discovering New Responses to Conflict
Session 7 Practicing Nonviolent Responses
Session 8 Creative Power: Expanding Our Vision of Peacemaking

PART THREE: Community Power
Session 9 Powerful Communities: Creating Circles of Equality
Session 10 The Earth is Our Mother: Our Connection to Creation

PART FOUR: Sisterhood
Session 11 Sisterhood is Still a Powerful Force: Women and Social Change
Session 12 Acting for Peace
Session 13 Celebrating Our Power as Women!

Ask the group:

> What did you like about this process? What worked and why?

Record the responses on the side of the sheet of paper where you have written Liked or Worked.

Then ask the group the following question:

> What could be improved and how?

Record the responses on the side entitled: Could Be Improved.

Written Evaluation — *15 min*

Pass out the written evaluation forms found at the end of this session and ask the participants to fill them out. If people need more time, they can complete the forms at home and send them to us as soon as possible.

Sending Forth — *30 min*

Bring out the small table and place it in the center of the circle. Light the larger candle. Say in your own words:

> Thank you for filling out the evaluation forms. Let us now move into our sacred ritual space as we prepare to conclude this part of our journey together. *Ring the bell.*
>
> Take a few deep breaths and relax.
>
> Look around the circle.
>
> We have traveled far, accompanied by the turtle who symbolizes the wisdom and power that we possess as women. We will continue to travel with her, taking with us all that we have shared and learned together.
>
> It is now time to return to our families, our communities, our world. Let us commission each other to go forth, claiming that awesome beauty, strength, tenderness and compassion, that yearning for justice that lives within each of us as women. Let us send each other forth to continue to be peacemakers.

Read the following story:

> When a woman in a certain African tribe knows she is pregnant, she goes out into the wilderness with a few friends and together they pray and meditate until they hear the song of the child. They recognize that every soul has its own vibration that expresses its unique flavor and purpose. When the women attune to the song, they sing it out loud. Then they return to the tribe and teach it to everyone else.
>
> When the child is born, the community gathers and sings the child's song to [her or] him. Later, when the child enters education the village gathers and chants the child's song. When the child passes through the initiation to adulthood, the people again

come together and sing. At the time of marriage, the person hears [her or] his song. Finally, when the soul is about to pass from this world, the family and friends gather at the person's bed, just as they did at their birth, and they sing the person to the next life....There is something inside each of us that knows we have a song, and we wish those we love would recognize it and support us to sing it.

Source: Alan Cohen, *"Singing Your Song."*

Then share:

We are here to sing this song for each other. What song do you need to hear? What message do you need to speak to yourself or others in this moment in your journey in order to go forth from this group and continue to be a presence for peace and love in our world? (*Pause*)

When you are ready, come forward and relight your candle, the candle that you lit when we first gathered and you shared why you had chosen to embark on this pilgrimage. After you have spoken or sung your message or mantra—or simply stood in silence— we will proclaim it back to you beginning with your name.

When everyone has shared her song, say:

Remember this song, this message, and our group singing it to you when you need to hear it.

Gather in a final circle. Join hands. Say in your own words:

Gaze upon each other, each of us a revelation of the Divine, our Mother who rocks us gently in her arms. Bless us, Holy One, as we venture forth from this room. Help us to imagine, to know, that we are that woman who loves herself—her body, mind, and spirit—who seeks healing for herself and others, a woman who longs for the creation of a new world. Are there any final intentions, hopes, or prayers that you would like to share at this time? (*Pause*)

Let us celebrate ourselves and our power as women! Let us conclude by saying together:

We are strong, beautiful, good, and holy. We are women of spirit. We are women of peace. We seek healing and wholeness—we *are* healing and wholeness—for our world. So be it!

Today's Assignment, A Prescription From: Dr. E.
By Clarissa Pinkola Estés

I assign you to be a beautiful, good, kind, awakened soulful person, a true work of art as we say, ser humano, a true human being. In a world filled with so much darkness, such a soul shines like gold; can be seen from a far distance; is dramatically different.

Want to help? Show your deepest most divine self to the world. There is nothing more rare, more strange, more needed. Why would you wait? Not worthy? Oh piffle. Not ready? Okay, so when? Next lifetime? Don't be silly with me about this. Inferiority complex? Okay, let me put it this way to you: you're not good enough to think you're not good enough. And you can quote me to yourself whenever you have need to. Dr. E. said so.

Have you forgotten that you made promises to your Beloved before you ever came to earth? The time to fulfill these is truly now. You want to cease feeling helpless, and you want to help the aching world? Serve someone and something. Everyone on earth serves someone and something. This means being your truest self now, fulfilling the promises you made to heaven long ago.

Anything you do from the soulful self will help lighten the burdens of the world. Anything. You have no idea what the smallest word, the tiniest generosity can cause to be set in motion. Be outrageous in forgiving. Be dramatic in reconciling. Mistakes? Back up and make them as right as you can, then move on. Be off the charts in kindness. In whatever you are called to, strive to be devoted to it in all aspects large and small. Fall short? Try again. Mastery is made in increments, not in leaps. Be brave, be fierce, be visionary. Mend the parts of the world that are "within your reach." To strive to live this way is the most dramatic gift you can ever give to the world.

Consider yourselves assigned. No lack of love,
tu abuelita,
Clarissa Pinkola Estés, Ph.D

Source: Clarissa Pinkola Estés, "Today's Assignment, A Prescription From: Dr. E."

Traveling with the Turtle:
A Small Group Process in Women's Spirituality and Peacemaking
Final Evaluation Form

Thank you for sharing your feedback with us to help us improve our process. We encourage you to be as open and honest as possible in your constructive feedback. Feel free to add additional pages.

Name _____

Facilitator_____ Participant_____ (check)

Group_____

E-mail _____

What did you like about *Traveling with the Turtle*? What were the most engaging, useful, or helpful aspects of this process? Why?

What, if any, changes did your group make in the curriculum?

Did you have any significant revelations or learnings during this process? Explain.

What could be improved and how would you improve it? Are there any topics you would like to have seen explored more, or topics you feel did not need to be included?

What did you think of the readings? How did they strengthen or complement the sessions, or did you find them unhelpful?

Add any comments you would like to make.

Describe your group's nonviolent action if you did one.

Thank you for your feedback! Send these forms to Traveling with the Turtle, 2501 Harrison St. Oakland, CA 94612 or to turtle@paceebene.org.

Traveling with the Turtle
Facilitation Guidelines

Traveling with the Turtle is a small group process in women's spirituality and peacemaking designed for a wide range of contexts and settings. It can be led either by people with a minimum of facilitation experience or by those with significant background in leading group process.

The facilitator is provided with the objectives for each session ("In This Session We Will") and directions for every element and exercise. There are directions for the participants' "home work": a Life Practice, journaling, and readings for the next session. Participants will do this work on their own and, therefore, will not usually need to refer to their manual during each session. They will be listening to the facilitator as she gives instructions or asks reflective questions.

All facilitators, regardless of experience, are asked to do two important things:

- Be prepared. This means reading the session text and readings carefully ahead of time, taking the time to grasp the intent and flow of the content, and following the instructions for the session preparations found at the beginning of each session.
- Do one's best to create a safe and productive environment so that participants can explore both the struggles and challenges they have encountered in their peacemaking journeys and ways they can further their healing and ability to act peacefully in their lives and the world.

The following facilitation guidelines—which have emerged from the experience of hundreds of trainings, workshops, and small group study programs led by Pace e Bene since 1997—are designed to help the facilitator accomplish these two objectives.

The Structure and Content of *Traveling with the Turtle*
Co-Facilitation

Though not absolutely necessary, it is best to have two co-facilitators lead this process. (Or you may choose to rotate the facilitation role among all of the participants.) Not only will this share the responsibilities between two people, it will also allow the person not immediately facilitating to be a "vibes watcher": to gauge the mood of the group and its needs and to intervene if necessary. The person not facilitating is available to:

- Add pieces that the facilitator may miss
- Provide support in challenging situations (e.g., broken agreements)
- Offer personal attention and accompaniment if a participant becomes emotionally overwhelmed during a session

- Carry out logistical tasks (for example, take notes), and
- Be available to take over if necessary
- When there are two facilitators, the process is shaped by the wisdom and experiences of two people, it keeps both people fresh, and it models power-sharing and nonviolent collaboration, important aspects of women's spirituality for the group. Both facilitators should also feel free to participate in each session's activities. Generally speaking, cultural diversity also strengthens *Traveling with the Turtle* co-facilitation.

Thirteen Sessions

The *Traveling with the Turtle* small group process is comprised of 13 sessions. The value and impact of the program comes from the cumulative momentum of all of the sessions that unleash and integrate the power and dynamics of personal, interpersonal, communal, and social change. We recommend scheduling and completing the entire program. The sessions can be held once a week, once every two weeks, or once a month. For some groups, however, it will not be possible to complete all of the sessions consecutively for various reasons.

Our recommendation is that one begins the series and works through it sequentially, even if a group decides that it is unable to complete more than four, five, or six sessions. The most important thing is to begin—as people participate, they may discover the importance of scheduling the entire study program.

The Structure of Each Session

Each session is expected to take two hours. In general, each session has the following structure:

- Begins with a short introduction where the facilitator welcomes everyone and gives an overview of the session.
- Participants discuss with a partner insights or relevant issues since the previous session.
- An opening ritual gathers the group back together and focuses on the session's theme.
- Each session then offers multiple formats: large group exercises, story-telling, reflection in pairs or small groups, times of creative expression (using various art media), guided meditations, role-plays, and debriefing. In all of these segments, we encourage participants to reflect on, and honor their own life experience.
- Every session closes with a ritual.
- The final part of each session focuses on closure and preparation for the next session.

Each participant is asked to do a Life Practice and journaling before the next session. They are also asked to read the material for the next gathering (found at the end of each session.)

Preparing Each Session

- Each session has an agenda that outlines the elements of the gathering, each with suggested times. Certain topics, reflections, or activities, however, may lead to long but valuable group discussion. Feel free to adjust the agenda.
- Review the agenda beforehand and read through the entire session (including the readings). Gather needed materials (candles, easel, felt markers, art supplies, a bell, etc.) and prepare necessary logistics as suggested in the session preparation section.
- Have the room set up before people arrive.
- For all sessions, you will need a flip chart with easel paper and non-toxic, felt-tip markers. If a flip chart is not available, tape large pieces of paper on the wall.
- Consider using appropriate music between exercises.
- Throughout this process there are activities encouraging participants to express their feelings or thoughts. Art supplies (crayons, colored pencils, clay, pastels, wire, drawing paper, etc.) are helpful. These supplies might be purchased with fees collected for the course or from a special collection during the first session.

Personal Preparation for Each Session

In addition to session preparation, being a facilitator requires personal preparation. It is best to be centered and grounded when facilitating. If a facilitator typically practices a particular spiritual discipline or regimen (for example, meditation, art-work, singing, writing, or mindful walking) she is encouraged to partake in this practice prior to facilitating each session.

Specific Elements of Facilitating

Creating a Centered Environment

Create a tone and atmosphere in the room where the group will meet by preparing a prayer table, covered with a colorful cloth and any objects on it—candles, etc.—that the session suggests.

Putting Instructions and Comments into Your Own Words

In each session there are:
- Instructions for the facilitator, and
- Instructions, presentations, and comments that the facilitator is to convey to the participants

The instructions for the facilitator are un-indented italicized text. The facilitator's instructions, presentations and comments to be conveyed to the participants are indented regular text. Many times the facilitator is prompted to put the comments or instructions into her own words.

Here is an example from Session 7:

Share in your own words:

Women's spirituality greatly values power-within, that power we tap into when we listen to and act from our deepest self. It also values power-with. Power-with seeks what is best for both ourselves and for those with whom we experience conflict.

"Share" means literally that the more you can present the comments or instructions to the participants naturally and in your own way, the better the flow will be. It is a good idea to read these instructions, presentations, or comments over several times if necessary.

Creating Flow by Building Bridges Between the Segments

One way to prepare one's facilitation is to notice the flow from one agenda item to the next and to be prepared to help connect these items smoothly by building bridges between them. Flow helps participants move smoothly and not feel disjointed or jarred when a new agenda item is introduced. One way to do this is to repeat previous material and connect it to the new exercise or issue. This provides an anchor for participants to build on as new material is added.

Balancing "Experiential Learning" with Presentations

Much of the *Traveling with the Turtle* process encourages participants to reflect on their own experience. This method is called *experiential learning*.

At the same time, in the *Traveling with the Turtle* process, the book and the facilitator provide input to the participants. This input is important because there is a rich history of women's spirituality and peacemaking containing stories and principles that participants can learn from and apply to their lives. Some examples of presentation include:

- Bringing out key values of women's spirituality and peacemaking related to an exercise
- Teaching a way to practice a nonviolence skill

Using Humor

Humor is important for several reasons. Since discussions of violence, conflict, and nonviolence are serious and heavy issues, humor helps to lighten things and helps people from getting overwhelmed. Humor is often important in nonviolent engagement as it helps to shift the dynamic away from a potentially violent conflict and it lightens the mood. Ways of incorporating humor include using funny stories, jokes, short and simple games, or nurturing an atmosphere where participants can be humorous. It is equally important not to use humor violently (for example, put-down humor).

Using The Diversity of Learning Channels

There are four primary learning channels: visual, auditory, kinesthetic (or learning through body movement), and emotional (or heart learning). Learning happens through all of these channels, but each person tends to process primarily through one or two of the channels. Vary the channels as much as possible in order to make the process more inclusive. Also, try to attend to multiple channels at one time. For example, write notes on the flipchart paper during large group reflection and debrief to attend to the visual along with auditory channels.

Creating a Safe and Productive Environment

The *Traveling with the Turtle* process explores the healing power of women's spirituality through stories, readings, group discussion, exercises, and journaling. These activities encourage participants to come to a deeper understanding of how the values and practices of this spirituality further such healing by reflecting on their own experience, learning from other participants, and taking action at whatever level they feel comfortable. Each session is structured to create space conducive to attentive learning, reflection, and honest sharing.

The facilitator creates this environment through the structure and rhythm of each of the sessions and the sensitivity and respect they display and cultivate.

Facilitating, Not Dictating

This process honors everyone's contribution. It is not about people winning debating points. There may be sharp differences of opinion in the group but the facilitator should encourage people to listen and wait to see how it all unfolds over the course of the thirteen sessions.

This process is therefore most successful when the facilitator is facilitating, which literally means, "helping to make things go easily." The facilitator does not dominate the conversation. She does not jump in and say, "You're wrong, and here's the right answer." Instead, the facilitator helps all people to participate and helps keep the rhythm of the process moving with a pace that's appropriate. The facilitator does not need to lecture or spend a long time explaining these lessons.

When a participant shares something that is unclear during the debrief, don't respond by making an interpretation of what the participant said. Use a question to gather more information. For example, ask the participants, "Can you say more about that?"

Traveling with the Turtle facilitators are not experts who have all the information, but co-learners who support the growth of the group. Finally, facilitators should not pressure themselves to be perfect—it is all right to make mistakes. The main thing is to learn and be an active participant in the group.

Creating Safe Space

A key dimension of this process is sharing personal stories, feelings, and other information that require trust and safety. The facilitator therefore needs to create an environment where all the members of the group feel comfortable and safe to share in this way. There are several building blocks for creating this environment. The first is a set of Group Agreements.

Making Agreements

One important way to establish safety is through the "Shared Agreements" presented in Session 1 and reproduced here:

Proposed Agreements

I agree to share and participate at whatever level I feel safe and comfortable.

- I will share what I want to share. If I choose not to share…or to share a little, that's fine. If I want to share more, that's fine. Together we will create an environment where our feelings and thoughts are respected.

- While I have the opportunity always to share at whatever level I feel safe and comfortable, I may be open to take opportunities voluntarily as they arise to feel uncomfortable when that might help facilitate my growth. In every case, this is up to me.
- The facilitators are not acting in the capacity of professional psychotherapists or counselors. They are ordinary people helping us explore alternatives to the violence in our lives and the larger world. If something comes up for me during our time together that would warrant or benefit from consulting with an appropriate health professional, I am encouraged to do so.

I agree to maintain confidentiality about personal stories or experiences shared in my small group or in the large group, unless I have been given permission to share them with others.

- In this process we work in small and large groups. I will not share a story or experience that someone else has shared in either small or large groups unless she has given her permission. When in doubt I will err on the side of caution and not share the story or experience. I will feel free, however, to share any insights that this story or experience may have stimulated.

I agree to Step Up/Step Back—to try to speak up if I tend to be more hesitant and to step back and give others the opportunity to speak if I tend to share often in groups.

- I will listen with my full and complete attention when others are speaking, and wait until a person has completed her thoughts before I speak.
- I will allow silence and accept space for various forms of communication.

I will strive to appreciate and honor our differences.

- Diversity is an opportunity for me to grow and learn in a new way. I will try to nurture an openness to, and celebration of, persons, approaches, and ways of being that are different from mine.
- As part of this, I recognize that there are power dynamics in every group, including this one. I will do my best to be sensitive to the use of power based on race, ability, sexual preference, money, or class. If someone uses power over someone else like this in this group (for example, if someone discounts another person's experiences), I will try to respond to this situation in a clear and loving way.

These agreements serve as a kind of container for the group process, in the way a bowl of water contains water and prevents it from spilling. The agreements act as a container that creates boundaries and safety beyond which one's sharing will not be "spilled."

The agreements are made at the beginning of the group process. Participants will first share what they need from the group to feel safe and comfortable. The facilitator then adds any of the above agreements that were not articulated. The Shared Agreements are then written on flipchart paper and posted on the wall throughout the series. When exercises require more personal sharing, it can be helpful to restate the agreements.

Reestablishing Safety When an Agreement is Broken

A broken agreement provides the facilitator and the participants with an opportunity to practice nonviolence in a real-life scenario. When an agreement is broken, raise the issue with the group and share what you are feeling. (If a participant notices the broken agreement, ask that person to share her feelings.) In either case, get some feedback from the rest of the group by asking what they are feeling or noticing. After receiving feedback, if you have an idea about what to do next, suggest it to the group for feedback. If you are not sure what to do, ask the group for ideas.

Here is an example. When someone shares an experience and another participant says, *"No, it's not like that. It's this way..."* The second person is denying the experience of the first person. The facilitator response might be something like, "I am feeling uncomfortable with what just happened. Dorothy shared her story and Alicia denied that person's experience." [Then follow the process outlined above. Try to re-fashion the agreement in light of the current situation.]

Paying Attention to the Comfort, Discomfort, and Alarm Zones

It is important to support participants in the growing process while ensuring that participants don't feel overwhelmed and end up shutting down. Encourage sharing within the group at whatever level feels comfortable. At the same time, encourage participants to be voluntarily and freely open to potentially experiencing discomfort when the opportunity for stretching and growth may create those feelings. If it appears that a participant is going into what is called the "alarm zone," in which she might shut down or leave the group, check-in with that person as soon as possible. If it happens in the middle of a session, check in with the person on the spot by giving the person the opportunity to share or not share what is happening. Or stop the process by taking a break. Then talk one-on-one with that person immediately.

Ensuring Everyone's Participation

Encourage participants to honor the Step Up/Step Back agreement. If some individuals begin to dominate the conversation, invite others to share. At times the facilitator might want to use a process called "mutual invitation" to encourage everyone's participation in the process. The facilitator either speaks first or invites someone else to do so. After the first person has spoken, she invites the next person to speak and so on. Of course, anyone can pass when she is invited and ask another person to speak. The process concludes when everyone has had the opportunity to speak if they so desire.

Some people require more time to process their thoughts than others. It is important to allow silence to let these people collect their thoughts.

Facilitation Challenges

Facilitating is both rewarding and challenging. The following is a list of challenges that facilitators often have to negotiate.

Keeping on Schedule

One of the most difficult facilitator challenges is adhering to the times scheduled in the Session Agenda. The facilitator must balance adhering to the schedule with allowing time for an array of learning elements *and* for the deep reflection and sharing that the material often unleashes.

The *Traveling with the Turtle* process integrates many different elements: reflection, exercises, meditation, etc. It uses these multiple elements for two reasons. First, because people learn in multiple ways. While some people learn by reading, others learning by doing, and still others by engaging in group discussions. We have created a process that seeks to address these different ways of processing and learning material. Second, learning is enhanced when multiple methods are integrated. Powerful results come from processing material in many different ways that reinforce and deepen one another. The problem is that using several different learning modes can sometimes take more time than using only one.

Even more challenging is the deep reflection and sharing some topics can provoke. The temptation is to spend significantly more time than is allotted for that segment. What do you do?

Time allotted for exercises are the best estimates based on experience. Try to remain within the time frame suggested. If an activity is going over time, decide whether or not to continue with it. If an activity is continued, a later activity may need to be reduced or eliminated altogether. Either decision is acceptable. In general, it is better to complete fewer activities well than to rush through the session in order to cover every activity. Depth is better than superficial understanding. Nevertheless, it is important to stay basically on track. Here are some ways to accomplish this.

First, gauge the energy or sharing in the group. If participants maintain a great deal of energy in an activity, or they continue deep sharing, consider continuing an activity that is exceeding its time limit.

Second, if the group is larger (more than five women), consider having participants share more frequently in pairs or small groups, rather than spend as much time in the large group. When doing this, it can be helpful to remind participants of how much time they have left to speak by ringing a bell at certain intervals. For instance, if partners have twenty minutes to share, ring the bell after ten minutes have passed.

Third, while it is good to maximize participation, this doesn't mean calling on everyone who wishes to speak during an activity. Acknowledge the raised hands and ask if it's all right to move on since time is running over. Encourage participants to continue to reflect on the material between sessions in their journals.

As time in an activity is running down, one good thing to do is to announce, "I'll take one or two more hands." This lets people know time is running out so they won't feel as jarred when the activity is stopped. If you're really stuck, ask the group by saying something like, "This is really important sharing *and* we are going over time. If we continue with this sharing, some parts of the agenda will be cut out. What would you like to do?" This empowers the group to make the decision. If it is at the end of the workshop, contract with the group to go over time. If people are going off the topic on hand, bring them back to it. This often signals that it's time to move on.

Balancing time requirements with growth opportunities is a skill that is learned over time.

Balancing Individual Growth and the Growth of the Group

A facilitator must consider whether one individual's transformation is helpful or harmful to the rest of the group's process. If something benefits only one person and leaves others frustrated, move the process along. One way to deal with that is to acknowledge and appreciate that one person's contribution, then say "It's time to move on," and offer to check in more with that one person after the session.

Being Transparent

In general, a good facilitator empowers the group whenever possible or when in doubt. Facilitators are not experts on the subject but co-learners with the participants. A good facilitator does not need to be the expert on every problem or issue that arises. A good rule of thumb is, "When in doubt, ask the group and decide what to do together."

Situations come up where it is unclear how to handle a situation. A good strategy is to consult with one's co-facilitator. Instead of talking with her in private, though, discuss the issue with the co-facilitator in front of the whole group so that everyone can hear the exchange. This models nonviolent teamwork by embodying openness and transparency in co-facilitation, and how facilitators resolve issues together. It dispels the myth that the facilitator is supposed to have the solution to every situation.

Varying Interaction Modes

Although *Traveling with the Turtle* is a group process, it also incorporates individual meditation and reflection time in order to pursue deeper introspection. This is especially important for more introverted individuals who may be more comfortable processing the material in this way.

Generally, there is a natural movement between individual, small group, and large group activities. If there are too many consecutive large group activities, the group may need to do a small group or individual activity. For example, if during a large group debrief no one is responding to a question and the energy is low, consider asking each participant to turn to the person sitting next to her and respond to the question. Usually, the energy will increase dramatically. Likewise, too many small group activities may diffuse the energy of the group and require a large group activity.

Emphasize, as well, that participants can offer their reflections in a variety of ways—by drawing images, moving, singing, as well as through spoken or written word.

Getting Support

Thank you for your willingness to facilitate this small group process on women's spirituality and peacemaking. The *Traveling with the Turtle* coordinators are available to consult with you about this process before a session and to assist along the way.

Feel free to give us any feedback based on your experience of facilitating this process. Don't hesitate to contact us.

Source: Adapted from Slattery, Butigan, Pelicaric, and Preston-Pile, *Engage: Exploring Nonviolent Living.*

Resources

Adleman, Jeanne, MA, and Gloria Enguidanos, Ph.D., eds. *Racism in the Lives of Women: Testimony, Theory, and Guides to Antiracist Practice*. Binghampton, NY: Harrington Park Press, 1995.

Benjamin, Medea and Jodie Evans, eds. *Stop the Next War Now: Effective Responses to Violence and Terrorism*. Maui, Hawaii: Inner Ocean Publishing, Inc., 2005.

Bolen, Jean Shinoda. *The Millionth Circle: How to Change Ourselves and the World*. Newbury Port, MA and Berkeley: Conari Press, 1999.

_____. *Urgent Message from Mother: Gather the Women, Save the World*. Newbury Port, MA and Berkeley: Conari Press, 2005.

Cane, Patricia Mathis, Ph.D. *Living in Wellness—Trauma Healing: A Capacitar Manual of Body Mind Spirit Practices for Stress, Trauma and Compassion Fatigue*. Santa Cruz, CA: Capacitar International, Inc., 2005.

_____. *Trauma Healing and Transformation: Awakening a New Heart with Body Mind Spirit Practices*. Watsonville, CA: Capacitar, Inc., 2000.

Castilla, Ana, ed. *Goddess of the Americas*. New York: Riverhead Books, 1997.

Chittister, Joan. *Heart of Flesh: A Feminist Spirituality for Women and Men*. Grand Rapids, MI: Eerdmans, 1998.

Chodron, Thubten. *Working with Anger*. Ithaca, New York: Snow Lion Publications, 2001.

Christ, Carol P. *Rebirth of the Goddess: Finding Meaning in Feminist Spirituality*. New York: Routledge, 1997.

Cooper-White, Pamela. *The Cry of Tamar: Violence Against Women and the Church's Response*. Minneapolis: Fortress Press, 1995.

Craighead, Meinrad. *The Mother's Songs: Images of God the Mother*. Mahwah, NJ: Paulist Press, 1986.

Eisler, Riane and David Loye. *The Chalice and the Blade: Our History, Our Future*. San Francisco: HarperSanFrancisco, 1987.

_____. *The Partnership Way: New Tools for Living and Learning Healing For Our Families, Our Communities and Our World*. San Francisco: HarperSanFrancisco, 1990.

Ellison, Sharon. *Taking the War Out of Our Words: The Art of Powerful, Non-Defensive Communication*. Berkeley: Bay Tree Publishing, 2003.

Hillesum, Etty. *An Interrupted Life: The Diaries of Etty Hillesum 1941-43*. New York and Washington. D.C.: Square Press, 1981 (reprinted by Pocket Books).

hooks, bell. *Feminism Is for Everybody: Passionate Politics*. Cambridge, MA: South End Press, 2000.

Galland, China. *The Bond Between Women: A Journey to Fierce Compassion*. New York: Riverhead Books, 1998.

Gottlieb, Lynn. *She Who Dwells Within: A Feminist Vision of a Renewed Judaism*. New York: HarperCollins, 1995.

Kidd, Sue Monk. *The Dance of the Dissident Daughter: A Woman's Journey from Christian Tradition to the Sacred Feminine*. San Francisco: HarperSanFrancisco, 1996.

King, Ruth. *Healing Rage: Women Making Inner Peace Possible*. Berkeley: Sacred Spaces Press, 2004.

Kirk, Gwyn and Margo Okazawa-Rey. *Women's Lives: Multicultural Perspectives*. Third edition. New York: McGraw-Hill, 2004.

Macy, Joanna and Molly Young Brown. *Coming Back to Life: Practices to Reconnect Our Lives, Our World* . Gabriola Island, British Columbia: New Society Publishers, 1998.

McAllister, Pam. *The River of Courage: Generations of Women's Resistance and Action*. Philadelphia: New Society Publishers, 1991.

_____. *You Can't Kill the Spirit*. Philadelphia: New Society Publishers, 1988.

Meehan, Bridget Mary. *Delighting in the Feminine Divine*. Kansas City, MO: Sheed & Ward, 1994.

Petracek, Laura J., Ph.D., LCSW. *The Anger Workbook for Women*. Oakland, CA: New Harbinger Publications, Inc., 2004.

Plaskow, Judith and Carol P. Christ, eds. *Weaving the Visions: New Patterns in Feminist Spirituality*. San Francisco: Harper and Rowe, 1989.

Reilly, Patricia Lynn. *A God Who Looks Like Me: Discovering a Woman-Affirming Spirituality*. New York: Ballantine Books, 1995.

Slattery, Laura, Ken Butigan, Veronica Pelicaric, and Ken Preston-Pile. *Engage: Exploring Nonviolent Living*. Oakland, CA: Pace e Bene Press, 2005.

Zappone, Katherine. *The Hope for Wholeness: A Spirituality for Feminists*. Mystic, CT, Twenty-Third Publications, 1991.

Useful web sites: www.codepink4peace.org; www.peacexpeace.org; www.interplay.org

www.capacitar.org; www.pndc.org; www.climatecrisis.net.

Resources for Healing

National Domestic Violence Hotline, 1-800-799-SAFE, 1-800-787-3223, www.ndvh.org

National Coalition Against Domestic Violence (NCADV), (303) 839-1852,www.ncadv.org

Institute on Domestic Violence in the African-American Community www.dvinstitute.org (612) 624-5357.

National Latino Alliance for the Elimination of Domestic Violence (the Alianza), www.dvalianza.org, (646) 672-1404.

Communities Against Violence (415) 333-HELP, www.cuav.org

Works to end violence against and within lesbian, gay, bisexual, trangender and queer/questioning (LGBTQ) communities.

Rape, Abuse and Incest National Network, 1-800-656-4673.

About the Authors and Artist

Cindy Preston-Pile is co-coordinator of Traveling with the Turtle: Women's Spirituality and Peacemaking Program. Through her affiliation with Pace e Bene Nonviolence Service she has offered numerous From Violence to Wholeness/Engage workshops across the country. Cindy has worked with Pax Christi, the Nevada Desert Experience, and the Catholic Worker movement; she co-founded Magdalene House for homeless women and children. She has also acted as a community organizer for low-income seniors. Cindy is a creator of ritual and a leader of prayer; she edited *Our Prayers Rise Like Incense: Liturgies for Peace*. Her spiritual practice integrates meditation with embodied practices such as InterPlay and Yoga. Cindy holds a Master of Divinity from the Jesuit School of Theology at Berkeley.

Irene Woodward was on the faculty of philosophy at Holy Names University for 40 years, serving as President of the university for ten years. She holds a doctorate in philosophy from the Catholic University of America. Irene co-founded and was the Executive Director of the Anawim House of Hope in Oakland, CA. Since her retirement, she is involved as a spiritual director and mentor, volunteers for Pace e Bene Nonviolence Service, and enjoys playing the violin.

Pamela Falkowski, D.Min., is a spiritual director and supervisor, retreat facilitator, teacher, musician, artist, certified leader of InterPlay, and a licensed massage therapist. She is the Creator-Director of Sunrise Ruby Ministries®, supporting and facilitating personal transformation through contemplative prayer and community. Body Sacred Body Mine® is the division of Sunrise Ruby Ministries® that encourages the conversation between our spirituality, sexuality/physicality, and creativity through a variety of therapeutic massage modalities. She is also Co-Director of the Interfaith Spiritual Guidance Program at The Chaplaincy Institute for Arts and Interfaith Ministries, an adjunct staff member of Mercy Center's Body Consciousness Program in Burlingame, California, and a staff member and administrator of the Pacific Center for Spiritual Formation. Pam received her spiritual direction and supervision training with the Sisters of the Cenacle and the Shalem Institute for Spiritual Formation. She has degrees from the Pacific School of Religion and DePaul University.

Works Cited

Frontmatter
Page iv. L.R. Berger, *As Rains Enter Rivers,* unpublished poem.

Session 1
15. Phil Porter and Cynthia Winton-Henry, *Leading Your Own Life: The InterPlay Leadership Program. Secrets of InterPlay I* (Oakland, CA: Body Wisdom, Inc., 2003), p. 27.
17. Laura Slattery, Ken Butigan, Veronica Pelicaric, and Ken Preston-Pile, *Engage: Exploring Nonviolent Living* (Oakland, CA: Pace e Bene Nonviolence Press, 2005), p. 9.
19. *Woman of Power* (Cambridge, MA: Woman of Power, Inc., 1984-1995) (out of print).
22. Clarissa Pinkola Estés, in Ana Castillo, ed., *Goddess of the Americas* (New York: Riverhead Books, 1997), pp. 34-35.
26. Carol Christ, *Rebirth of the Goddess: Finding Meaning in Feminist Spirituality* (New York: Routledge, 1997), pp. 50-67.
28. Patricia Mathes Cane, *Trauma Healing and Transformation: Awakening a New Heart with Body Mind Spirit Practices* (Watsonville, CA: Capacitar, Inc., 2000), pp. 190-191.
29. Joan Chittister, OSB, *Heart of Flesh: A Feminist Spirituality for Women and Men* (Grand Rapids, MI: Eerdmans, 1998), pp. 3-4.

Session 2
37. Lynn Gottlieb, *She Who Dwells Within: A Feminist Vision of a Renewed Judaism* (New York: HarperCollins, 1995), p. 17.
39. Jose Luis Stevens, *Praying With Power* (London: Watkins Publishing, 2005), p. 107.
40. Bridget Mary Meehan, *Delighting in the Divine Feminine* (Kansas City, MO: Sheed & Ward, 1994), p. 32.
43. Audre Lorde, *Sister Outsider* (Berkeley: The Crossing Press, 1984), pp. 53-59.
45. Nicholas D. Kristof, Op-ed, *The New York Times* (September 29, 2004).

Session 3
53. Pamela Cooper-White, *The Cry of Tamar: Violence Against Women and the Church's Response* (Minneapolis: Fortress Press, 1995), p. 33.
54. Patricia Lynn Reilly, *A God Who Looks Like Me: Discovering a Woman-Affirmative Spirituality* (New York: Ballantine Books, a division of Random House, 1995), pp. 120-121.
55. Starhawk, *Truth or Dare: Encounters with Power, Authority and Mystery* (New York: Harper Collins, 1990), pp. 110-111.
56. Maria da Silva Miguel, in Mev Puleo, ed., *The Struggle is One: Voices and Visions of Liberation,* (Albany, New York: SUNY Press, 1994), p. 249.
58. Patricia Mathes Cane, *Trauma, Healing and Transformation: Awakening a New Heart with Body Mind Spirit Practices* (Watsonville, CA: Capacitar, Inc., 2000), pp. 80-83.

61. Sue Monk Kidd, *The Dance of the Dissident Daughter* (New York: HarperCollins, 2002), pp. 28-32.

63. Laura Petracek, *The Anger Workbook for Women* (Oakland, CA: New Harbinger Publications, 2004), pp. 21-35 (adaptations).

63. Thubten Chodron, *Working with Anger* (Ithaca, NY: Snow Lion Publications, 2001), pp. 43-143 (adaptations).

65. Dorothy Samuels, "The Violence in Ourselves," *Fellowship Magazine,* 1976.

Session 4

78. Thubten Chodron, "The Ball of Light," *Working With Our Anger* (Ithaca, NY: Snow Lion Publications, 2001), pp. 142-143 (adaptation).

80. Patricia Mathes Cane, *Living In Wellness—Trauma Healing: A Capacitar Manual of Body Mind Spirit Practices for Stress, Trauma and Compassion Fatigue* (Watsonville, CA: Capacitar International, Inc., 2005), p. 30.

81. John Dear, *Disarming the Heart: Toward a Vow of Nonviolence* (Scottsdale, PA: Herald Press, 1993).

81. Hussein Bulhan, in *Frantz Fanon and the Psychology of Oppression* (New York: Plenum Books, 1985), p. 135.

81. Laura Slattery, Ken Butigan, Veronica Pelicaric, and Ken Preston-Pile, *Engage: Exploring Nonviolent Living* (Oakland, CA: Pace e Bene Nonviolence Press, 2005), p. 34.

Session 5

88. Iyanla Vanzant, *One Day My Soul Just Opened Up: 40 Days and 40 Nights Toward Spiritual Strength and Personal Growth* (New York: Simon & Schuster, 1998), pp. 9-10.

89. Laura Slattery, Ken Butigan, Veronica Pelicaric, and Ken Preston-Pile, *Engage: Exploring Nonviolent Living* (Oakland, CA: Pace e Bene Nonviolence Press, 2005), pp. 28-29.

91. Ibid., p. 31.

93. Ibid., p. 37.

95. L.L. Heise, J. Pitanguy and A. Germain, *Violence Against Women: The Hidden Burden* (Washington, D.C.: The World Bank, 1994), p. 5.

98. Barbara Deming, *On Revolution and Equilibrium* (New York: War Resisters League, 1990).

99. J'Ann Schoonmaker Allen, written for *Traveling with the Turtle.*

100. Thich Nhat Hanh, "Creating True Peace." Reprinted with the permission of The Free Press, a Division of Simon & Schuster Adult Publishing Group, from *Creating True Peace: Ending Violence in Yourself, Your Family, Your Community* by Thich Nhat Hanh. Copyright © 2003 by The Venerable Thich Nhat Hanh. All rights reserved, pp. 13-15.

Session 6

109. Pamela Cooper-White, *The Cry of Tamar: Violence Against Women and the Church's Response* (Minneapolis: Fortress Press, 1995), p. 42.

113. Isabel Allende, www.peacexpeace.com.

113. Thich Nhat Hanh, "Cultivating the Flower of Nonviolence: An Interview with Thich Nhat Hanh," for *Fellowship Magazine* (January/February 1999).

113. Angie O'Gorman, "Defense Through Disarmament," in *The Universe Bends Toward Justice: A Reader on Christian Nonviolence in the U.S.* (Philadelphia: New Society Publishers, 1990), p. 242.

113. Laura Slattery, Ken Butigan, Veronica Pelicaric, and Ken Preston-Pile, *Engage: Exploring Nonviolent Living* (Oakland, CA: Pace e Bene Nonviolence Press, 2005), p. 91.

115. Ibid., pp. 56-58.

118. Sharon Ellison, *Taking the War Out of Our Words: The Art of Powerful, Non-Defensive Communication* (Berkeley: Bay Tree Publishing, 2003).

121. Bill Hewitt, Paige Bowers, Siobhan Morrissey, Lori Rozsa, Steve Helling, Jeff Truesdell, Liza Hamm, *People Magazine* (March 28, 2005), pp. 54-59.

Session 7

129. Ruth King, "The Buddhist Practice of LovingKindness," in *Healing Rage: Women Making Inner Peace Possible* (Berkeley: Sacred Spaces Press, 2004), pp. 171-173.

131. Laura Slattery, Ken Butigan, Veronica Pelicaric, and Ken Preston-Pile, *Engage: Exploring Nonviolent Living* (Oakland, CA: Pace e Bene Nonviolence Press, 2005), pp. 90-93.

134. Katherine Zappone, *The Hope for Wholeness: A Spirituality for Feminists* (Mystic, CT: Twenty-Third Publications, 1991), p. 84.

138. Darlene Thomas, "My Story," written for *Traveling with the Turtle*.

140. Julia Occhiogrosso, "Our Creative Power," written for *Traveling with the Turtle*.

142. Sue Monk Kidd, *Dance of the Dissident Daughter: A Woman's Journey from Christian Tradition to the Sacred Feminine* (New York: HarperCollins, 2002), pp. 219-222.

144. Matthew Artz, "Bulgarian Tile Projects Have Roots in Berkeley," *Berkeley Daily Planet,* September 7, 2004), pp. 1-2.

Session 8

151. Sister Mary Mattias Ward, "Hand Meditation," unpublished.

153. Diana Neu, "A Hand Blessing," in *WATERwheel*, Vol. 2, No. 1, Winter 1989.

155. Women in the Options Program of the Riverside Correctional Facility in Philadelphia, Tonya McClary, "Poetry as Healing," in *The Vision* (New York: American Friends Service Committee), Fall, 2005, p. 4.

159. Cecilia Trang Le, "From War I Dance," in Cynthia Winton-Henry, with Phil Porter, *What the Body Wants* (Kelowna, BC Canada: Wood Lake Books, Northston Publishing, an imprint, 2004), pp. 214-215.

161. Jean Shinoda Bolen MD, *The Millionth Circle: How to Change Ourselves and the World* (Newburyport, MA and San Francisco: Conari Press, 1999), pp. 11-18.

164. Linda F. Weiskoff, "Karuna Counseling: Transitions Within a Collective," in *Racism in the Lives of Women*, Jean Adleman, MA and Gloria Enguidanos, PhD, eds. (Binghampton, NY: Harrington Park Press, an imprint of The Haworth Press, Inc., 1995), pp. 261-270.

168. Marta Donayre, "Mandorla Denied" written for *Traveling with the Turtle*.

Session 9

178. Elaine Huegel, "Remembering September 11, a Dialogue," in *United Church News* (Cleveland, OH) (September 2002).

181. Jean Shinoda Bolen, M.D. "A Circle of Equals," in *The Millionth Circle: How to Change Ourselves and the World* (Newburyport, MA and San Francisco: Conari Press, 1999), pp. 39-42.

183. Inez, Talamantez, "Women of All Nations," in *Radically Speaking: Feminism Reclaimed*, Diane Bell and Renate Klein, eds. (North Melbourne Victoria, Australia: Spinifex Press, 1996), p. 3.

186. Winona LaDuke, "The Indigenous Women's Network: Our Future, Our Responsibility: Statement of Winona LaDuke," in United Nations Fourth World Conference on Women (Beijing, China) (August 31, 1995).

188. Sharon Abercrombie, "WAGES trains women for eco-friendly cleaning co-op," in *The Oakland Catholic Voice—Online edition*, Vol. 44, No. 7 (April 3, 2006).

190. Abraham McLaughlin, "Nobel Redefines What it Means to Be a Peacemaker," in *The Christian Science Monitor* (October 12, 2004), p. 7.

Session 10

198. Joanna Macy and Molly Brown, *Coming Back to Life: Practices to Reconnect Our Lives, Our World* (Gabriola Island BC, Canada: New Society Publishers, 1998), pp. 150, 160-165.

203. Joyce Rupp, *The Cosmic Dance: An Invitation to Experience Our Oneness* (Maryknoll, NY: Orbis Books, 2002), pp. 9-12.

205. Michael Nagler, "Using Right Means," in *The Steps of Nonviolence* (Nyack, NY: Fellowship Publications, 1999), pp. 15-19.

207. Janet Chisholm, "Constructive Program—Reflections," in *Fellowship Magazine* (September/October, 200).

209. Emily Wax, "A Place Where Women Rule," *Washington Post Foreign Service* (July 9, 2005), p. A1.

Session 11

221. Pam McAllister, *This River of Courage: Generations of Women's Resistance and Action* (Philadelphia: New Society Publishers, 1991), pp. 199-202, and *You Can't Kill the Spirit: Stories of Women and Nonviolent Action* (Philadelphia: New Society Publishers, 1988), pp. 203-225; Aruna Gnanadason, Musimbi Kanyoro and Lucia Ann McSpadden, eds., *Women, Violence and Nonviolent Change* (Geneva: WCC Publishers, 1996), and Lisa Schirch, ed., *Women in Peacebuilding: Resource and Training Manual* (unpublished, 2004).

220. Carol Etzler, "Standing Before Us," *Sisters Unlimited* (Vergenes, VT).

225. Peggy Gish, "Iraq: 'The Invasion Has Brought Us Poverty'—Economic Nonviolence Empowers Women," in CPTNET on MennoLink, server@MennoLink.org (January 22, 2005).

226. American Friends Service Committee and Fellowship of Reconciliation, "The Women's Path of Peace," in *Building from the Inside Out: Peace Initiatives in War-Torn Colombia*.

229. Monica Elizondo, "Interview of Dolores Huerta," from Pace e Bene's First Annual Nonviolence Award Ceremony (Oakland, CA) (October 22, 2005).

230. Sumaya Farhat-Naser and Gila Svirsky, "We Refuse to Be Enemies" in *Stop the Next War Now!: Effective Responses to Violence and Terrorism* (Maui, Hawaii: Inner Ocean Publishing, Inc., 2005), pp. 96-97.

231. Sister Christine Vladimiroff, "Statement to the Vatican of Community Support for Sister Joan Chittister," press release issued by Sisters of St. Benedict of Erie, PA in Summer 2001 (September 20, 2004).

Session 12

238. Laura Slattery, Ken Butigan, Veronica Pelicaric, and Ken Preston-Pile, "Engage Study Program Facilitation Guidelines, in *Engage: Exploring Nonviolent Living* (Oakland, CA: Pace e Bene Nonviolence Press, 2005), pp. 185-186.

239. Ibid., 186-187.

240. Ibid., p. 206.

241. Ibid., p. 207.

240. "Women's Spirituality," in *Woman of Power* (Cambridge: Woman of Power, Inc., 1984-1995) (out of print).

Session 13

247. Phil Porter and Cynthia Winton-Henry, "Walking, Stopping and Running," adapted from *InterPlay* (Oakland, CA: Body Wisdom, Inc., 2003), p. 35.

249. Laura Slattery, Ken Butigan, Veronica Pelicaric, and Ken Preston-Pile, *Engage: Exploring Nonviolent Living* (Oakland, CA: Pace e Bene Nonviolence Press, 2005), pp. 238-239.

253. Alan Cohen, "They're Playing Your Song," as published in *From the Heart,* syndicated column on www.alancohen.com.

254. Clarissa Pinkola Estés, "Today's Assignment, A Prescription from Dr. E.," 2001-2004, C.P. Estés.

Facilitation Guidelines

257. Laura Slattery, Ken Butigan, Veronica Pelicaric, and Ken Preston-Pile, "Engage Study Program Facilitation Guidelines, in *Engage: Exploring Nonviolent Living* (Oakland, CA: Pace e Bene Nonviolence Press, 2005), 250-258.

Acknowledgements

We are grateful for permission to use copyrighted materials from the following publishing companies and individuals. Citations listed below are ordered as they are found in the book.

L.R. Berger, "The Odds." Published by permission of the poet.

Phil Porter and Cynthia Winton-Henry, "Babbling," adapted from *Leading Your Own Life: The Inter-Play Leadership Program. Secrets of InterPlay 1*," p. 27. Published by Body Wisdom, Inc. 2003, 2273 Telegraph Ave., Oakland, CA 94612 (510) 465-2797, info@interplay.org, www.interplay.org. Reprinted by permission of Body Wisdom, Inc.

Laura Slattery, Ken Butigan, Veronica Pelicaric, and Ken Preston-Pile, *Engage: Exploring Nonviolent Living* (Oakland, CA: Pace e Bene Press, 2005.) The following selections were adapted and reprinted with permission of Pace e Bene Press: Shared agreements; Descriptions of Violence; The Violence Spectrum; Sharing an Experience of Violence; CARA: The Four-Step Process for Nonviolent Engagement; Nonviolent Engagement Real-Play Exercise; Nonviolent Action Preparation; The Nonviolent Action Checklist; Next Steps; Facilitation Guidelines.

Patricia Mathes Cane, Ph.D., "Ritual," from *Trauma Healing and Transformation: Awakening a New Heart with Body Mind Practices* (Watsonville, CA: Capacitar, Inc., 2000), www.capacitar.org. Reprinted by permission of Capacitar, Inc.

Lynn Gottlieb, "YHVH Giving Birth," from *She Who Dwells Within: A Feminist Vision of a Renewed Judaism* (New York: HarperCollins, 1995.) Reprinted by permission of HarperCollins Publishers.

Jose Luis Stevens, "On Being a Woman," from *Praying With Power* (London: Watkins Publishing, 2005.) Reprinted by permission of Watkins Publishing.

Bridget Mary Meehan, excerpted and adapted from "The Feminine Divine in the Hebrew Scriptures" and "The Feminine Divine in Sophia and Jesus-Sophia" in *Delighting in the Divine Feminine* (Kansas City, MO: Sheed & Ward, 1994.) Reprinted by permission of Sheed & Ward.

Audre Lorde, "The Erotic As Power," from *Sister Outsider* (Berkeley: The Crossing Press, 1984.) Reprinted by permission from *Sister Outsider* by Audre Lorde, Copyright © 1984 by Audre Lorde. The Crossing Press is a division of Ten Speed Press, Berkeley, CA, www.tenspeed.com.

Nicholas D. Kristof, "Sentenced to Be Raped," from *The New York Times,* Sept. 29, 2004. Copyright © 2004 by The New York Times Co. Reprinted by permission.

Patricia Lynn Reilly, "Imagine a Woman," from *A God Who Looks Like Me: Discovering a Woman-Affirmed Spirituality (*New York: Ballantine Books, 1995). Copyright © 1995 by Patricia Lynn Reilly. Used by permission of Ballantine Books, a division of Random House, Inc.

Starhawk, "Personal Power Place Meditation," from *Truth or Dare: Encounters with Power, Authority, and Mystery*, paperback edn. (New York: HarperCollins, 1990.) Reprinted by permission of HarperCollins Publishers.

Maria da Silva Miguel, "The People as Poet," from *The Struggle is One: Voices and Visions of Liberation,* Mev Puleo, ed. (Albany, NY: SUNY Press, 1994). Copyright © 1994 by the State University of New York. All rights reserved.

Patricia Mathes Cane, Ph.D., "Salute to the Sun," adapted from *Trauma Healing and Transformation: Awakening a New Heart with Body Mind Practices* (Watsonville, CA: Capacitar, Inc., 2000). Reprinted by permission of Capacitar, Inc.

Sue Monk Kidd, "The Feminine Wound," from *The Dance of the Dissident Daughter: A Woman's Journey from Christian Tradition to the Sacred Feminine* (New York: HarperCollins, 2002). Reprinted by permission of HarperCollins Publishers.

Laura Petracek, "Working with Our Anger," adapted from *The Anger Workbook for Women* (Oakland, CA: New Harbinger Publications, Inc., 2004), www.newharbinger.com. Reprinted by permission of New Harbinger Publications, Inc.

Thubten Chodron, "Working with Our Anger," adapted from *Working With Anger* (Ithaca, NY: Snow Lion Publications, 2001). Reprinted by permission of Snow Lion Publications.

Dorothy Samuels, "The Violence in Ourselves," from *Fellowship Magazine,* 1976. Reprinted by permission of *Fellowship* magazine (www.forusa.org/fellowship).

Thubten Chodron, adapted from "The Ball of Light," from *Working With Our Anger* (Ithaca, NY: Snow Lion Publications, 2001). Reprinted by permission of Snow Lion Publications.

Patricia Mathes Cane, Ph.D., " Fingerholds to Manage Emotions," adapted from *Living in Wellness—Trauma Healing: A Capacitar Manual of Body Mind Spirit Practices for Stress, Trauma and Compassion Fatigue* (Watsonville, CA: Capacitar International, Inc., 2005). Reprinted by permission of Capacitar, Inc.

Gemmia L. Vanzant, "One Day my Soul Just Opened Up," from *One Day my Soul Just Opened Up: 40 Days and 40 Nights Toward Spiritual Strength and Personal Growth* by Iyanla Vanzant (New York: Simon & Schuster, 1998). Copyright © 1998 by Iyanla Vanzant. Reprinted by permission of Simon & Schuster Adult Publishing Group.

Laura Slattery, Ken Butigan, Veronica Pelicaric, and Ken Preston-Pile, "Zones of Learning," adapted from *Engage: Exploring Nonviolent Living* (Oakland, CA: Pace e Bene Press, 2005). Originally adapted from a handout, "Using Discomfort Zones for Learning," by Future Now: A Training Collective, which incorporated ideas first developed by Training for Change. Reprinted by permission of Pace e Bene Press.

L.L. Heise, J. Pitanguy and A. Germain, "Gender Violence Worldwide, Throughout the Life Cycle," from *Violence Against Women: The Hidden Burden* (Washington, D.C.: The World Bank, 1994.) Reprinted by permission of the World Bank.

Barbara Deming, "Two Hands," from *On Revolution and Equilibrium* (New York: War Resisters League, 1990.) Reprinted by permission of War Resisters League.

J'Ann Schoonmaker Allen, "Two Hands in North Carolina." Written for this book. Reprinted by permission of author.

Thich Nhat Hanh, "Creating True Peace." Reprinted with the permission of The Free Press, a Division of Simon & Schuster Adult Publishing Group, from *Creating True Peace: Ending Violence in Yourself, Your Family, Your Community* by Thich Nhat Hanh. Copyright © 2003 by The Venerable Thich Nhat Hanh. All rights reserved.

Janet Chisholm, "Closing" in Session 6. Reprinted by permission of author.

Sharon Ellison, "Communication: An Introduction to a Historical Model and to The New Powerful, Non-Defensive Communication Model," adapted from *Taking the War Out of Our Words: The Art of Powerful Non-Defensive Communication* (Berkeley: Bay Tree Publishing). Reprinted by permission of the author.

Bill Hewitt, Paige Bowers, Siobhan Morrissey, Lori Rozsa, Steve Helling, Jeff Truesdell, Liza Hamm, "Seven Hours of Terror," from *People Magazine*, March 28, 2005. Reprinted by permission of *People Magazine*.

Ruth King, "The Buddhist Practice of LovingKindness," from *Healing Rage: Women Making Inner Peace Possible* (Berkeley: Sacred Spaces Press, 2004). Reprinted by permission of author.

Katherine Zappone, "The Habits of Mutuality." Reprinted by permission of the author.

Darlene Thomas, "My Story as told to Cindy Preston-Pile." Written for this book. Reprinted by permission of author.

Julia Occhiogrosso, "Our Creative Power." Written for this book. Reprinted by permission of author.

Sue Monk Kidd, " A Spirituality of Naturalness," from *The Dance of the Dissident Daughter: A Woman's Journey from Christian Tradition to the Sacred Feminine* (New York: HarperCollins Publishers, 2002.) Reprinted by permission of HarperCollins Publishers.

Sister Mary Mattias Ward, adapted and quoted from "Hand Meditation." Reprinted by permission of author.

Diann L. Neu, "A Hand Blessing," from *WATERwheel*, Vol. 2, No. 1, Winter 1989. Diann L. Neu, Co-director of WATER, The Women's Alliance for Theology, Ethics and Ritual, 8121 Georgia Ave., Silver Spring, MD 20910 USA, phone 301 589-2509; fax 301 589-3150; dneu@hers.com. Reprinted by permission of WATER.

Written by women in the Options Programs at Riverside Correctional Facility in Philadelphia, who participated in a poetry workshop organized by the American Friends Service Committee National Criminal Justice Program. "*Poetry Alive Tribe*," from "Poetry as Healing" by Tonya McClary in *The Vision*, Fall 2005. Published by the American Friends Service Committee National Criminal Justice Program. Permission granted by AFSC.

Cecilia Trang Le, "From War I Dance," in Cynthia Winton-Henry, with Phil Porter, *What the Body Wants* (Kelowna, BD, Canada: Wood Lake Books, Northstone Publishing, an imprint, 2004). Reprinted by permission of Wood Lake Books, Inc.

Jean Shinoda Bolen, M.D., excerpted from "How to Change the World: The Millionth Circle," in *The Millionth Circle: How to Change Ourselves and the World* (Newburyport, MA and San Francisco: Conari Press, imprint of Red Wheel/Weiser, 1999.) Reprinted by permission of Conari Press. To order please call 1-800-423-7087.

Linda F. Weiskoff, "Karuna Counseling: Transitions Within a Collective," from *Racism in the Lives of Women*, Jean Adleman, MA and Gloria Enguidanos, PhD, eds. (Binghampton, NY: Harrington Park Press, an imprint of The Haworth Press, Inc., 1995, pp. 261-270. Reprinted by permission of The Haworth Press, Inc.

Marta Donayre, "Mandorla Denied." Written for this book. Reprinted by permission of author.

Jean Shinoda Bolen, M.D., "A Circle of Equals," from *The Millionth Circle: How to Change Ourselves and the World* (Newburyport, MA and San Francisco: Conari Press, imprint of Red Wheel/Weiser, 1999). Reprinted by permission of Conari Press, Imprint of Red Wheel/Weiser. To order please call 1-800-423-7087.

Inez, Talamantez, "Women of All Nations," from *Radically Speaking: Feminism Reclaimed*, Diane Bell and Renate Klein, eds. (North Melbourne Victoria, Australia: Spinifex Press, 1996.) Reprinted by permission of Inez Talamantez.

Abraham McLaughlin, "Nobel Redefines What it Means to Be a Peacemaker," from *The Christian Science Monitor*, October 12, 2004. Copyright © 2004, The Christian Science Monitor. All rights reserved. Reprinted by permission of The Christian Science Monitor.

Winona LaDuke, "The Indigenous Women's Network: Our Future, Our Responsibility: Statement of Winona LaDuke," from United Nations Fourth World Conference on Women, Beijing, China, August 31, 1995. Reprinted by permission of author.

Sharon Abercrombie, "WAGES Trains Women for Eco-Friendly Cleaning Co-op," from *The Oakland Catholic Voice—Online edition*, April 3, 2006, Vol. 44, No. 7. Reprinted by permission of The Oakland Catholic Voice.

Joanna Macy and Molly Brown, "The Council of All Beings," from *Coming Back to Life: Practices to Reconnect Our Lives, Our World* (Gabriola Island, BC, Canada: New Society Publishers, 1998). Reprinted by permission of the publisher.

Joyce Rupp, "The Cosmic Dance," in The Cosmic Dance: An Invitation to Experience Our Oneness (Nyack, NY: Fellowship Publications, 1999). Reprinted by permission of the publisher.

Michael Nagler, "Using Right Means," from *The Steps of Nonviolence* (Nyack, New York: Fellowship Publications, 1999.) Reprinted by permission of the author.

Janet Chisholm, "Constructive Program—Reflections," from *Fellowship Magazine*, September-October, 2004. Reprinted by permission of *Fellowship* magazine (www.forusa.org/fellowship).

Emily Wax, "A Place Where Women Rule," from Washington Post Foreign Service, Saturday, July 9, 2005. Copyright © 2005, The Washington Post. Reprinted by permission of The Washington Post.

Peggy Gish, "Iraq: The Invasion Has Brought Us Poverty—Economic Nonviolence Empowers Women," from CPTNET on server@MennoLink.org, January 22, 2005. Christian Peacemaker Teams, Chicago, IL.

Monica Elizondo, "Interview of Dolores Huerta," from Pace e Bene's First Annual Nonviolence Award Ceremony, October 22, 2005, Oakland, CA. Reprinted by permission of author.

Sumaya Farhat-Naser and Gila Svirsky, "We Refuse to Be Enemies" from *Stop the Next War Now!: Effective Responses to Violence and Terrorism* (Maui, Hawaii and San Francisco: Inner Ocean Publishing, Inc., 2005.) Reprinted by Permission of Inner Ocean Publishing, Inc.

Sister Christine Vladimiroff, "Statement to the Vatican of Community Support for Sister Joan Chittister" (Date of Statement, Summer 2001). September 20, 2004. Reprinted by permission of author.

Phil Porter and Cynthia Winton-Henry, "Walking, Stopping and Running," adapted from *InterPlay*™ (Oakland, CA: Body Wisdom, Inc., 2003), cynthia@interplay.org. Reprinted by permission of Body Wisdom, Inc.

Alan Cohen, "They're Playing Your Song," as published in his column, "From the Heart." Reprinted by permission. All rights reserved.

We earnestly tried to contact all publishers or authors to secure necessary permissions for printing. We regret any errors, but gratefully acknowledge use of the following texts:

Woman of Power, out-of-print.

Clarissa Pinkola Estés, Ph.D., "Guadalupe: The Path of the Broken Heart," from *Goddess of the Americas*, Ana Castillo, ed.

Joan Chittister, OSB, excerpt from *Heart of Flesh: A Feminist Spirituality for Women and Men* (Grand Rapids, MI: Eerdmans Publishing Co., 1998).

Carol Christ, " History of the Goddess" adapted from *Rebirth of the Goddess: Finding Meaning in Feminist Spirituality* (New York: Routledge, 1997).

Matthew Artz, "Bulgarian Pile Projects Have Roots in Berkeley," from *Berkeley Daily Planet* (September 7, 2004).

Elaine Huegel, "Remembering September 11, a Dialogue," from *United Church News* (September 2002).

Carol Etzler, "Standing Before Us," in *Sisters Unlimited* (Vergenes, VT).

Clarissa Pinkola Estes, Ph.D., "Today's Assignment, a Prescription from Dr. E., " Copyright © 2001-2004. C.P. Estes

Stay in Touch with the Turtle

Traveling with the Turtle and Pace e Bene Nonviolence Service are developing a growing network of individuals and groups in the United States and around the globe committed to creating a more peaceful world. We invite you to be part of this network by staying connected with us. To do so, please fill out the following form:

- o Yes, send me Pace e Bene's free quarterly newsletter.
- o Yes, send me free online updates and Pace e Bene's e-newsletter.
- o I am interested in facilitating a Traveling with the Turtle group.
- o I would like to host a Traveling with the Turtle workshop or retreat.
- o I want to offer my skills/volunteer to help spread the word about Traveling with the Turtle. (Areas of expertise needed include: outreach, publicity, fundraising, translation, etc.)
- o I want to make a tax-deductible donation to help Traveling with the Turtle thrive.

    o $25   o $50   o $100   o $250   o $500   Other:

Name: _____

Address: _____

City/State/Zip: _____

Organization or Affiliation: _____

Phone: _____

E-Mail: _____

Send this form to
Traveling with the Turtle
Pace e Bene
California Office
2501 Harrison Street, Oakland, CA 94612
510-268-8908

turtle@paceebene.org

Peacemaking Resources from Pace e Bene

Traveling with the Turtle: A Small Group Process in Women's Spirituality and Peacemaking by Cindy Preston-Pile and Irene Woodward. A thirteen-session process that explores the values and practices of women's spirituality and their contribution to peacemaking. Paperback, 283 pages.

From Violence to Wholeness by Ken Butigan with Patricia Bruno, OP. A ten-part curriculum for group study in the spirituality and practice of active nonviolence. Available in English andpanish, Paperback, 170 pages

Franciscan Nonviolence: Stories, Reflections, Principles, Practices and Resources by Ken Butigan, Mary Litell, OSF and Louis Vitale, OFM. Acollection of reflections on the stories of St. Francis and St. Clare that illuminate nonviolence as a relevant spiritual practice in today's world. Available in English and Spanish, Paperback, 124 pages

Engage: Exploring Nonviolent Living by Laura Slattery, Ken Butigan, Veronica Pelicaric and Ken Preston-Pile. A twelve-part curriculum for group study in the spirituality and practice of active nonviolence. Paperback, 300+ pages

Peace Grows! by Rosemary Lynch, OSF and Mary Litell, OSF. This packet of materials developed as part of Pace e Bene's Nurturing a Culture of Peace program for use in workshops and retreats. Includes a curriculum, music CD, and a video (VHS or DVD). May be ordered separately or as a package.

Roots of Violence in the U.S. Culture: A Diagnosis Toward Healing by Alain Richard, OFM. A groundbreaking book exploring the origins and current causes violence in US culture today. Paperback, 156 pages

ORDER FORM

Traveling with the Turtle	____ @$25.00	____
Ordering 5 or more	____ @$21.00	____
Franciscan Nonviolence	____ @ $12.95	____
Engage: Exploring Nonviolent Living	____ @ $22.00	____
Ordering 5 or more:	____ @ $18.00	____
From Violence to Wholeness	____ @ $19.95	____
Ordering 5 or more:	____ @ $15.95	____
Roots of Violence	____ @ $14.95	____
Pilgrimage Through a Burning World	____ @ $21.95	____
Peace Grows! Curriculum only:	____ @ $17.95	____
Ordering 5 or more:	____ @ $14.95	____
Curriculum w/ CD and DVD:	____ @ $49.95	____
Curriculum w/ CD and VHS:	____ @ $44.95	____
Peace Grows! CD	____ @ $12.95	____
Peace Grows! DVD	____ @ $24.95	____
Peace Grows! VHS	____ @ $19.95	____
Packet of ten identical Peace Cards	____ @ $12.00	____

Please select one: o Mahatma o Gandhi o Mother Teresa o Albert Camus o Nelson Mandela o Wendell Berry o Thich Nhat Hanh

Six assorted Peace Cards	____ @ $8.00	____
Six "Be the Change..."	____ @$12.00	____
Cards (Blank inside)	____ @ $12.00	____
Six "Be the Change" Cards	____ @ $12.00	____

Name _____

Organization _____

Address _____

City _____

State ____ Zip _____

Phone _____

E-mail _____

Enclosed: o Check (payable to **Pace e Bene**)
Charge my: o Visa o Mastercard
Account # _____
Expiration Date _____
Signature _____

(mail order) Pace e Bene Nonviolence Service
1420 W. Bartlett Ave.,
Las Vegas, NV 89106

Phone and fax order: (702) 648-2281
E-mail order: paceebene@paceebene.org

Shipping and handling for all books:
Add $4.00 for first copy, $1 for each additional copy.
Prices subject to change without notice.